A Western Horseman Book

LEGENDS
VOLUME 3

Outstanding Quarter Horse Stallions and Mares

Contributors

Diane Ciarloni
Jim Goodhue
Kim Guenther
Frank Holmes
Betsy Lynch
Larry Thornton

Edited by Kathy Swan

D1533196

LEGENDS
VOLUME 3

Published by
Western Horseman Inc.

3850 North Nevada Ave.
Box 7980
Colorado Springs, CO 80933-7980

Design, Typography, and Production
Western Horseman
Colorado Springs, Colorado

Cover painting by
Orren Mixer

Printing
Publisher's Press
Salt Lake City, Utah

©1997 by Western Horseman Inc.
All rights reserved
Manufactured in the United States of America

Copyright Notice: *This book is copyrighted by Western Horseman Inc., and therefore protected by federal copyright law. No material may be copied, FAXed, electronically transmitted, or otherwise used without express written permission. Requests must be submitted in writing.*

Fifth Printing: September 1999

ISBN 0-911647-40-6

INTRODUCTION

THIS MARKS the third volume in our series of *Legends* books profiling well-known Quarter Horse stallions and mares, and several Thoroughbred stallions. Like the first two, this one has been a labor of love—loads of work, but very rewarding.

Because it would be extremely difficult and time-consuming for any one person to write about all of the horses chosen for this book, we asked six free-lance writers to help us out. These writers are profiled in the back of the book. But in brief, Jim Goodhue knows the early-day horses perhaps better than any other contemporary writer. Diane Ciarloni, who authored the first *Legends* under the name Diane Simmons, is well-versed with the Quarter running horses. Betsy Lynch and Kim Guenther are well-acquainted with performance horses. Larry Thornton is widely recognized for his pedigree knowledge. And Frank Holmes is a walking-talking encyclopedia of horses past and present, not only Quarter Horses, but also Paints and Appaloosas.

Kathy Swan, our associate editor, coordinated the efforts of the free-lancers, helped them procure photographs, and edited their copy. She, as well as everyone involved with the book, has worked hard to ensure accuracy, but we realize there might be mistakes. In the early days of the AQHA, record-keeping was not what it is today, and so there are some mistakes in pedigrees in the early AQHA studbooks. That's why some of the pedigrees in this book might not jibe with those early studbooks. With a number of horses, and not necessarily any in this book, their exact breeding will never be known.

In the first *Legends*, Jim Goodhue wrote a piece titled "A History of Early AQHA Registration." It's a handy reference if you would like to know more about this subject.

If you spot any errors, send a letter to us pointing out the mistakes. We will correct them in the next printing of the book.

AQHA Titles

Many Quarter Horse owners, trainers, and enthusiasts today might not be familiar with AQHA's first system for grading

Western pleasure classes have changed drastically since this photo was taken in 1960 at the Thunderbird Ranch in Woodstock, Illinois. The ranch offered a number of instructional western pleasure classes that summer.

WH File Photo

INTRODUCTION

Quarter race horses. Before AQHA came up with today's speed index ratings, running horses were graded with a D, C, B, A, or AA according to their speed at specified distances. The latter was the fastest. As both horses and tracks became faster, a faster grade—AAA— was added. Still later, top AAA was added, and this was indicated by either TAAA or AAAT following a horse's name. You will see these grades used with several of the horses in this book.

Another AQHA term no longer used is that of Honor Roll, which designated the year-end high-point horse in an event. For example, Poco Lena was the Honor Roll cutting horse for several years. Now, AQHA simply uses the term *high point*. Both terms are used throughout this book.

A horse can still earn the title of AQHA Champion today, but it is no longer as coveted as it was in the "olden days." Back then, many owners and trainers worked hard and traveled many miles to win enough halter and performance points so they could earn AQHA Championships for their horses. It was considered to be the most prestigious of titles, especially before the World Championship Quarter Horse Shows began. In those early years, many great horses showed at halter in the morning and in performance in the afternoon to earn points toward their AQHA Championships.

You might also wonder how some horses may have earned a half-point in performance. For example, a horse's total points might be, say, 145.5. Well, in the early years such classes as western pleasure and western riding were not considered as competitive as, say, calf roping and reining. Therefore a horse placing in a pleasure or western riding class might only have earned ½ point. That was also in the days when about 98 percent of the western pleasure exhibitors were women, and 98 percent of the reiners were men. The times, they have changed.

Will there be a *Legends Volume 4*? Yes, but not right away. We already know most of the horses we want to include, but the list is not finalized.

Credits

We would very much like to thank those who helped us by providing photographs to use in the book. The many great, old photos used in all three of the *Legends* books are a big reason why they are so popular. For this particular book, we would especially like to thank Darol Dickinson of Ellicott, Colo., and the staff of *The Quarter Horse Journal* for providing so many photographs, and Ray and Joyce Bankston of Dalco photography for allowing us to use a number of their photographs.

Special appreciation goes to Orren Mixer for creating the outstanding cover painting—as he also did for the first two *Legends* books.

I would also like to thank members of our *WH* crew who worked behind the scenes to help us produce this book. Jeanne Mazerall, assistant to our art director, did the layout and design. Marilyn Petrenas, typesetting manager, handled the typesetting. And Bert Anderson, production manager, and his assistant, Glenn Mattingly, often came to the office early and stayed late to get the book ready to send to the printer.

Patricia A. Close, Editor
Western Horseman Inc.

CONTENTS

1

STEEL DUST

By Jim Goodhue

This extraordinary horse and his descendants helped to provide the basis for the Quarter Horse of today.

THERE WAS a time (particularly in the middle to late 1800s) when the horses we know today as Quarter Horses were known almost universally throughout the West as Steel Dusts, or Steel Dusters, or Steel Dust Horses. As recently as the 1930s, when the preeminent breeder Jack Casement wrote an article for *Western Horseman* magazine in which he advocated the registry that was to become the American Quarter Horse Association, he titled it "Why A Steel Dust Stud Book?"

These days, our question might be "Why was this breed of horses so completely identified with a name that means so little to us today?" Legend has it that there was a stallion in the middle of the 19th century who was so superior and whose offspring were such outstanding performers that everyone wanted to have a part in the phenomenon.

Mare owners from far and wide bred their mares to this extraordinary horse named Steel Dust. People who needed top horses acquired mounts and breeding animals who were as closely descended from Steel Dust as possible. Horse traders found that they could demand higher prices if they claimed their horses were members of the Steel Dust family. Some owners took the simple expedient of naming their own horses Steel Dust, regardless of whether they were related to the original Steel Dust. These latter two practices naturally added to the confusion that was to follow.

And confusion there is. The name of this great horse has been listed as Steel Dust and Steeldust. He has also been referred to as Steele, Blind Steele, Blind Steel Dust, Old Blind Steel Dust, and Runafter. The state in which he was bred has been given as Illinois, Kentucky, Missouri, Tennessee, or Texas. His foaling date is thought to have been about 1845, but has been given as early as 1843 and as late as 1856. His height has been given as a compact 14.2 hands, as well as a rangier 16 hands.

Because records from that era are scanty and because memories aren't always accurate, there have been claims for all of these "facts."

There even was one self-appointed authority who stated there was no such horse as Steel Dust, and that the whole family developed from a Thoroughbred horse brought from England to Texas by way of New Orleans. Others were equally convinced that Steel Dust was a Morgan. Since the original Justin Morgan, from whom that breed sprang, was said by many to have been an ideal Quarter Horse in both conformation and performance, it seems a plausible claim.

Whatever its source, there were definite, highly desirable attributes for which the Steel Dust horses were universally credited. In the book *They Rode Good Horses,* which is the official history of the first 50 years of the American Quarter Horse Association, Don Hedgpeth wrote, "They were heavy-muscled horses, marked with small ears, a big jaw, remarkable intelligence and lightning speed up to a quarter of a mile."

The late Robert M. Denhardt, one of the breed's best historians, wrote about Steel Dust: "The startling uniformity of his descendants gives us a rather clear picture

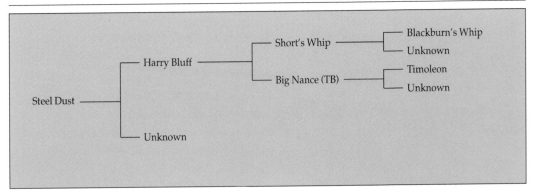

```
                                         ┌─── Blackburn's Whip
                         ┌─── Short's Whip ───┤
                         │               └─── Unknown
          ┌─── Harry Bluff ───┤
          │              │               ┌─── Timoleon
          │              └─── Big Nance (TB) ───┤
Steel Dust ───┤                          └─── Unknown
          │
          └─── Unknown
```

of his appearance" despite the fact that no reliable description has been kept of the old horse himself. Nor are there any known photographs of the horse. Denhardt also wrote that the cross of Steel Dust on Texas mares produced "the best cow horse the Southwest had known."

Because of this reputation, horsemen and others began to think that the name Steel Dust referred to an entire breed and not just one horse and his descendants. It seemed less and less important to differentiate between one strain of horses and an entire breed.

Despite all of the discrepancies and scantiness of records, reliable documentation indicates there really was a prepotent and prolific stallion named Steel Dust. In the November-December 1939 issue of *Western Horseman* magazine, Denhardt wrote that a long-time Quarter Horse breeder in Colorado had given him an old handbill advertising Dan Tucker, the sire of Peter McCue. This not only gave concrete evidence of Steel Dust's existence, it also was among the first indications of his breeding. The handbill showed that Dan Tucker traced twice to Steel Dust and three times to Harry Bluff, who was shown to be the sire of Steel Dust.

Denhardt concluded that the veracity of the pedigree on this handbill could hardly be questioned because "when it was printed, too many people knew the facts." Also, the flier was printed for Thomas Trammell, of the famed partnership Trammell and Newman, Sweetwater, Texas. They were well-known breeders "who could not afford to be considered dishonest."

The first stockman who bred Quarter Horses on a large scale and attempted to research the background of these horses was William (Billy) Anson. A member of

Steel Dust traced to the legendary Thoroughbred Sir Archy, who was the sire of Timoleon.

the English aristocracy, Anson bought horses throughout the Southwest for the British army during the Boer War and established a large ranch near Cristobal, Tex., keeping a select band of breeding horses for himself. He wrote that he had traced Quarter Horses to the early chronicles of Virginia and "there seems little doubt that they were the original racing animals of the early planters and country gentlemen of Virginia and the Carolinas."

Anson and others found evidence that the pedigrees of many of the greatest

Peter McCue was one of the most famous descendants of Steel Dust.

Photo Courtesy of Walter Merrick

Balleymooney, foaled in 1914, was by Concho Colonel, who traced back to Steel Dust. Balleymooney was owned by Dan Casement of Colorado. The Casements were enthusiastic about Steel Dust bloodlines.

Quarter Horses in the early 1900s traced at least once and often several times to Steel Dust. For example, through his sire, Dan Tucker, Peter McCue traced back to Steel Dust. Peter McCue's son Hickory Bill had three or more indications of Steel Dust in his pedigree. Old Joe Bailey (of Weatherford) is believed to have traced at least

four times to that fountainhead; and his son Yellow Wolf inherited more of the valuable blood through his dam, Old Mary.

Other notable progenitors from that era who could legitimately claim Steel Dust as an ancestor include such individuals as Little Joe, Possum, Lock's Rondo, Pid Hart, Old Fred, Dogie Beasley, Texas Chief, Tubal Cain, (Billy Anson's) Jim Ned, and Old Billy, who is credited with starting a family of his own.

These and other Steel Dust descendants, then, helped provide the basis of the modern Quarter Horse as registered by the American Quarter Horse Association. Steel Dust figures in the pedigrees of 17 of the 18 stallions still living at the time of the association's organization and who were designated as foundation sires. Through them and other fine members of the family, the blood of the legendary Steel Dust has been passed down almost 150 years later to such recent notables as Refrigerator, CD Olena, Down With Debt, BR Peppy Smoke, Noblesse Six, Docs Arky Sug, Mr Jess Perry, Bar J Jackie, and Heza Fast Man.

The accomplishments of these modern horses are known and can be relied on because of the efforts of the AQHA in recording bloodlines, standardizing names,

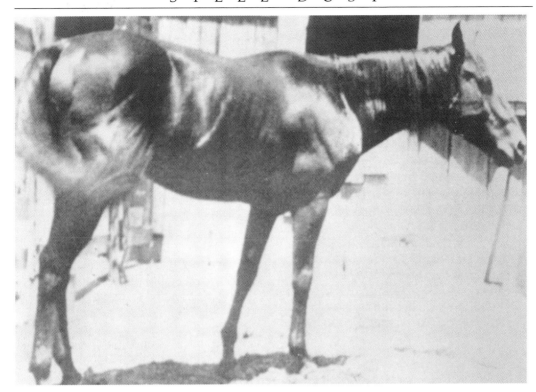

Old Joe Bailey, also known as Weatherford Joe Bailey, is believed to have traced at least four times, and possibly seven times, to Steel Dust.

Photo Courtesy of the American Quarter Horse Heritage Center & Museum, Amarillo, Texas

recognizing sanctioned races and shows, and keeping records of those events. Such was not the case in the middle of the 1800s, however, and we are left to wonder which of the two remarkable versions of Steel Dust's racing record is true.

According to one story, Steel Dust never raced until he was about 13 years old. Until then, he had been used simply as a saddle horse (and perhaps a breeding animal). Despite Steel Dust's somewhat advanced age, his owner, Middleton (Mid) Perry, loaned him to a race-horse man named Jack Batcheler. Batcheler was to train him and then match him against a horse named Brown Dick, owned by Alfred Bailes. Brown Dick was the most outstanding of a successful string of runners campaigned by Bailes. He was believed to be almost unbeatable at a quarter of a mile.

At this time, Dallas was just a small jumble of log cabins; Fort Worth was not yet even an army outpost. But a village named Lancaster (about 10 miles south of Dallas) was a thriving, up-and-coming settlement. It was at a straightaway 2 miles west of Lancaster that the race took place about 1857.

Before a large, holiday-minded crowd, Steel Dust came off as a decided victor. It

Red Dog, owned by Jack Casement of Colorado, was a descendant of Steel Dust. In addition to being a good broodmare sire, Red Dog also sired the outstanding Appaloosa stallion Joker B.

was said that Steel Dust's quiet disposition and lack of reputation completely disarmed the betting denizens of Lancaster, who made him a definite underdog in the wagering. So, Steel Dust's triumph almost bankrupted the town, while the winner's connections went back to the ranch on Ten Mile Creek with a wagonload of money. It

Squaw, a daughter of Peter McCue, was said to have ideal Steel Dust conformation. She was owned by Coke Roberds of Colorado.

also was related that Bailes almost immediately sold Brown Dick to a man from another part of Texas.

The race and subsequent sale of Brown Dick do not end this version, however, as the race was followed by an argument over something to do with the event. This quarrel was between a relative of Jack Batcheler, named Jack Lilley, and a man known down through the ages only as Lightfoot. It is said that Lightfoot backed down from an actual physical encounter; but during the night that followed, he slipped into the room where Lilley was sleeping and discharged both barrels of his shotgun at close range to Lilley's heart.

On hearing of the killing—according to this account—Mid Perry was so upset by the violence that he decreed Steel Dust was never to race again. One race, one conquest, and the end.

Now, the other explanation of Steel Dust's popularity, believed by many people, was that Mid Perry had been a noted race-horse man in Illinois before moving to Texas, and he had campaigned Steel Dust as much as he could.

Most of the people who have passed along this variation of Steel Dust's story have agreed that he was a great race horse and a consistent winner over such speedsters as the Kentucky-bred Monmouth. One old-timer reported that Steel Dust could run a quarter of a mile in 22 seconds "any time." The famous Shiloh also may have been among his defeated opponents.

According to the stories that list numerous races, Steel Dust's career was ended not by a murder, but by an accident. When starting in a race from a chute made of poles, Steel Dust's legendary lunge at the beginning threw him into the side wall and a large splinter rammed into his shoulder. This injury not only disabled him and prevented his running the course, but also eventually caused him to go blind.

In either case, it has been reliably reported that mares were brought to Steel Dust's court by prominent breeders from hundreds of miles away—a considerable distance in those days. Even after he reached an advanced age, he continued to sire the "speedy, low, stocky, well-built, well-muscled, and high-spirited" sons and daughters for whom he was famous.

Among all the conflicting facts about Steel Dust, two seem generally accepted as true. These refer to color and breeding.

It is generally agreed that he was bay or brown, and many reliable authorities list him specifically as blood bay. His foals, too, are believed to have been predominantly bay or brown.

The only written records that have been passed down concerning the breeding of Steel Dust list his sire as Harry Bluff, a son of Short's Whip (or Short Whip) and a Thoroughbred mare named Big Nance. Through this mare, Steel Dust was a descendant of Timoleon, a son of the famous Sir Archy. A Thoroughbred imported from England, Sir Archy was a particularly important source of short speed despite his own connections to longer distances.

Shiloh, another from the Sir Archy line, was probably the most important cross on Steel Dust blood. This combination produced a large portion of the most successful individuals who were known as Steel Dust horses.

The breeding of Steel Dust's dam is unknown, but her name may have been Katrina.

The most widely accepted version of this history starts with Steel Dust resulting from the mating given and being foaled in Illinois. His exact foaling date is not known, but it was about 1845. Then, as a yearling or 2-year-old, he was taken to Texas.

It seems that sometime during the 1840s, there were several families from the counties of Sangamon and Greene in Illinois who decided to make the long move to Texas. These included the families of Thomas Ellis and two of his sons-in-law, Mid Perry and Jones Green (or Greene). These two younger men are believed to have spent the previous year in newly independent Texas and their accounts of the new country may have been the cause of this mass migration. For one thing, good farm land could be purchased for 25 to 50 cents an acre.

Some of the newcomers, including Thomas Ellis, settled in Lamar County where they resumed farming. Mid Perry and Jones Green, with some of the others, pushed on farther west to the prairie country where grazing was better. They found their spots on Ten Mile Creek in southern Dallas County, between Five Mile Creek and Bear Creek.

Perry and Green had been horse and mule breeders and dealers in Illinois, and it was natural for them to bring parts of their herds to Texas. Perry's group included the young stallion Steel Dust. The most widely accepted version of this history has Steel Dust being bred by Perry in Illinois, but there were those who reported Perry previously had lived in Kentucky and had bred Steel Dust in that state.

As Helen Michaelis has written, neither historians nor writers bestowed fame on Steel Dust for originating a distinguished group of Quarter Horses. He earned the reputation himself through his deeds and "through his celebrated sons and daughters and his descendants after them." Horsemen, themselves, recognized the value of these descendants and passed along this knowledge to later generations.

Whatever the whole truth may be con-

Pedigree   of

Dan Tucker,

The famous racing-stallion now owned and kept by Thos. Trammell, Sweetwater, Texas.

Dan Tucker was sired by Barney Owens. 1st dam, Butt Cut, by Jack Traveller, he by Steel Dust, out of Queen, who was sired by Pilgrim, by Lexington. 2nd dam, June Bug, by Harry Bluff the sire of Steel Dust. 3rd Dam, Munch Meg, by Snow Ball. 4th Dam, Monkey, by Boanerges.

Jack Traveller was sired by old Steel Dust. Dam, Queen, by Pilgrim, by Lexington. Harry Bluff is Whip and Timoleon stock, and was sired by Short Whip, out of Big Nance, a thoroughbred mare. Barney Owens was sired by Cold Deck, and out of the Overton mare. Cold Deck was by Billy Boy, he by Shiloh, and out of a Steel Dust mare. Cold Deck's dam was Dolly Coker, by Old Rondo.

For further information in regard to this famous breed of racers, address.

Thos. Trammell,   Sweetwater, Texas.

This old handbill advertising Dan Tucker gave concrete evidence of Steel Dust's existence.

cerning Steel Dust and the Steel Dusters, there is one undeniable fact about these horses. Whether the Quarter Horse champions of today actually benefit genetically from being able to trace their bloodlines back to Steel Dust, it is a fact that they and the entire modern breed of Quarter Horses have profited from the ideal on which the Steel Dust legend is based: horses universally recognized for speed and other abilities, as well as the willingness to use those talents when asked.

The date of Steel Dust's death is not known, but it may have been in the 1870s.

2 OLD SORREL

By Jim Goodhue

Even today, more than 50 years later, his bloodline can be found in the winners of every working event for which the Quarter Horse is acclaimed.

THE KING RANCH of Kingsville, Tex., according to its ad in the first volume of the AQHA Stud Book, had in mind the production of "an ideal horse for ranch, remount, polo, and pleasure purposes."

From this program evolved a Quarter Horse who consistently has been successful in each of those fields. "These results were obtained," the ad continued, "by working from a superb individual that had perfect action and a wonderful disposition."

That superb individual was a stallion we have come to know as Old Sorrel. His characteristics were enhanced and "fixed" by the application of scientific breeding principles and by careful selection of his descendants. These methods were so successful that every King Ranch Quarter Horse carried the blood of Old Sorrel (often in multiple crosses) by the time the AQHA was established.

Even today, more than 50 years later, his bloodline can be found in the winners of every working event for which the Quarter Horse is acclaimed. One still finds his name in the pedigree of many current winners and champions.

The King Ranch was founded when Richard King paid $300 in 1853 for 15,550 acres of a Spanish land grant recorded as the "Rincon de Santa Gertrudis." There on

Old Sorrel founded a dynasty of performance horses for the King Ranch.

Photo Courtesy of *The Quarter Horse Journal*

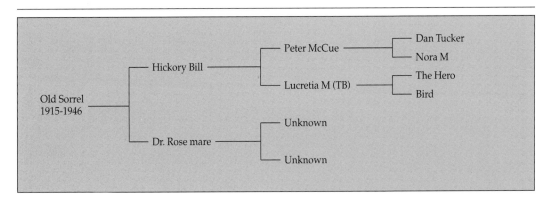

Old Sorrel
1915-1946
├── Hickory Bill
│   ├── Peter McCue
│   │   ├── Dan Tucker
│   │   └── Nora M
│   └── Lucretia M (TB)
│   ├── The Hero
│   └── Bird
└── Dr. Rose mare
    ├── Unknown
    └── Unknown

the banks of the Santa Gertrudis creek, he established a livestock operation with a partner, Gideon K. (Legs) Lewis, who was later killed. By the latter part of the 20th century, the ranch occupied more land than the entire state of Rhode Island.

By the time of King's death on April 14, 1885, he had accumulated 600,000 acres of land and thousands of cattle and horses. His widow, Henrietta, was determined to continue the success of the ranch. One of her first actions was to make her son-in-law, Robert Justus Kleberg, the ranch's full-time manager. For the next 40 years, this partnership followed the dream of Captain King by using more productive methods of managing the land and the livestock.

Kleberg, an attorney, had come to the attention of Captain King during a case when Kleberg trounced the attorneys who represented King. King hired the young attorney the next day. While becoming more and more involved with the activities of the ranch, Kleberg met and married the Kings' daughter, Alice.

It was their sons, Richard M. "Dick" and Robert Justus Jr. "Bob," who took charge of the ranch in 1916 when their father became too ill to maintain the heavy schedule required to run the huge operation. With the example of their grandfather and father before them, they proceeded to use the most progressive methods available for ranch management.

Dick, who later served in the Congress of the United States, earned a law degree from the University of Texas. Then in 1911 he returned to the ranch to help manage the growing operation.

Bob, however, had completed only 2

Halter and Performance Record: None.

Progeny Record:

Foal Crops: 22   Race Starters: 2
Foals Registered: 116

years of study at the University of Wisconsin School of Agriculture when he was called home in 1916. Among the first tasks assigned to Bob was the continued improvement of the ranch's cattle. But he also turned his attention to improving the ranch's horses. Several Thoroughbred and Standardbred stallions had been used over the years. Some Arabian, Saddlebred, and Morgan stallions also had been placed with broodmare bands who traced back to the mustang stock running on the land when King bought it. Although improved, the horses still didn't meet the standards set by the ranch. They weren't sufficiently sound and hardy, and they weren't even good cow horses.

The Clegg Horses

Ever alert for improved methods or livestock on other ranches, Bob particularly had an eye on the horses coming from the nearby ranch of George Clegg. Clegg's particular pride was a band of

Wimpy, by Old Sorrel's son Solis, earned the right to hold AQHA registration #1 by being named grand champion at the 1941 Fort Worth Stock Show. He was one of the first equine inductees in AQHA's Hall of Fame.

Courtesy of *The Quarter Horse Journal*

broodmares carefully selected for both exceptional looks and ability. These mares, whom he called his "wax dolls," had to have both.

Clegg was equally astute in selecting stallions to breed to those mares. At the beginning of the century, he used Little Rondo, who was sired by Sykes' Rondo. In 1905, Clegg bought the yearling Little Joe by Traveler. After a very successful racing career, Little Joe was put with Clegg's broodmares for several years before being sold to Ott Adams, another neighboring rancher noted for his fast horses.

Next, Clegg turned to the promising young Hickory Bill, a son of the spectacular runner Peter McCue. *Legends, Volume 2* has the complete story of Peter McCue,

who was bred by Samuel Watkins on his Little Grove Stock Farm. Watkins also bred Hickory Bill.

Hickory Bill's dam was Lucretia M, who was sired by The Hero (a Thoroughbred son of Iroquois, out of Ontario, a daughter of the great fountainhead of brilliant speed *Bonnie Scotland). His second dam was another one of Watkins' homebreds named Bird. She was sired by Jack Traveler and was out of Kitty Clyde.

Jack Traveler was a Texas-bred, sired either by Steel Dust (by Harry Bluff) or by a son of Steel Dust. His dam was Queen by Pilgrim (TB). After racing for A.W. Green in Texas, he became the property of Little Grove Stock Farm.

Kitty Clyde was a speedster who was raced from her home state of Kentucky to Texas and back to Illinois, where she eventually was given to Samuel Watkins. According to an early Thoroughbred stud book, which was the precursor to the American Stud Book (of Thoroughbreds), she was sired by Star Davis (TB) and was out of Margravine by the imported Thoroughbred Margrave. She proved to be as

Peppy, a son of Little Richard by Old Sorrel and out of a daughter of Cardinal by Old Sorrel, was an example of the line breeding the King Ranch practiced. Peppy was the King Ranch's first successful show horse. His genes later figured in the pedigree of the great cutting horse Peponita. This photo is the horse's AQHA registration picture.

Courtesy of the American Quarter Horse Heritage Center & Museum, Amarillo, Texas

good a broodmare as she was a runner. In addition to Bird, she was the dam of Nora M—an accomplished half-miler who capped her racing career by producing Peter McCue.

Among Clegg's "wax dolls" were four mares with an unusual background. Dr. Rose was a dentist in Del Rio, Tex., who owned and operated ranches in Mexico. Unsatisfied by the horses in his remudas, Rose went to Kentucky and bought a carload of mares. Turned out on his Mexican ranches, they lost their individual identity, but they and their offspring retained the quality he had been seeking. When the mares proved to be abundant producers, he found it necessary to sell off some horses—including a carload to rancher J.C. McGill, a partner of Clegg in the cattle business.

Clegg spotted four older mares in the group that he thought would fit into his herd. He got them by trading younger, fatter mares for them. One of those matrons, believed by some to be one of the original Kentucky-bred mares, foaled a promising-looking sorrel colt in 1915, sired by Hickory Bill. In the pedigree of the sorrel colt, the mare is listed as a Dr. Rose mare having unknown breeding. That doesn't mean, though, that she didn't contribute her share of superior genes to his makeup.

El Alazan

At Kleberg's suggestion, his cousin Caesar Kleberg went shopping among Clegg's horses that year. Caesar, an excellent judge of horseflesh and active in managing the King Ranch, spotted the powerful looking Dr. Rose mare and her sorrel colt. After some dickering he bought the colt for $125 and borrowed the mare to lead the colt back to the King Ranch.

As this colt matured and developed into an outstanding horse, he was known simply as "The Clegg Horse" to the ranch owners. To the *kinenos*, he was *El Alazan*

Rey Jay, a son of Rey Del Rancho, was best known as a broodmare sire, especially when bred to daughters of Jewel's Leo Bars.

Courtesy of *The Quarter Horse Journal*

Old Sorrel also had two other attributes appreciated by the ranch management.

(Spanish for The Sorrel). As he aged, they modified that name to *El Alazan Viejo* (The Old Sorrel). When he was registered with the AQHA at a ripe old age, he had to be given a name. The decision was made to Anglicize his nickname to Old Sorrel.

The King Ranch has a tradition of requiring their stallions and mares to earn their way into the breeding herd by proving their abilities through regular cattle work on the ranch. Old Sorrel was no exception. Bob Kleberg has written that "Old Sorrel proved to be outstandingly the best cow horse we had ever had on the King Ranch. He was exceptional as to

beauty, disposition, conformation, smoothness of action, and fine handling qualities."

He has added that Old Sorrel was "the best cow horse I ever rode, but he was also a damn good running horse. He had that well-balanced look and the feel of a race horse."

A well-known anecdote illustrates Old Sorrel's versatility and all-around athletic ability. When Mrs. Bob Kleberg became interested in Thoroughbred jumping horses, she had a regulation jumping course built on the ranch. Bob informed her that he had an old cow horse who could take those jumps. So, after tying Old Sorrel's lead shank to his halter, the story relates that Bob rode the 14-year-old stallion bareback over the obstacles, including 4-foot oxers. Evidently Kleberg felt a horse

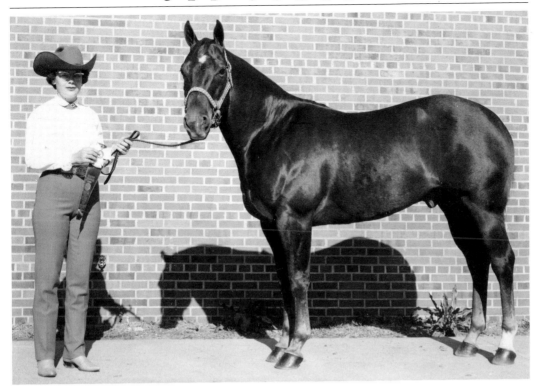

Sonora Sorrel was by Lauro, by Wimpy, and out of a daughter of Old Sorrel. This gelding was one of the all-time leading halter point-earners, winning 198 in 1964.

who could readily jump prickly pear and mesquite as a part of a day's work could handle the artificial barriers on a level surface just as easily.

Old Sorrel also had two other attributes appreciated by the ranch management. First, he had a rich, dark sorrel or chestnut color. Being a recessive characteristic, this sorrel color is easy to breed true. In addition, he had no white on his feet. With the alkaline and sand soils of the ranch, which tend to cause sand burns, it was important to have as little white on the feet as possible.

Dr. J.K. Northway went to work for the King Ranch as a young veterinarian in 1916. His decades of service to the ranch were important factors in the development of the ranch's superior livestock. Northway wrote, "Old Sorrel was a beautiful chestnut horse of medium size and weight. I would say maybe just a little long in the barrel, but otherwise a wonderfully balanced, versatile horse at all times." He stated that Old Sorrel stood about 14.3 and had a wonderful disposition.

"I saw Richard Kleberg and George Clegg rope off him and ride him all morning and then race him in the afternoon,"

Shown here as the grand champion mare at the 1962 Fort Worth Stock Show, Anita Chica was one of the King Ranch's greatest show horses. **Western Horseman** Photo

Gitana Chica was an excellent show mare by Old Sorrel's son Tomate Laureles. T.C. Jinkens is at the mare's lead and Robert Kleberg is accepting the grand champion mare trophy.

Northway stated. "You could rope, cut, or do any other ranch work on him and he was not just adequate—he was superior in all his actions."

The Lazarus Mares

When used for breeding, Old Sorrel's foals were watched and screened carefully. Fifty of the best-handling and best-riding mares on the ranch were selected for Old Sorrel's harem. Mostly mares of considerable Thoroughbred blood, some of these were home-bred, and some were known as "Lazarus mares." Later, mares acquired from George Clegg and Ott Adams were added to the mix when it was discovered that Old Sorrel crossed very well on daughters of Little Joe (the son of Traveler who had been used in both herds).

In a striking parallel to the Dr. Rose mares, the Lazarus mares had been purchased from Sam Lazarus of Fort Worth. Lazarus, president of the Quanah,

Acme, and Pacific Railroad Company, had put together a band of racing Thoroughbreds. When he became disillusioned with racing, he wanted to get out of the business, but find a good home for his horses. In 1910 he wrote and offered them to the King Ranch, but was informed that the ranch didn't need them. When he persisted, Caesar Kleberg again made a major contribution to the ranch's breeding program.

Going to Fort Worth on other business, Caesar decided to have a look at what Lazarus was offering. Impressed with what he found, Caesar decided the ranch might use these horses after all. Lazarus agreed to sell the horses for $100 apiece if the King Ranch agreed to two unusual stipulations. The new owners were not to race any of the horses or make known to the public the pedigrees of any of these well-bred horses.

Among them was a stallion named Martin's Best. Northway recalled that Bob Kleberg believed that this horse was "probably the best in conformation and type of the early foundation Thorough-

18

Babe Grande, a 1928 foal, traced top and bottom to Hickory Bill. His sire, Old Sorrel, was by Hickory Bill, and his dam was a Dr. Lawrence mare by the Strickland Horse by Hickory Bill. This is the horse's registration photo.

Courtesy of the American Quarter Horse Heritage Center & Museum, Amarillo, Texas

breds that went into the great family of the Old Sorrel horses." His daughters were particularly productive additions to the broodmare band placed with Old Sorrel.

From the geldings in his first crop, two were carefully selected for the task of proving Old Sorrel's ability to sire horses capable of meeting the ranch's standards for cattle work. One of these was named Tino (not to be confused with his stallion full brother, also named Tino). Tino, the gelding, was produced by Brisa, a daughter of Martin's Best who had been Bob's favorite mount until she was put in the broodmare band. The other gelding was called Melon.

Tino then was ridden by Bob Kleberg and Melon by Lauro Cavazos, an exceptional horseman who was a foreman of the ranch at the time. These two riders tried those two geldings on every kind of work needed on the ranch and competed with each other in trying to prove his mount was the better of the two. Both geldings came through with excellent results and gave great hope for the prospects of Old Sorrel as a sire.

Bob Kleberg, with his knowledge of genetics learned at the University of Wisconsin and practical experience on the ranch, felt it was possible and necessary to preserve Old Sorrel's attributes through future generations. He and the geneticist A.O. Rhoad wrote in *The Journal of Heredity*, "Having seen other stallions, even after they had proven their merits for breeding, carry on for only one generation, we determined, if possible, to perpetuate the wonderful qualities of this stallion."

Typical of the King Ranch's progressive methods, one of the first steps was to round up 1,200 head of undesirable mares, geldings, and jacks and ship them across the river into Mexico. Northway reported that "We didn't get anything back, but I believe it was the best day's work we ever did." Room had been made for the horses of the future.

Old Sorrel was first bred to the best of his daughters from the original 50 mares. The ranch found these foals to be encouraging, but not exceptional.

A decision was made to practice less intense line breeding by breeding Old Sorrel's daughters to his sons and also breed the sons' daughters to other sons. This

Old Sorrel was first bred to the best of his daughters from the original 50 mares.

Macanudo resembled his sire more than any other son. Foaled in 1934, he was another double-bred Hickory Bill. He was sired by Old Sorrel by Hickory Bill and was out of Canales Bell. This photo was used for Macanudo's AQHA registration.

Courtesy of the American Quarter Horse Heritage Center & Museum, Amarillo, Texas

plan immediately began producing foals who not only were good performers but also maintained the type and other fine qualities of Old Sorrel.

From Old Sorrel's first crop in 1922 only one son was kept as a stallion. This was Little Richard, who later sired Peppy and other fine horses. Because of these fine contributions to the breed, the AQHA gave Little Richard the registration number 17. This was one of 18 numbers reserved for outstanding foundation sires. Little Richard was mated with the ranch mares from 1927 until 1937.

From the second crop (1923) came two more top-quality stallions, Solis and Cardinal (sometimes spelled Cardenal). After proving themselves under saddle, they joined the stallion battery in the long-range program.

Cardinal and Peppy

Though they were very similar in type, Cardinal had better handling abilities than Little Richard, but in disposition he wasn't as even-tempered, and he wasn't as big. An attempt was made to combine their attributes by mating each of them with daughters of the other. This paid off when Little Richard sired Peppy from a daughter of Cardinal in 1934.

Peppy was the first horse to be exhibited extensively by the King Ranch. It was reported that Peppy stood slightly more than 15 hands and weighed about 1,200 pounds. Shown throughout the Southwest from 1936 until 1941, Peppy successfully promoted both the King Ranch horses and the Quarter Horse breed.

In 1940, Peppy was the grand champion at both Fort Worth and Beeville. In 1941, he was judged champion stallion, champion cow-horse type, and best horse in show at

Because of his bay color, Silver King was not a desirable breeding prospect for the King Ranch sorrel herd. He was sold, and his owner at the time this photo was taken was Percy Turner of Water Valley, Texas. Silver King sired many good running and performance horses and was the great grandsire of the great Two Eyed Jack.

From *The American Quarter Horse Association Stud Book and Registry, Vol. 1, Number 1, 1941.*

Tucson, Arizona. In addition, he had worked a quarter-mile in 22.2 seconds.

Peppy sired some of the finest horses ever produced on the ranch. Two of his early show winners were Peppy Jr. and Rosal. Peppy Jr. later sired Pepper Girl, the second dam of the spectacular cutting horse Peponita. The winner of two NCHA world championships, Peponita also won two AQHA world championships in cutting.

Later, Peppy's show-winning offspring were led by the AQHA Champion Peppy's Pokey. This son of Peppy also sired arena ROM qualifiers after his own show career.

Peppy's son Cuero became an important sire in California. He sired many working horses, including ROM-qualifiers, while his daughters added AQHA Champions and racing ROM foals as well as more arena ROM performers to the family.

Another son of Peppy who left the ranch but became an important sire in other hands was Tamo. The versatile Tamo sired racing ROM-qualifiers, working ROM performers, and halter champions.

His daughters later were to make him a leading sire of AQHA Champions.

Solis and Wimpy

Although he wasn't used for breeding until a couple of years after Cardinal, Solis probably had an even more important effect on the King Ranch horses. He proved to be an important contributor to the line-breeding program by siring outstanding horses from daughters of Old Sorrel. One of these double-bred foals was the great Wimpy.

Wimpy quickly gained fame by being named grand champion stallion at the 1941 Fort Worth Stock Show. The AQHA had agreed to hold registration number 1 for the stallion who won that show. Wimpy then went on to prove that the number had

The King Ranch won a produce-of-dam class with two sons of Water Lilly, both sired by Old Sorrel. Hired Hand is on the far left and Little Man is in the foreground with Loyd Jinkens at his lead.

Photo by Neal Lyons, Courtesy of *The Quarter Horse Journal*

been given to a truly worthy individual.

His reputation was acknowledged by the AQHA when Wimpy was one of the four inductees the first year horses were added to its Hall of Fame. Old Sorrel was added to that roster the following year, 1990.

Bred to daughters of Old Sorrel, Wimpy got such foals as Wimpy II, Lauro, Bill Cody, and Silver Wimpy (sire of the brilliant Marion's Girl, the 1954 and 1956 NCHA World Champion Cutting Horse). Another son who became a leading sire was Showdown. Wimpy's son Kip Mac was an early AQHA Champion.

Taken to Oklahoma and bred to John Dawson's intensely Missouri Mike-bred mares, Wimpy II became a leading sire and leading maternal grandsire of AQHA Champions. His get also included two racing ROM foals. In addition he sired

Wimpy III, who also was to become another leading sire and leading maternal grandsire of AQHA Champions.

Lauro also left the King Ranch before establishing his considerable reputation. Settled in west Texas, Lauro sired several AQHA Champions, including Sonora Sorrel and Sonora Monkey. During a career that made him one of the all-time leading halter-point winners, Sonora Sorrel earned 198 points in 1964 to be named Honor Roll halter horse. In 1959, Sonora Monkey was both the Honor Roll calf roping horse and reining horse.

The record books also show that Lauro was listed as both the paternal grandsire and the maternal grandsire of the mare Revision. This mare was the dam of Pass Over, the brilliant Champion Quarter Running 2-Year-Old Filly of 1973 and Champion Quarter Running 3-Year-Old

The broodmare Water Lilly gave the King Ranch two of its best Old Sorrel sons, Little Man and Hired Hand.

Filly of 1974 who earned more than a half-million dollars.

For additional information about Wimpy and his family, see *Legends, Volume 1*.

Ranchero and Rey Del Rancho

According to Bob Kleberg, the other major contribution made by Solis came when he sired Ranchero from an Old Sorrel mare. Ranchero was a favorite of the foreman Lauro Cavazos, who got his knowledge of the ranch's horses from actually working them on the ranch.

Ranchero's tradition was carried on by his son Rey Del Rancho. This younger stallion, who had five crosses to Old Sorrel in the first four generations, was out of a Babe Grande mare. He became a favorite of Dick Kleberg Jr. and the cowboys on the ranch. They appreciated the early speed and intelligence of his foals. Bob, however, was not as fond of the horse because of his smaller size. He described Rey Del Rancho as a "well-balanced horse that stood 14.3 hands, but light behind; a trim horse that was very quick."

Rey Del Rancho left his mark in the breeding herd through both his daughters and sons. He was the sire of Anita Chica, one of the greatest show horses campaigned by the King Ranch. In turn, she produced the ROM-qualifier and NCHA money-winner El Pobre. Used extensively in the ranch breeding ranks, El Pobre proved to be quite successful.

Among the influential sons of Rey Del Rancho were Callan's Man (an NCHA top 10 horse and sire of the good cutter Mr Linton) and El Rey Rojo , sire of El Bandido Rojo, a top show horse until his untimely death at 3 in a fire.

Another major contribution to the reputation of Rey Del Rancho as possibly the best King Ranch progenitor of cutting horses was made by his son Rey Jay (one of Rey Del Rancho's three AQHA Champions). The sire of good performers himself, Rey Jay became best known when his daughters were bred to Jewel's Leo Bars, better known as Freckles. The resulting foals included such stars as

Another major contribution to the reputation of Rey Del Rancho as possibly the best King Ranch progenitor of cutting horses was made by his son Rey Jay.

Hired Hand is generally considered to be Old Sorrel's best son. Loyd Jinkens is the handler.

Courtesy of *The Quarter Horse Journal*

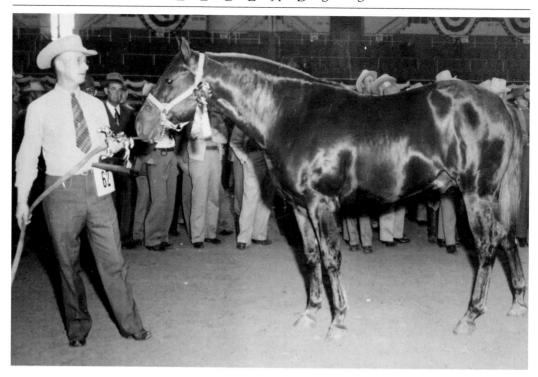

Colonel Freckles, Freckles Playboy, and Freckles Hustler.

Tomate Laureles

From Old Sorrel's 1927 crop came the fine stallion Tomate Laureles. Robert Denhardt wrote that Tomate Laureles was "unexcelled as a producer of female stock." For instance, one of his daughters was the dam of the highly acclaimed show mare Gitana Chica. For his siring abilities, the AQHA awarded Tomate Laureles with the foundation sire registration number 19.

In 1928, Old Sorrel had another outstanding foal, named Babe Grande, out of a Hickory Bill mare. Babe Grande, as well as his sons and daughters, were exceptional for their cow sense and action. His daughters produced both Saltillo and Rey Del Rancho. Saltillo sired the very capable cutting mare Alice Star.

Among Babe Grande's top foals was the stallion Brown Ceasar. His name appears in the pedigrees of horses prominent in both racing and shows. His ROM running

daughter Lassie Caesar produced the famous runner Blonde Joan (the 1957 Champion Quarter Running Filly and dam of the race horse Brigand).

In 1932, the talented mare Brisa produced another Old Sorrel son named Tino. This Tino, however, was left a stallion and proved to be exceptionally prepotent. Something of an oddity in the King Ranch herd, Tino was a bay. Northway has reported that Tino "became a wonderful individual" and was "certainly an intelligent individual" with plenty of size.

Macanudo

The great Macanudo was from the 1934 Old Sorrel crop. He was out of the Hickory Bill and Texas Chief-bred mare Canales Bell. It was said that Macanudo looked more like his sire than any other son of the old horse, and may have been the best cow horse from that generation. Macanudo's conformation made him the grand champion stallion at the 1940 South Texas Livestock Show.

Macanudo's combination of ability and conformation was passed on to his son Babe Mac C, one of the earliest AQHA Champions. Babe Mac C continued the line by siring four AQHA Cham-

Wax Doll, by Hired Hand's Cardinal, was a top reining and halter mare. The information on the back of this photo says she was the grand champion mare at Columbus, Ohio, in 1960, and she was owned by Eddie Porath, Northville, Michigan.

Photo by Don and Pearl Stickney, Courtesy of *The Quarter Horse Journal*

pions and several working ROM foals. Macanudo also demonstrated considerable early speed.

Kingwood was another son of Macanudo who helped prove that King Ranch blood could have a beneficial influence even when taken off the ranch. Bred to mares with all kinds of pedigrees, Kingwood sired horses with conformation, with working ability (two ROM), and with speed (fourteen ROM). His AA daughter Old Folks produced seven ROM runners, including Klondike (AAA) and Tonto's Time (AAA and sire of AAA).

Silver King and Water Lily

Old Sorrel's son Silver King was foaled in 1937. Possibly because of his color, which was bay rather than the King Ranch uniform chestnut, this notable individual was allowed to leave the King Ranch. Silver King sired a large number of both

running and working horses, including the AQHA Champion Baldy Silver.

Silver King's sons further enhanced the family reputation. Possibly the best known was the ROM racer Double Diamond, who sired the AQHA Champion Two D Two and other ROM working horses.

Two D Two gained immortality by siring the great Two Eyed Jack, an AQHA Champion and all-time leading sire of AQHA Champions. Two D Two also sired Tookie's Two, the 1967 Honor Roll Reining Horse.

Silver King's daughters also did their share. They produced many well-known horses—including AQHA Champion Eternal Sun and AAA racers Mr Magic Bar, Sugar Nicky, and the stakes-winning Miss Davril.

Water Lilly was said to be the best mare on the King Ranch by the time the AQHA

Hand was the grand champion stallion and Little Man was named reserve champion. In 1942, Water Lilly's Chicaro-sired daughter, Delicatesa De Texas, produced Tejano, another son of Old Sorrel who was to sire many good horses for the King Ranch remuda.

Hired Hand

With the aid of Water Lilly, Old Sorrel had sired, at the end of his breeding career, what many people believe was his greatest son, Hired Hand. Dr. Northway described Hired Hand as being about 15 hands, well-balanced, and wonderfully muscled in his forearms and hindquarters, with good, straight hind legs. He went on to state that Hired Hand came equipped with a particularly good disposition and temperament and could do anything that was desirable of an all-around Quarter Horse.

Hired Hand was just as good in the breeding herd. For example, though only 32 of his foals were exhibited in AQHA-recognized shows, 3 earned their AQHA Championships. He and his foals were so exceptional that the decision was made to build the ranch's entire breeding program around him. This was done by using him in a program very similar to the one designed for Old Sorrel.

First, Hired Hand was mated with mares who were several generations removed from Old Sorrel. These foals and their descendants then were crossed among themselves in such a way as to concentrate the blood of Hired Hand and perpetuate his type and abilities.

Among Hired Hand's many successful show horses were the AQHA Champions H H Dee, Henry's Bullet, and Strawboss T. In addition, Fistful and Strawboss T were named Superior performance horses.

Some of Hired Hand's sons used successfully in the ranch's program were King Hand, Hired Hand's Cardinal, El Shelton, Tipo De Norias, and Hired Hand II.

Based on the records of his foals, Hired Hand's Cardinal must be judged one of the best in this group of outstanding horses. Out of a daughter of Peppy, Hired Hand's Cardinal added luster to both branches of the family.

Among the noted foals of Hired Hand's

Strawboss T. was one of Hired Hand's AQHA Champions. He is shown here after winning a cutting.   **Photo by Al Roth**

was formed. This mare was shown in pedigrees to be a daughter of the Waggoner Ranch's Yellow Jacket, but some claimed that she was actually a daughter of Peter McCue's son Buck Thomas.

Water Lilly lived up to her reputation by producing the good stallion Little Man in 1941 and the great stallion Hired Hand in 1943. Both were sons of Old Sorrel and both were top show horses. At the 1948 State Fair of Texas, for instance, Hired

Cardinal was the AQHA Superior cutting horse Chick Jay. With a grand total of more than 250 points in AQHA events, Chick Jay also was an AQHA Champion.

Two top performing daughters of Hired Hand's Cardinal proved that his talents weren't passed only to his sons. His filly Wax Doll was the 1962 AQHA High-Point Reining Mare and also earned a Superior in halter. The superb cutting mare Laura Felicis was the 1976 AQHA World Champion Junior Cutting Horse and the 1977 AQHA Reserve World Champion Senior Cutting Horse.

Pep Up

In the early 1940s, the Waggoner Ranch of Vernon, Tex., bought two young stallion prospects from the King Ranch. One was sired by Macanudo and the other was a son of Peppy named Pep Up. Years later, after the horse known to the Waggoner Ranch as Pep Up had become a highly successful sire, testimony was received by the AQHA that in the shipping of the two youngsters and their arrival in a rainstorm, their identities had been switched.

In those days before widespread blood or DNA testing, the association had to make a judgment based on the facts at hand. After due deliberation, it was decided to switch the breeding of the two stallions. So, the official records were changed to show that Pep Up was a son of Macanudo and the other horse was listed as the son of Peppy. In either case, of course, Pep Up was strong in the blood of Old Sorrel.

Although Pep Up sired many capable foals, his primary fame has come as a broodmare sire. Through such daughters as Shady Dell, producer of five AQHA Champions including Poco Dell and Peppy Belle, Pep Up will live in Quarter Horse history, regardless of his actual parentage. Peppy Belle earned her acclaim as dam of two of the greatest names in the cutting horse field, Peppy San and Mr. San Peppy.

Peppy San was not a King Ranch horse, but has helped continue the reputation of this family. Two of his outstanding foals,

Peppy's Desire and Chunky's Monkey, were both out of the world champion Stardust Desire. Since she was sired by Stardust Red, by Macanudo Jr, these two cutters had two crosses to Macanudo.

Mr. San Peppy won the 1972 NCHA Derby and then was named NCHA open world champion in both 1974 and 1976. He was the first horse to win, in 1976, both the NCHA title and the AQHA world championship in cutting. The first horse to win $100,000 in open cutting horse events, Mr. San Peppy was the youngest horse ever to be inducted into the NCHA Hall of Fame.

The King Ranch first leased this great competitor and then bought him to add to its stallion battery. In this way the ranch brought in some outside blood, but through a horse who had a direct link to Old Sorrel.

As a sire, Mr. San Peppy was equally as dominant. Among his foals were the 1976 AQHA Reserve World Champion Junior Cutting Horse, Beats Workin; 1982 NCHA World Champion Cutting Horse Tenino San; and NCHA Super Stakes Reserve Champion Miss Peppy Also.

Mr. San Peppy also sired the noted Peppy San Badger (best known as Little Peppy). An NCHA Hall of Fame member, Peppy San Badger won the 1977 NCHA Futurity, the 1978 NCHA Derby, and became the 1980 NCHA Reserve World Champion. Bred by Joe Kirk Fulton of Lubbock, Tex., Peppy San Badger also was acquired by the King Ranch to add to the ranch's dynasty. He, too, became an eminent sire of cutting horses.

So, the blood of Old Sorrel lives on. Every new generation finds more talented horses who can trace back to this immortal horse, who died at age 31 in July 1946.

3 FLYING BOB

By Jim Goodhue

He was not only a great race horse, but also sired many successful speedsters.

A PORTION OF Louisiana has been designated officially as Acadiana—in honor of the Acadian people of French ancestry who settled there in southern Louisiana when they were forced to leave their homes in Nova Scotia—but it is best known as Cajun Country. Derived from Acadian, of course, the word Cajun has come to stand for good food, dance-provoking music, a charming people with a soft-spoken dialect, hospitality, and fast horses.

This story may have begun when those last two attributes came together one day near the end of the 1890s. The Cajuns say that on that occasion, a stranger traveling west stopped at the home of Francois Abadie near Carencro. He offered to breed two mares to the fine-looking stallion he had hitched to his wagon in payment for accommodations for himself and his horses.

Quickly, Abadie located two mares who were in the mood. Of the two mares who took part in this exchange, one belonged to his friend Aurelien Brasseaux. In due course, Brasseaux's mare produced a male foal who was named Dewey. When Dewey became well-known in the racing

Jack Randle, shown here with Flying Bob, said the stallion was big, strong, beautifully built, kind, gentle, and intelligent.

Photo Courtesy of *The Quarter Horse Journal*

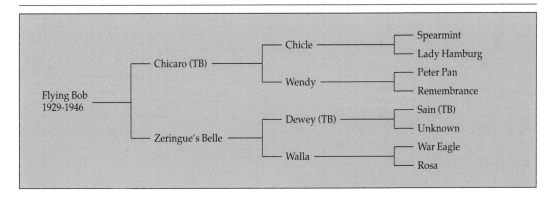

```
                                                    ┌─── Spearmint
                                      ┌─── Chicle ───┤
                                      │              └─── Lady Hamburg
                   ┌─── Chicaro (TB) ─┤
                   │                  │              ┌─── Peter Pan
                   │                  └─── Wendy ────┤
Flying Bob ────────┤                                 └─── Remembrance
1929-1946          │                                ┌─── Sain (TB)
                   │                  ┌─── Dewey (TB)┤
                   │                  │              └─── Unknown
                   └─ Zeringue's Belle ┤
                                      │              ┌─── War Eagle
                                      └─── Walla ────┤
                                                     └─── Rosa
```

circles of Cajun Country, people in that area began referring to his mysterious sire as Sain, which roughly means brownish.

The young Dewey received no special attention. It is believed that, when he reached maturity, he was ridden and hitched to a wagon and used in everyday chores just like any other stallion of his time.

Cajun horsemen were known then, as now, as skilled trainers and producers of short-distance speed and were also known for breeding some of the sturdiest and fastest Quarter Horses known to racing. So, even everyday activities would include some relationship to speed. When Cajun-bred sprinters dominated Quarter Horse racing all the way to the West Coast throughout the 1930s and 1940s, it was because short-distance racing had been a strong part of the culture for many decades.

In *Foundation Sires of the American Quarter Horse*, though, Robert M. Denhardt recorded a less romantic (though equally exciting) account of Dewey. Denhardt believed that Dewey was a registered Thoroughbred sired by the imported Sain, a son of St. Serf, and was out of a mare with the unusual name of Sister To Uncle Bob. She was by Luke Blackburn. Denhardt was told that Dewey was brought to Louisiana by a traveling racehorse man to run against the fast mare Louisiana Girl. After defeating her, Dewey was sold to the mare's owners who, like all good Cajun breeders, were ever alert for an opportunity to improve the speed of their horses.

In either case, it was only natural that some of Dewey's offspring were tried at sprinting matches (as might be expected in

Halter and Performance Record: None.

Progeny Record:

Foal Crops: 12	Race Starters: 55
Foals Registered: 125	Race Money Earned: $26,239
Halter Point-Earners: 1	Race Registers of Merit: 36
Halter Points Earned: 2	Race World Champions: 3
Leading Race Money-Earner: Diamond Bob ($3,697)	

a region that sported so many small, straightaway tracks). Their speed soon caused the Cajun community to look on Dewey as something special. A gelding named Currency and a mare we have come to know as Zeringue's Belle were two of the fastest and best-known foals by Dewey, but they certainly weren't his only claim to fame.

Zeringue's Belle was the pride and joy of Noah Zeringue, who farmed sugar cane near the town of Erath. Zeringue supplemented his meager farm income with the money he made as a farrier and as the owner of a consistently good race mare. This mare, Zeringue's Belle, is said to have won 24 of her 27 matches, run 2 dead heats, and lost only 1 race.

The big Fair Grounds Race Track in New Orleans was a different matter from the short straightaways, which seem to have sprouted near every community in the region. Some of the finest horses from

Queenie, by Flying Bob and out of Little Sis, was a three-time world champion on the track. The information on the back of this photo gives the jockey as F. Figueroa and the owner as J. R. Jelko.

Photo by James M. Leinenkugel, Courtesy of *The Quarter Horse Journal*

all over the country competed at the Fair Grounds on the large oval track. Fortunately, racing season at the Fair Grounds was a slack time for sugar cane farmers, so Zeringue was able to put his farrier skills to use at the big course.

At a meet there in 1927, Zeringue was called on to set the racing plates for a superb-looking Thoroughbred stallion named Chicaro. This 4-year-old's breeding was as outstanding as his appearance. He was sired by the very successful imported stallion Chicle, who was a son of the immortal Spearmint; and was out of Wendy, by Peter Pan, a son of Commando, who was noted as a progenitor of brilliant sprinters.

Chicaro had raced successfully on tracks in the eastern United States before he started having problems. These included what was believed to be a throat

restriction, and he had undergone an operation for that condition. He was attempting a comeback at the Fair Grounds. A disappointing out in his first race quickly put an end to the hopes for more glory on the racecourse.

Encouraged rather than discouraged, Zeringue knew that a race horse who couldn't run was not a hot commodity. He felt that the background of Chicaro was sufficient to warrant a chance at stud, and so he approached the bay stallion's owner, Bob Carter, with a proposition.

The idea was that Chicaro should be put at stud so he could still show the worth of his bloodlines and previously demonstrated abilities. Carter agreed with Zeringue's reasoning and an arrangement was reached to put Chicaro in the hands of Paulenare Broussard, a retired black racehorse trainer who had settled at the small community of Nunez.

In another version of the story, Denhardt reported that Chicaro was owned by John Dial of Goliad, Texas. In this version,

Queenie proved that great race mares could also become great broodmares. After her illustrious career on the track, she produced eight foals who qualified for the Racing Register of Merit.

Photo from *Great Moments in Quarter Racing History,* **by Nelson C. Nye**

strongly reminiscent of the story about Sain covering a Brasseaux mare to get Dewey, Denhardt wrote that when Dial took Chicaro from New Orleans to Goliad, they spent the night in Abbeville. Zeringue's Belle was mated with the Thoroughbred stallion that night.

Zeringue's Belle was among the first of the many good Cajun mares taken to Chicaro. As often happens when mares are raced extensively, however, it was said in the Cajun version that she had some problem getting in foal. Finally, she produced a fine-looking bay colt on June 12, 1929. The colt was called Bob in honor of Chicaro's owner.

He was originally registered with The Jockey Club as a Thoroughbred by the name of Royal Bob and raced under that name as a 2-year-old. His dam was listed as Erath Queen. Later, it became public knowledge that he was a son of Zeringue's Belle.

Unlike the one version of Dewey's history, the young Bob got plenty of attention. He got all of the milk one cow could produce and frequent grooming. Bob was sent to the races at 18 months and immediately proved his worth against horses near his own age. Soon he was matched with a

mature horse and again was the winner. Jack Hebert, the owner of this older horse, is said to have been so impressed with the youngster that he told Zeringue, "Your colt had to be flying." With that, his name became Flying Bob.

Although the young horse did not race in official races after his 2-year-old year, Cajun legend has it that Flying Bob did not stop his sprinting career there. He kept on winning races and mare owners began clamoring to breed their good race mares to him. So, for the next 13 years, Flying Bob had two successful careers—as a winning matched-race sprinter and as a sire of running foals. The foals, too, showed brilliant speed and caused him to become even more admired.

This thriving stud career prompted Zeringue to build a horse trailer, a novelty in those days, to carry the popular stallion to many of the best mares in the region. Flying Bob became so sought-after that his

Flying Bob became so sought-after that his owner eventually raised his stud fee to $25—or $25 worth of livestock!

31

*Joe Queen was as good-
looking as he was fast. His
dam was Queenie, a daugh-
ter of Flying Bob, and his
sire was the famous Joe
Reed 2. Joe Queen was a
stakes winner on the track
before becoming a highly
successful sire.*

Photo by Darol Dickinson

owner eventually raised his stud fee to
$25—or $25 worth of livestock!

This dual career brought about an
unusual race that turned out to be a loss
for the stallion, but a gain for his owner.
Zeringue matched Flying Bob against Joe
Dugas' famous mare Black Annie in a race
that was won by the mare. Dugas wanted
to make a broodmare of Black Annie,
sometimes known in Cajun country as La
Negress, and he was so impressed with
Flying Bob that he chose him to be her first
suitor. According to reports, the owners

then agreed that in place of a stud fee they
would make a sporting arrangement over
the resulting foal. If it turned out to be a
male, Dugas would keep it for 6 months
and then sell it to Zeringue for $200. If it
was a filly, Dugas would retain ownership
and no money would change hands.

The foal was a colt who was named Bob
Jr. and became the property of Zeringue
after the stipulated 6 months. Bob Jr.
became well-known to the racing industry
and added further distinction to the growing legend of Flying Bob.

According to F.S. LeBlanc in his excellent book, *Cajun-Bred Running Horses*,
Flying Bob was still running against top
competitors at the age of 15. At that time,
he was matched against Bow Way, a
highly successful sprinting Thoroughbred.

"DEE DEE"
A.Q.H.A. # 2512
SIRE: FLYING BOB ... DAM: EMERGENCY
LS WORLD CHAMPION QUARTER RUNNING STALLION

Dee Dee, a son of Flying Bob, was indeed the 1945 World Champion Quarter Running Stallion, but his dam was not Emergency as the information on the front of this picture says. According to the AQHA Stud Book, his dam was Sis, a mare by Doc Horn (TB).

Photo Courtesy of *The Quarter Horse Journal*

The race was run at St. Martinville over a distance of 10½ arpents, a rather long race for the Quarter-bred race horses of Cajun Country. (An arpent is a French measurement roughly 192 feet. Flying Bob's previously mentioned match with Black Annie was at 4 arpents, for instance.) This recollection holds that Flying Bob won the race before a large crowd and took his final bow on the track.

LeBlanc also stated that in 1944, Bob Randle of Richmond, Tex., convinced Zeringue that Flying Bob would have even more opportunities at stud if the Texan could buy the horse and take him back to his family's Huisache Ranch. Largely because of Zeringue's desire to enhance the horse's contribution to racing, he agreed to the sale.

However, an article in the September 1947 issue of *The Quarter Horse by the National Quarter Horse Breeders Association* reported that the Randle family bought Flying Bob in October 1942, after spending several years driving back and forth to Abbeville, La., trying to make the

purchase. The closest they had come was in 1940 when Zeringue agreed to a sale but changed his mind before money could be put up. They had to settle, though, for his definite promise that if he ever sold Flying Bob, it would be to them. He kept the promise, and the horse changed hands, according to this version, in October of 1942.

Though not entirely conclusive, the official records show that Flying Bob's foals of 1944 and 1945 were primarily bred by Texans. Of course, some of these Texans had been known to haul mares to Louisiana to mate with Flying Bob in previous years.

Jack Randle recalled that Flying Bob was a big, strong, beautifully built horse who

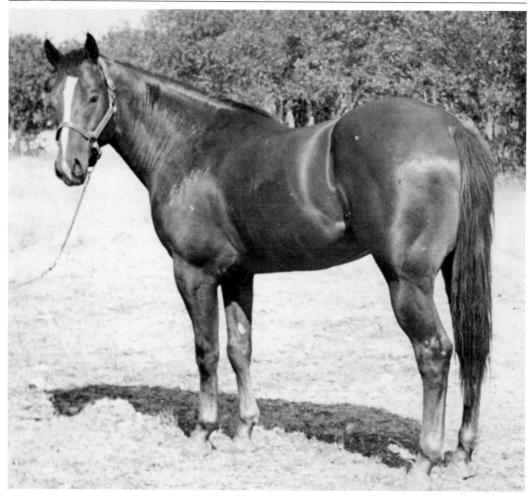

Diamond Bob (by Flying Bob and out of Escoba) was the 1949 World Champion Quarter Running Stallion.

Not only Flying Bob, but his sons and daughters also were producing top-caliber speedsters.

was kind, gentle, and intelligent. Other sources elaborated that he stood 15.1 hands and weighed about 1,100 pounds. The old stallion died on February 18, 1946, and was buried at the Huisache Ranch.

By the time the American Quarter Racing Association was formed (February 1945) and published its first official *Year Book* (dated 1945), the Flying Bob horses were well established as track-burners. Not only Flying Bob, but his sons and daughters also were producing top-caliber speedsters.

That first year book listed Lady Lee, sired by Flying Bob's son Babe Ruth, as a

recognized track record-holder. Flying Bob's own foals who held track records at that time were Queenie, Dee Dee, Punkin, Effie B, and Billie Too. Flying Bob was already acclaimed as the leading sire of racing Register of Merit-qualifiers.

No world champion was named for the 1944-45 racing season. Instead, Flying Bob was given recognition as the sire of both Dee Dee, champion Quarter running stallion for the season, and Queenie, champion Quarter running mare. Since Dee Dee and Queenie both were out of mares who traced quickly to Dedier (also known from the Cajun pronunciation of his name as Old DJ), perhaps that illustrious sire of broodmares should have been singled out for attention too.

In the following season, Queenie was named as the world champion Quarter

running horse and, of course, won the mare championship.

Although recognized Quarter Horse racing was not organized until late in Flying Bob's life, he sired a total of 36 Register of Merit-qualifiers (all in racing). The official records of the AQHA show that his 55 starters earned a total of $26,239. This does not include money from those earliest days of Quarter Horse racing before the AQRA was absorbed into the AQHA (1949). Although the AQRA was not formed until 1945, it kept records of recognized races going back to 1940, based on the files of the Southern Arizona Horse Breeders Association.

Included among Flying Bob's later foals were such outstanding race horses as Diamond Bob (champion stallion for 1949), Mayflower W, Bay Annie A, Mayfly, Shu Shu Baby Doll, and Bob E.

The illustrious Queenie, a foal of 1937, won 10 times and had 6 thirds in her 16 official starts. These included a win in the World Championship Quarter at the Rillito Track. She beat such good horses as Squaw H, Jeep B, and Blackout despite the fact that she was handicapped. Her right front foot was badly deformed because she was stepped on as a foal by her dam, the unregistered Little Sis. The old injury

Bay Annie A, a 1941 daughter of Flying Bob out of Fannie, never ran slower than third in her 45 races. She earned a racing ROM and so did three of her foals.

Photo Courtesy of *The Quarter Horse Journal*

was said to pain Queenie noticeably after every race.

It was expected that Queenie would win the title of world champion in 1944-45 as well as champion mare until she was defeated by Dee Dee in a matched race. The outcome of that race may have been affected by her gate opening early by mistake. She ran about 300 yards before she could be brought back to run the actual race.

Then Queenie upset the theory that great race mares cannot become great broodmares. She consistently produced outstanding offspring. Eight of her foals qualified for the racing ROM.

Queenie's most noted son was Rukin String, the 1953 World Champion Stallion and World Champion 2-Year-Old Colt of 1952. A multiple stakes winner and track record-holder, he earned $21,894 from the small purses available then. Rukin String continued the glory of the bloodline by becoming an important sire.

Joe Queen was a stakes-winning son of Queenie and a track record-holder before his successful career as a sire. The gelding Gunny Sack was another stakes-winner.

Queenie's fillies, Queen O' Clubs J (later a valuable producer) and Miss Queenie, placed in important futurities at Rillito and Los Alamitos. Queenie's other ROM speedsters were Bond Issue, Alliance, and Little Queeny.

Dee Dee, foaled in 1939, outran such horses as Jeep B, Chester C, and Noo Music, as well as Queenie during his campaign for the stallion championship. His track records were earned at 440 yards (Corona, Calif.) and 300 yards (Rillito). He displayed further versatility by beating Idleen at 220 yards. The *AQRA Year Book* reports that Dee Dee contested five races that season, including the Pacific Coast Championship, and won them all.

At stud, Dee Dee continued his success. As late as 1963, he figured among the leading sires of money-earning runners with earnings of more than $83,000. He crowned his breeding career by siring the famed "gray ghost," Bart B.S.

Bart B.S., a foal of 1947, was a crowd-pleasing speedster who often came from behind to win. Never out of the money, he won 12 of his 15 official starts. Bart B.S., like his sire, seemed to win at any distance and under any weight. These wins were over such noted horses as Savannah G, Clabbertown G, War Star, Clabber II, and Black Easter Bunny. For his efforts, he was acclaimed Co-Champion Quarter Running Stallion of 1951.

In the breeding pen, too, Bart B.S. added even more to his family's reputation. Among his many ROM-qualifiers, top AAA, and AAA race horses were plentiful. Bart B.S. soon joined Dee Dee on this list of leading sires of money-earners and stayed there for many years. His starters accumulated more than $121,000.

Bart B.S.'s daughter Fiance upheld the family honor. She is the second dam of the excellent runner and sire Ichibon.

Flying Bob's track record-holding daughter, Effie B, was first, second, or third in each of her five official starts. As a broodmare, Effie B produced three ROM-qualifiers, including notable producing daughters Bit (stakes-placed) and Piggy Wiggy (dam of the good sire Wiggy Bar).

Flying Bob's son Diamond Bob equaled a 440-yard track record and placed in three stakes (all at 440 yards). As a 3-year-old in 1949, he won four of his nine races and was in the money three other times. Diamond Bob was racing against and beating such horses as Maddon's Bright Eyes, Stymie, and Little Sister W. For his efforts, he was named

Flying Bob's track record-holding daughter, Effie B, was first, second, or third in each of her five official starts.

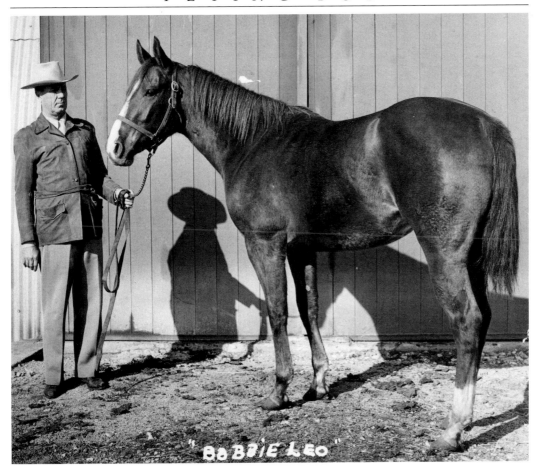

"BOBBIE LEO"

Bobbie Leo was out of Frye's Breeze, an unraced daughter of Flying Bob who became one of his best-producing get. Bobbie Leo, who was by the famed race horse and sire Leo, was named the 1954 World Champion 2-Year-Old Filly. She earned a speed index of 100 and was stakes-placed at five distances from 300 to 440 yards.

Photo Courtesy of *The Quarter Horse Journal*

1949 Champion Quarter Running Stallion. He later proved to be a capable sire.

Bob E by Flying Bob not only qualified for the racing ROM, he twice equaled the 220-yard track record at Vessels Race Track.

Another son, Flying Bob Jr, was not raced in recognized races, but proved his royal blood by siring some very capable runners. His early ROM get include the stakes-placed Danger Boy C, as well as Jim Bob, Teejo, and Doc.

Other sons of Flying Bob, who proved very early that Flying Bob was a sire of sires, include Bob Randle (sire of Little Sis), Jimmy (sire of Pep), and Bob KK.

Breezing Bobby placed second in her only official race, but proved to be one of Flying Bob's best-producing daughters. She was the dam of the stakes winners Breezing Johnny and Bobby Dial. Her stakes-placed son Bar None Bob set a track record at La Mesa Park and went on to become a popular sire of winning sprinters.

Another lightly raced daughter, Rosedale, qualified for the ROM with only two starts. As a broodmare, she also proved to be top-notch. She was the dam of Mackay Boy, a stakes winner and then an important sire. Her stakes-placed foals were Mackay Jimmie and Jay Joe II. Rosedale's other ROM-qualifier was Black Dale, winner of some $10,000 in 1950, a considerable sum back then.

The excellently conformed Punkin was first or second in each of her five races. She added to Flying Bob's reputation by outrunning Prissy, Miss Bank, and Squaw H. She later produced ROM racers Mud Mender and Top Maxie.

The heavily campaigned Bay Annie A, a 1941 daughter of Flying Bob, was first, second, or third in 45 races. She finished ahead of such well-known sprinters as

Miss Bank, Hank H, Buster, Senor Bill, Punkin, and Prissy. When retired, she produced ROM racers Triple Bay, Bachari, and Good Buddy.

The good mare Mayflower W combined the blood of two leading families of the day. She was by Flying Bob, and out of Texas Pride W by My Texas Dandy. She made ROM as a 2-year-old and set a track record at 300 yards. At 3, she established a track record at 330 yards. At 4, she won the Eagle Pass Championship Stakes and set a 440-yard record for that track.

Mayflower W produced May's Pilgrim, who earned the title of Superior race horse. May's Pilgrim also was a successful sire.

Flying Bob's daughter Mayfly qualified for the racing ROM at 2. As a 5-year-old, she equaled the 350-yard track record at the Vessels Race Track (which became Los Alamitos). Mayfly was the dam of the ROM-qualifiers Sharp Chick and Lil Bar Breeze. Sharp Chick also earned points in halter classes.

Though unraced, Frye's Breeze became one of Flying Bob's better-producing daughters. Her top foal was the filly Bobbie Leo, 1954 World Champion 2-Year-Old Filly. Bobbie Leo equaled Centennial Park's 330-yard record and placed in stakes at 300 yards, 330 yards, 350 yards, 400 yards, and 440 yards. She earned a speed rating of 100.

Other running ROM foals of Frye's Breeze were Frye's Brand, Frosty Girl, Gloleo, Leo

Bobbie, Bar Lisa, and Red Bee Breeze. She also was the dam of the stakes-placed Top Gage and Breezing Jag, who earned points both at halter and in performance.

Della Rose, a racing ROM daughter of Flying Bob, continued her winning ways as a broodmare. She was the dam of four ROM runners, including Over Charge, Preferred Stock, and Rose Room.

The stakes-winning Bar The Door was the top foal produced by Della Rose. After earning a speed rating of 100, Bar The Door won 4 halter points and became a noted sire.

Sailor Bob, another unraced daughter of Flying Bob, distinguished herself in the broodmare band. Her ROM foals include Le Bob (stakes winner and sire), Sailor Bob B (ROM at both racing and performance), and Bobbie Lee (equaled 350-yard track record at Santa Rosa). Her daughter Della Bob was the dam of the AAA-AQHA Champion Bar Bob, himself a proven sire.

Flying Bob's daughter Sue Bob made ROM with two wins, two seconds, and two thirds. She then produced ROM foals Bobbie Bruce (stakes-placed and set 400-yard record at Columbus), Yendis (set a track record at 350 yards), and Ridgetta.

Another ROM running and producing daughter of Flying Bob was Miss America Eckert. A winner of two recognized races, she later was the dam of five ROM runners. These included the Superior race horse Buster's Chick as well as Flying Barzal (speed rating of 100), Fly High, Flying Charge, and Miss Palm Bar.

Baby Shot, by Flying Bob, scored two wins and a third from only three starts. She also made ROM from those starts before becoming a ROM producer. Her racing foals include Bar Gemini (ROM in both racing and performance), Mackay Chick (racing ROM), and Red Bee Bars (racing ROM).

Flying Bob's Annie O only ran a second and a third from her two starts, but she made up for it as a broodmare. Her five ROM runners were stakes-

Many speedsters on the track today can be proud of the part Flying Bob fills in their pedigrees.

Bart B. S. was one of Flying Bob's best sons. As outstanding a sire as he was a runner, the gray stallion was a leading sire of money-earners for many years.

Photo from *Great Moments in Quarter Racing History,* **by Nelson C. Nye**

winning Dial Ann, stakes-placed Dazzling Dial, stakes-placed Hi Dow, Denise Dial, and Gingy Dial.

Unraced Lady Bob R added to Flying Bob's broodmare-siring record by producing three ROM speedsters. These were the Superior race horse Okie City Bob, the good-producing mare Jody B Reed, and Leo Dale.

Lady Heart was unplaced in her three starts, but she blossomed as a broodmare. She made Flying Bob the maternal grandsire of Hy Adventure (ROM and a good money-earner for his day) and Speck Deck (ROM and a very capable sire).

Dona Dee was ROM on the track herself and was a ROM producer. This daughter of Flying Bob was the dam of Miss Troxell, a ROM filly who placed in three stakes.

La Machine was second or third in six stakes—all at 440 yards or 510 yards. She was out of Flying Bob's unregistered daughter Annie. La Machine later established herself as the matriarch of a commendable family of speed horses.

All of these horses, of course, were near the beginning of Flying Bob's legend as a sire. Eventually, 36 of his sons and daughters ran their way into the racing Register of Merit and his daughters added 87 more qualifiers to the record. Flying Bob was at the top of the lists when organized racing began and many speedsters on the track today can be proud of the part Flying Bob fills in their pedigrees.

4 MADDON'S BRIGHT EYES

By Frank Holmes

"She knew she was something special from the day she was born."

THAT MADDON'S Bright Eyes was one of the greatest Quarter running horses of all time is indisputable. Her record-setting races and world champion titles attest to this fact.

But Bright Eyes was far more than just a great sprinter. She was a character, a personality. She was a bay bombshell with one blue eye who looked and acted like a movie star in the paddock, a ballerina going into the starting gates, and a runaway freight train leaving them.

She blazed a path across the short-horse racetracks in the late 1940s and early 1950s in a manner that was so convincing she attracted coverage by *Newsweek* magazine. She was a superstar.

Maddon's Bright Eyes was foaled in the spring of 1946 on the Albuquerque ranch of C.L. "Tess" and Cleo Maddon. She was sired by Gold Mount, and her dam was an

Maddon's Bright Eyes, twice world champion Quarter running horse, and three-time world champion Quarter running mare.

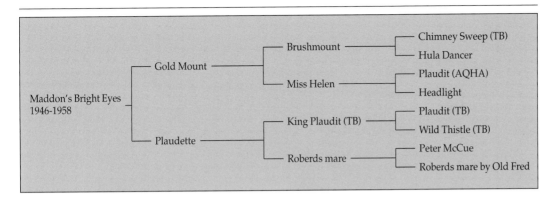

					Chimney Sweep (TB)
			Brushmount	
					Hula Dancer
	Gold Mount			
					Plaudit (AQHA)
			Miss Helen	
Maddon's Bright Eyes					Headlight
1946-1958					
					Plaudit (TB)
			King Plaudit (TB)	
	Plaudette			Wild Thistle (TB)
					Peter McCue
			Roberds mare	
				Roberds mare by Old Fred

unregistered daughter of King Plaudit (TB) named Plaudette.

Both Gold Mount and Plaudette traced to the famous Old Fred line of horses that had been popularized by Coke Roberds of Hayden, Colorado. These were solid horses—well-known in ranch, show, and racing circles.

It should be noted here that, despite the fact that Plaudette was quite a race performer in her own right and a superior producer, she remains a controversial subject to this day. This is due to her Appaloosa and cropout Paint markings. In addition to Bright Eyes, Plaudette also produced the well-known foundation Appaloosa stallion Bright Eyes Brother.

While she was carrying Bright Eyes, Plaudette was owned by Charlie Shoemaker of Albuquerque. Shoemaker had match-raced the oddly colored mare for years with considerable success. Apparently tiring of her, he gave her to Johnny Alonzo, of Laguna Pueblo, N.M., with the stipulation that the foal she was carrying was to remain his.

Shortly after acquiring her, Alonzo boarded Plaudette at Tess Maddon's. After she foaled, he tried to have her bred again, but she failed to settle. Eventually, he gave her to Maddon for the board bill. Shortly after Bright Eyes was foaled, Maddon purchased her from Shoemaker for $100.

Tess Maddon passed away in 1971, but his widow still lives on the family ranch outside Willard, New Mexico. Cleo Maddon vividly remembers the circum-

Halter and Performance Record: Race Register of Merit; 1949 World Champion Quarter Running Horse; 1949, 1950 World Champion Quarter Running Mare; 1951 World Co-Champion Quarter Running Horse; 1951 World Co-Champion Quarter Running Mare; Race Earnings, $16,577.

Progeny Record:

Foal Crops: 4	Race Starters: 3
Foals Registered: 4	Race Money Earned: $11,760
Halter Point-Earners: 3	Race Registers of Merit: 2
Halter Points Earned: 17	
Leading Race Money-Earner: Me Bright ($6,051)	

stances surrounding Bright Eyes' birth.

"Bright Eyes was foaled on May 12, 1946," she recalls. "She was a bay with a blue right eye, blaze face, and three white socks. She knew she was something special from the day she was born. And Tess sure never did anything to cause her to think otherwise."

Tess Maddon was first and foremost a horseman. He was born into a cotton farmer's family in Washington, Okla., but that lifestyle never held any appeal for him. To make a living, he tried his hand at several things over the years, including farming and ranching. But horse breeding and horse racing were always his first loves.

He was a good enough horseman to

Bright Eyes as a foal at the side of her controversial dam, Plaudette. Then-owner Johnny Alonzo is holding Plaudette in this photo.

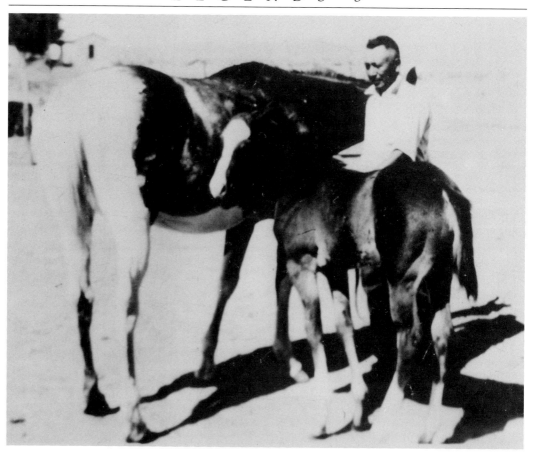

know that, in Bright Eyes, he had the kind of an animal who comes along but once in several lifetimes.

"Tess said from the beginning that Bright Eyes was going to be a champion," Cleo reminisced. "When she was still a weanling, he used to get on old Plaudette and pony Bright Eyes.

"He'd ride out, away from the place. When he'd get as far out as he was going, he'd turn the old mare around, turn Bright Eyes loose, and take off for home at a dead run. Bright Eyes would put her little head down, squeal and grunt, and take off for the barn as fast as her legs would carry her.

"Even as a baby, Bright Eyes loved to run."

The Maddon family handled all of Bright Eyes' early training and race prepa-

ration. When it came time to ride her, the chore was handled, in part, by Tess and Cleo's teenage daughter, JoAnn.

Finally, the time came for the mare to meet what had seemed to be her destiny from the very beginning.

Bright Eyes made her first race start in September of 1948, in a trial heat of the New Mexico Quarter Horse Futurity, which was held in Albuquerque during the state fair. She won handily, covering the 440 yards in :22.6. She was overlooked by the bettors in her racing debut, and paid $19.40 to win. In the finals, Bright Eyes served notice that she was, indeed, something special. Falling to her knees at the break, she recovered to win by ¾ of a length, once more in the time of :22.6.

Those two races were her only starts as a 2-year-old, but they were enough to earn her a AA race rating and a Register of Merit certificate.

One of the greatest races of Bright Eyes'

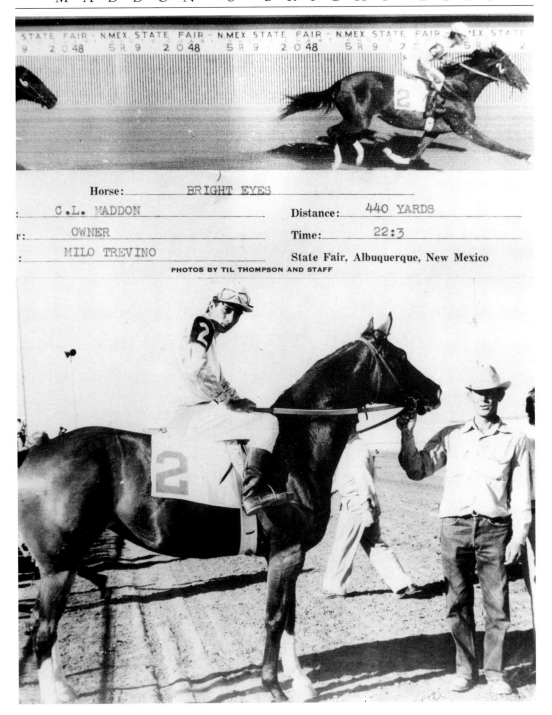

STATE FAIR - N.MEX. STATE FAIR - N.MEX. STATE FAIR - N.MEX. STATE FAIR - MEX. STATE
9 2 0 48   5 R 9   2 0 48   5 R 9   2 0 48   5 R 9   2   5 R 9   2

Horse: BRIGHT EYES

C.L. MADDON   Distance: 440 YARDS

OWNER   Time: 22:3

MILO TREVINO   State Fair, Albuquerque, New Mexico

PHOTOS BY TIL THOMPSON AND STAFF

At the 1948 New Mexico State Fair, Bright Eyes was named grand champion halter mare of the National Quarter Horse Show and won the 440-yard, 2-year-old racing futurity. Owner C.L. "Tess" Maddon is at Bright Eyes' head (below).

Photo by Thompson and Staff, Courtesy of Cleo Maddon

early career took place at Albuquerque in the fall of 1949. This was the 440-yard New Mexico Quarter Horse Championship, held during the state fair.

Just 3 days prior to this race, Bright Eyes had competed in the New Mexico Quarter Horse Derby. Acting up in the gate, she flipped over backwards and banged her head. She wound up running fourth in this race—beaten for the first time in her career.

In the championship, Bright Eyes drew the outside rail in an eight-horse field that included such tough competitors as Miss Bank, Diamond Bob, Raindrop, and Miss Pinkie. At the break, Miss Pinkie slammed

As this photo shows, Bright Eyes knew only one way to run—all out. She's on the far left.

Photo by Ralph Morgan

Bright Eyes kicked in her afterburners, caught, and passed the field as if it were standing still.

into Bright Eyes, spinning her almost completely around. By the time she got straightened out, the field was 3 lengths away.

Bright Eyes kicked in her afterburners, caught, and passed the field as if it were standing still. She was first to the wire by ¾ of a length, winning in the time of :22.2. This lowered the track record, which was held jointly by Shue Fly and Miss Bank; set a world record for 3-year-olds; and equaled the world record held by Woven Web (TB).

Largely as a result of this race, Bright Eyes was named the 1949 Champion Quarter Running Mare and 1949 World Champion Quarter Running Horse.

Bright Eyes' 1950 racing campaign began in Tucson, at Rillito Track. After easily winning a 330-yard allowance race there, she ran another of her super races.

The occasion was the 220-yard Cele Peterson Handicap, run on April 2. Assigned the top weight of 125 pounds, Bright Eyes broke slowly, then recovered to cross the finish line first. Her winning time of :12.1 set a track record and equaled the world mark.

Two weeks later, still at Rillito, Bright Eyes went to the post in the 250-yard Speed Stakes. Overtaken by Little Sister W 50 yards from the finish line, Bright Eyes took off like a house afire to win, going away, by a length and a half. In the process she equaled yet another world record and set yet another track record.

The next test for the "Blue-Eyed Queen of Sprint," as she was often called, was the 440-yard Rillito World Championship, held April 28.

Showing that she was truly at the top of her form, Bright Eyes took the feature event by 3 lengths over Osage Red and Tidy Step. Her time, over an off-track, was a blistering :22.3—once again a track record.

The final tally for Bright Eyes at Rillito read like this: four starts, four wins, three track records, and two world records.

After the Rillito meet, Bright Eyes took time off from approved competition to run a match race against the highly regarded West Coast speedster Tidy Step at the Agua Caliente Track in Tijuana, Mexico. Suffering through a less-than-perfect start, Bright Eyes came from a full length off the pace to nip Tidy Step at the wire. Her time for the 440-yard event was :22.1, $\frac{1}{5}$ of a second faster than the track record for Thoroughbreds set by Nuhat in 1932.

From Mexico, Maddon took Bright Eyes to Ruidoso, where she won two allowance races. Then it was on to Albuquerque and the state fair meet.

Here, Bright Eyes locked horns with Blob Jr., who was at the peak of his career. Sharing the top weight of 126 pounds with the stallion in the New Mexico State Fair Championship, Bright Eyes lost by $\frac{3}{4}$ of a length.

By virtue of this win, Blob Jr. was named the 1950 Champion Quarter Running Stallion and World Champion Quarter Running Horse. For the second year in a row, Bright Eyes was named Champion Quarter Running Mare.

In 1951, the Ott Adams-bred mare Monita rose from the ranks to challenge Bright Eyes.

By the time the two met, late in the racing season at La Mesa Park, in Raton, N.M., Bright Eyes had notched two victories in two starts at Centennial Park in Littleton, Colorado. In one of those she

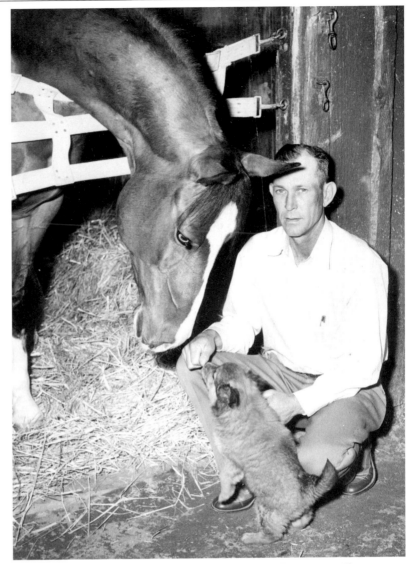

Wherever she went, Bright Eyes was accorded the status of a superstar. She was, according to Cleo Maddon, a horse who loved kids and small animals. This revealing picture of Bright Eyes and Tess Maddon was taken in 1952, at Bay Meadows in San Mateo, California.

had established a 440-yard world's record of :21.8, besting the old mark of 22 seconds flat that had been set by Miss Princess in 1948 in a match race against Barbra B.

In her first encounter with Monita, the 400-yard Raton Handicap, Bright Eyes came out on top. The pair met again, 2 weeks later, in a 440-yard handicap race at

After being forced to retire from racing due to injury, Bright Eyes was bred to Three Bars (TB) in 1953. Bright Bar, a brown colt, was the resulting foal. Rated AAA on the tracks, Bright Bar duplicated his famous dam's feat when he won the New Mexico State Fair Futurity in 1956 (above).

Trans-Photo Laboratories Photo, Courtesy of Cleo Maddon

Centennial. This one went to Monita. In fact, her 1¼-length victory over Bright Eyes marked the first time in the latter's career that any horse had ever daylighted her. Bright Eyes won her next outing at Centennial, and then headed home to New Mexico.

For the remainder of the year, the two brilliant race mares were pitted against each other in the quest for horse-of-the-year honors.

Back in Raton, Bright Eyes was beaten badly by Monita in a 440-yard event. In this race, the blue-eyed bay finished a dismal fifth—easily her poorest performance in three seasons of competition.

In Albuquerque, for her fourth state fair meet in a row, Bright Eyes locked horns once more with her nemesis. In the Shue Fly Stakes, it was Bright Eyes by a nose over Monita. In notching the victory, Bright Eyes covered the 350 yards in the world record time of :15.7. In the New Mexico State Fair Championship, Bright Eyes bested Monita for the second straight time, covering the 440 yards in :22.2, to almost equal her best time at that distance.

At the end of the racing season, Bright Eyes and Monita were named 1951 World Co-Champion Quarter Running Mares and 1951 World Co-Champion Quarter Running Horses.

In 1952, Bright Eyes traveled to Bay Meadows in San Mateo, California. Her arrival there was preceded by much fanfare. The track's general manager, Bill Kyne, challenged any horse in the world to match her at a quarter of a mile for $50,000. There were no takers.

In her first outing at Bay Meadows, Bright Eyes equalled the world record of :15.7 for 350 yards. This was followed by a 440-yard handicap, in which she conceded 7 pounds to the reigning champion Quarter running stallion Clabbertown G and lost to him.

Back in Colorado that fall, Bright Eyes notched a 330-yard win against Tonto Bars Gill and Leola. A week later, she gave up 9 pounds to Monita's paternal half-sister, Stella Moore, in the Raton Handicap, and was beaten by her.

On August 29, 1952, Bright Eyes went to the post in what was to be her final race. It took place at Centennial in the World Championship Quarter. As always, Bright Eyes was pitted against a field of top com-petitors, and, as always, she knew but one way to meet the competition—head on.

When the gates sprung open, Bright Eyes broke hard. So hard, in fact, that she tore the muscles of her right hind leg, ripping the tendon off her stifle joint and fracturing the bone. She finished the race on three legs, beaten only by the winner, Dalhart Princess, by half a length.

When the race was over, Bright Eyes could hardly walk. It took Tess Maddon 2 hours just to get her back to her stall. From there she was hauled to Colorado A&M (now Colorado State University) at Fort Collins. The veterinarian who examined her there predicted that she would never walk on the injured leg again.

There was nothing left for Maddon to do but haul Bright Eyes home. Eventually, she started to put weight on her injured leg and made a slow but steady recovery. As he did throughout her racing career, Tess Maddon literally lived with Bright Eyes as he nursed her back to health.

And although she finally did make a full recovery from her debilitating injury, Bright Eyes was through as a race horse. In five racing seasons, she went to the post 25 official times, winning 18 and finishing second 5 times. Her official earnings during an era of low purses was $16,577.

In seven of Bright Eyes' eighteen victories, she set records, and in three of her nine defeats, she pressed the victors to record times. She was officially rated AAA at five of the seven official distances and had an unofficial AAA at a sixth.

All that now remained as a challenge for Tess Maddon and Bright Eyes was to see if she could reproduce herself.

Maddon chose Three Bars (TB) to be the

As he did throughout her racing career, Tess Maddon literally lived with Bright Eyes as he nursed her back to health.

sire of Bright Eyes' first foal. Bred to him in 1953, she foaled Bright Bar, a good-looking brown colt with a big star, snip, and white on all four legs.

During the state fair race meet that fall, Bright Eyes made one final appearance, with Bright Bar at her side, at the track that had been the scene of some of her most memorable races.

Paraded before the grandstand, she was met with thunderous applause from her fans.

Cleo Maddon remembers that occasion, and many other similar ones, as if they had taken place just yesterday.

"People loved Bright Eyes," she recalls. "And she seemed to love people back. Anyone could approach her, whether she was in a box stall at the track, or in a corral at home, and she'd come up to them. And she loved children; whenever there were kids around, even when she was in race training, she'd put her head clear to the ground so that they could get at her.

"She grew up right with us, you know. She thought she was family; she thought she was people."

Although he was raced but lightly, Bright Eyes' eldest son, Bright Bar, showed that he had inherited at least a portion of his famous dam's speed and heart. Entered in the 1956 New Mexico Futurity, Bright Bar won it by several lengths after qualifying in the trials with a virus and a 103-degree temperature. He

went on to start a total of five times as a 2-year-old, winning three and earning his AAA rating.

Retired to stud, Bright Bar sired a total of 165 foals. Of these, 72 were race starters, with 33 earning ROMs. He also proved to be a superior sire of show and arena horses.

After Bright Eyes, Bright Bar was Tess Maddon's favorite. Although many offers to buy him were tendered, he was never for sale, and lived out his entire life with the Maddons, passing away in 1972.

Bright Eyes was barren in 1955. In 1956 she produced Bright Red, by Leo. Like all of Bright Eyes' foals, Bright Red was both good-looking and colorful. A bright red sorrel, he sported a full-blazed face and four stockings to the knees and hocks.

Bright Red was not raced as a 2-year-old. In five starts as a 3-year-old, he won twice. As a sire, he had 131 AQHA-registered get. Of these, 49 were performers and they accumulated 258 halter and 736.5 performance points in open and youth competition. Eight earned their ROMs in performance and one was an AQHA Champion.

In racing, seven of Bright Red's offspring qualified for their ROMs. Bright Red also made a positive impact on the Paint Horse breed.

In 1957, Bright Eyes produced Me Bright, also by Leo. Like her dam and eldest brother, Me Bright had her share of bad luck at home and at the track.

"When Tess was breaking Me Bright," recalls Cleo Maddon, "she fell in a gopher hole and hurt herself. We never really got her healed until we took her to Ruidoso for the first All-American Futurity in 1959.

"In her time trial, her jockey didn't even carry a bat. She won it easily, beating Galobar by 2 lengths. But the jockey had let her drift and race officials disqualified her. They placed her fifth and we collected fifth-place money.

"Because of her time, Me Bright was still qualified to run in the finals, but 2

"She grew up right with us, you know. She thought she was family; she thought she was people."

HORSE *BRIGHT RED*

OWNER *C. L. Maddon* DISTANCE *400 yds*

TRAINER *owner* TIME *21-3* DATE *10-1-59*

Trans-Photo Lab

JOCKEY *E. Armstrong* STATE FAIR, ALBUQUERQUE, NEW MEXICO

days later track officials gave her a 'no time' and placed her last. Tess never felt that we were treated fairly in that race, and neither do I."

Later that fall, Me Bright raced in the New Mexico State Fair Futurity and easily won it. In nine starts, she notched three firsts, two seconds, and one third. She had a speed index of 100.

In keeping with her family tradition, Me Bright proved to be a superior producer. She produced 10 foals, and 6 of

them earned their Registers of Merit on the track. Of these six, four had speed indexes of 95 or above.

Prior to producing her fourth and final foal in early 1958, Bright Eyes became paralyzed in her hindquarters. The Maddons tried in vain to discover the cause of her

Bright Red, a red sorrel colt by Leo and out of Bright Eyes, was foaled in 1956. Lightly raced, he earned his Register of Merit as a 3-year-old. In this winner's circle shot of him taken in October 1959, Tess Maddon is at his head and Cleo Maddon stands to the left with hand raised.

Photo Courtesy of Cleo Maddon

Me Bright, a 1957 bay mare by Leo and out of Bright Eyes, was the most like her dam in both looks and fleetness. Like Bright Eyes, she won the New Mexico State Fair Futurity and stood grand champion at halter in the Quarter Horse show.

Photo by Darol Dickinson, Courtesy of Cleo Maddon

malady. Her condition worsened.

After presenting the Maddons with a sorrel filly by Leo, Bright Eyes was unable to get around by herself. Maddon confined her to a box stall and rigged up a sling that prevented her from falling. Once more, he moved in with her and nursed her around the clock.

When the filly, who was named Lady Bright Eyes, was 3 months old, the pain overwhelmed Bright Eyes and she began to give in to it.

Maddon was often quoted in later years as saying that he had sworn an oath to himself while he was caring for Bright Eyes that, as long as she showed that she had the will to live—as long as she fought to stay alive—he would not give up on her. On June 29, 1958, when it became apparent to him that his famous mare had lost that will, he had her quietly put to sleep.

Before she died, Bright Eyes had given her last foal a healthy start on life. Lady Bright Eyes continued to prosper under the care of the Maddons and, as a yearling, she was generally considered to be the best-looking "Bright Eyes" of them all.

When she was 18 months old, the Maddons took Lady Bright Eyes to a vet to have a small navel hernia repaired. While tied up at the vet's, the filly threw a fit and injured herself so severely that she had to be destroyed. She was taken back home and buried beside Bright Eyes and Plaudette.

For years after the death of Maddon's Bright Eyes, the Maddon family continued to feature her blood in their breeding and race programs.

Initially through Bright Bar, Bright Red, and Me Bright, and then through a succes-

According to Cleo Maddon, Bright Eyes had the unusual habit, while parading to the post, of stopping and staring off into the distance. She did it before every race, and at other times as well. "It was as if she could see something that we could not," Cleo said. In this photo taken at La Mesa Park in Raton, N.M., in 1951, Bright Eyes strikes just such a pose.

Photo Courtesy of *The Quarter Horse Journal*

sion of speedy sprinters including Bar Bright, Bright Bardee, Bright Rebel, and Johnny Boone, the Maddons fashioned a family of Quarter Horse runners who were a force to be reckoned with wherever they appeared.

In March of 1997, Maddon's Bright Eyes was enshrined in the AQHA Hall of Fame. Although long overdue, the accolade came as no surprise to Cleo Maddon. "From the time we first heard about the Quarter Horse Hall of Fame, we felt that Bright Eyes would be in it someday," she said.

Then Cleo concluded, "Throughout her life, from the time she was a foal, Bright Eyes used to pause from time to time and look off into the distance. We could never figure out what she was doing.

"Before every race, while she was parading past the grandstand, she would stop and look away. If the jockey tried to keep her moving, she'd throw a fit. But if he'd just let her pause for a few seconds, she'd go on to the post on her own accord.

"She did the same thing on that day in Albuquerque, when we paraded her before the grandstand one last time. We never knew what she was looking at.

"Maybe she saw her future. Maybe she always knew her destiny."

5 SHOWDOWN

By Frank Holmes

This good-looking stallion was originally named Robert Kleberg.

WHEN O.G. Hill Jr. of Hereford, Tex., began showing Quarter Horses in the Texas panhandle in the early 1950s, he found the competition pretty stiff.

"When I started taking my Quarter Horses to the shows," he says, "I had to go up against such established breeders as Warren Shoemaker and Jimmie Randals in eastern New Mexico, and Glen Casey and E. Paul Waggoner in west

Texas. Those boys beat me pretty regular at first.

"But I told myself that someday I was going to own a horse who would enable me to have a showdown with those guys and come out on top my share of the time. In 1953 I located the stallion I felt had the potential to be that horse.

"At the time I bought him," Hill continues, "his registered name was

One of owner O.G. Hill's goals for Showdown was to do well at the New Mexico State Fair in Albuquerque. Here, Showdown was named grand champion in the mid-1950s.

Photo Courtesy of *The Quarter Horse Journal*

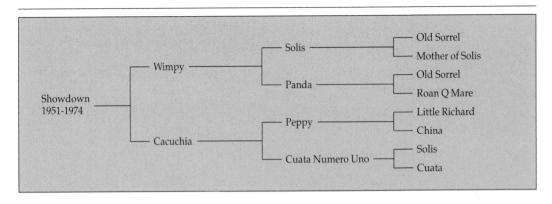

Halter and Performance Record: Halter Points, 45.

Progeny Record:

Foal Crops: 21	Performance Point-Earners: 45
Foals Registered: 395	Performance Points Earned: 1,035.5
AQHA Champions: 14	Performance Registers of Merit: 22
Halter Point-Earners: 67	Superior Performance Awards: 4
Halter Points Earned: 1,198	Race Starters: 1
Superior Halter Awards: 6	Race Money Earned: $25
Leading Race Money-Earner: Showdown Salty ($25)	

Robert Kleberg. For what I had in mind, I knew that would never do. I renamed him Showdown."

Robert Kleberg was foaled on the Hale Center, Tex., ranch of pioneer Texas lawman and Quarter Horse breeder J. Frank Norfleet in the spring of 1951. Although Norfleet had been breeding his own well-known line of Quarter Horses for a number of years, Showdown was of pure King Ranch breeding.

"In 1950, the King Ranch gave Mr. Norfleet a mare for services he had rendered them when he was a Texas Ranger," Hill says. "The mare was named Cacuchia and she was sired by Peppy and was out of Cuata Numero Uno, by Solis. At the time she was given to Mr. Norfleet, Cacuchia was in foal to Wimpy P-1. Showdown was the resulting foal.

"I wound up owning Cacuchia when she got to be a little older. She was a sorrel with no white markings—a good mare, but not a great one."

J. Frank Norfleet was in his 90s when Showdown was foaled. Worried that he wouldn't be able to develop the promising colt to his full potential, the ex-lawman gave him to his young friend and namesake, J. Frank Daugherty of nearby Oilton, Texas. It was while Showdown was under Daugherty's care that he came to the attention of Hill.

"I saw Showdown for the first time at the Tri-State Fair in Amarillo, in the fall of 1952," he says. "I liked him immediately and tried to buy him on the spot, but he wasn't for sale.

"I couldn't get him out of my mind

though, so I made a trip down to Daugherty's ranch every 6 weeks or so for the next 6 months until Frank finally agreed to sell him to me. I gave $5,000 for him, which was a lot of money for a horse in 1953."

Hill brought his new purchase along slowly, showing him only a handful of times in 1954 and 1955. By 1956 the rancher deemed Showdown ready for the big time.

"By the time Showdown got to be a 5-year-old," Hill says, "he was pretty much a model Quarter Horse. He was a nice deep chestnut in color, with a small star on his forehead and white on his left rear pastern. He stood 15 hands and weighed 1,250 pounds.

"Jimmie Randals of Montoya, N.M.,

O.G. Hill and Showdown after the chestnut stallion had garnered grand champion stallion honors at the 1956 Buffalo, Okla., Quarter Horse Show.

Photo Courtesy of *The Quarter Horse Journal*

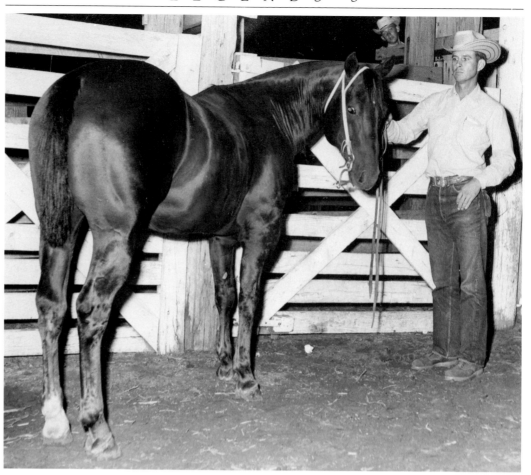

At the 1957 Tri-State Fair in Amarillo, Pandarita Hill, shown on the right, held by Curley Daugherty, was first in aged mares. Panzarita Hill, with J. Frank Daugherty at the halter, was second. Both were sired by Showdown.

At the 1959 Southwestern Exposition and Livestock Show in Fort Worth, Pandarita Hill (shown here) went grand. Her sister Panzarita Hill was reserve.

Photo by L.H. Launspach

was showing Poco Dell at this time, and Glen Casey, who lived right up the road in Amarillo, was showing his string of Bill Cody-bred horses. A little farther to the east, in Vernon, Tex., E. Paul Waggoner had a barn full of Poco Buenos and Pretty Bucks. But I knew I had a good horse, so I wasn't overly concerned.

"Showdown and Poco Dell were the same age," Hill continues, "and I'll have to admit that Dell wound up being our toughest competition. It was pretty much a tossup as to which one would walk off with the blue ribbon when those two horses met in a halter class. But Showdown came out on top his share of the time, and that was good enough for me."

According to AQHA records, Showdown earned 15 grands, 5 reserves, and 45 halter points in a 5-year show career. Although he was well-broke to ride, and a seasoned ranch horse, the stallion was never shown in performance.

"Gayle Borland, who owned and showed the great cutting mare Hollywood Lin, trained Showdown for arena cutting in 1960," Hill says. "Gayle rated him as a natural athlete, with a lot of cow sense. But I got too busy with ranch work, and Showdown got too busy as a breeding horse, and we just never made it to any cuttings."

Even before he was retired from show

ring competition, Showdown served notice that his strongest suit might not be as a show horse, but rather as a sire.

According to Hill, this was due in part to Showdown's superior conformation and breeding, and in part to the band of mares that the stallion bred.

"I bought my first registered Quarter Horse filly in 1947," Hill says. "From that time on, I always worked to improve the quality of my mares. I consistently went after the best mares that money could buy."

A number of Hill's initial purchases came from the same place that Showdown did.

"Frank Daugherty and his father, Curley, had already been in the Quarter Horse business for quite a few years by the time I started putting my program together. They had made liberal use of the blood of the famous west Texas sire Chubby over the years, and I was able to

"...I'll have to admit that Dell wound up being our toughest competition."

Excuse, owned by Monte Reger of Woodward, Okla., was Showdown's first AQHA Champion, earning the award in 1960.

Photo Courtesy of *The Quarter Horse Journal*

Showdown Rick, a 1961 stallion by Showdown and out of Miss Fizz, earned 30 halter and 12 performance points. He is shown here after winning grand champion stallion honors at a Quarter Horse show in Walnut Grove, Minn., in 1964. He was owned by Bob Beach, Chandler, Minnesota.

Photo Courtesy of *The Quarter Horse Journal*

acquire several mares of this breeding to add to my program," Hill continued.

"Because of their long-standing friendship with J. Frank Norfleet, the Daughertys also owned a number of descendants of Norfleet's famous race mare Panzarita. Again, I was able to add a few of those mares to my band.

"These mares, added to the ones I had already acquired, gave me what I felt was one of the best broodmare bands in the country."

With mares of this quality to work with, it didn't take Showdown long to began to make his mark as a sire.

Alibi Hill, a 1954 sorrel stallion out of Dutchie Chub, by Chubby, was Showdown's first registered foal, and his first show champion.

"Dutchie Chub was many times grand champion at halter," Hill says. "She was without a doubt one of the best conformation daughters of Chubby, and she turned out to be an excellent producer too. I showed Alibi quite a bit as a yearling and he won several big shows, including the Southwestern Exposition and Fat Stock Show in Fort Worth."

The next two Showdown get to make a splash in the show ring were the three-quarter sisters, Pandarita Hill and Panzarita Hill, who both traced maternally to Panzarita.

"Panzarita was a legendary mare in this part of the country in the 1930s," Hill says. "She was a mare of near-flawless conformation who could work cattle all week and then run the quarter in 22 seconds flat on the weekend. Jim Minnick, the well-known early AQHA inspector, called her the greatest Quarter mare that he'd ever seen.

"Curley Daugherty purchased Panzarita from J. Frank Norfleet and, in time, sold her to the Hepler Brothers of Carlsbad, New Mexico. One of the conditions of the sale was that Curley would get her third foal. That foal was Panzarita Daugherty," Hill explains.

"Like her dam, Panzarita Daugherty was a beautiful mare and a top performer. She was shown often and won a lot at halter and in performance. One of the better mares I ever bought from the Daughertys was Mayflower Daugherty. She was a 1950 chestnut mare by Hot Rock and out of Panzarita Daugherty."

Following his father's lead of several years earlier, Frank Daugherty sold Mayflower Daugherty to O.G. Hill with the understanding that he could have a foal out of her. The foal he chose was Pandarita Hill, a 1954 sorrel filly by Showdown who would become her sire's first show ring superstar.

Conditioned and shown by the Daughertys, Pandarita Hill accumulated 157 halter points and was the 1959 AQHA Honor Roll Halter Horse. On many occasions, her stiffest competition came from her three-quarter sister and trailer-mate, Panzarita Hill.

"Curley Daugherty was so impressed with Pandarita Hill as a baby that he bred Panzarita Daugherty to Showdown. She foaled a bay filly in 1955 that Curley named Panzarita Hill. Those two mares were tough to beat in halter competition."

The high point of the Daugherty mares' show careers came in early 1959, at the

Here is Showpond, a 1959 stallion by Showdown and out of Pondora. He followed his famous dam into the ranks of AQHA Champions in 1963.

Photo Courtesy of *The Quarter Horse Journal*

Southwestern Exposition and Livestock Show. There, in a class of 100 aged mares, Pandarita Hill placed first, and Panzarita Hill placed second. In competition against the winners of the other mare classes, Pandarita went grand and Panzarita reserve.

The two made additional headlines that year at Fort Worth when they sold to B.A. Skipper Jr. of Plainview, Tex., for $25,000.

As would be expected, their successes

Caliente Hill, foaled in 1962 and a full brother to Showdown Eloise, was arguably Showdown's greatest son. Campaigned to his AQHA Championship in 1967 by Billy Allen of Scott City, Kan., Caliente Hill is shown here after being named the grand champion stallion at the 1967 National Western Stock Show in Denver.

Photo by Darol Dickinson

added greatly to Showdown's growing reputation as a show-horse sire.

Excuse, the first of what would be 14 AQHA Champions sired by Showdown during his breeding career, was foaled in 1957. The bay stallion, who was out of Little Ethel, a Chubby granddaughter, was sold as a weanling to Monte Reger of Woodward, Oklahoma.

"Monte came by in the fall of 1957," Hill recalls, "and told me that he needed a top show colt he could use as an excuse to go to the horse shows. He picked out the Showdown colt he thought was the best, and named him Excuse. He got away to enough shows with the colt to make him an AQHA Champion by the time he was 3."

Showdown Nick, a 1958 palomino gelding out of Bird by Nick S., became Showdown's second AQHA Champion when he qualified for that award in 1961. Nick was one of several top Showdown get out of Warren Shoemaker-bred mares.

"Warren Shoemaker was the dean of the New Mexico Quarter Horse breeders at the time I got into the business," Hill says. "I made a trip to his ranch outside of Watrous in 1955 and bought several mares from him. Although they were a little leggier, and had more stretch than most of the mares I owned, they crossed well with Showdown.

"Showdown Nick was the most successful show horse I got from the Shoemaker mares. He was an AQHA Champion who earned 41 halter and 33 performance points. Showmount, a 1957 sorrel stallion out of Slipaway Mount by Cripple Mount, earned 18 halter points; and Showdown Tanna, a 1956 sorrel mare out of Lady Mount by Cripple Mount, earned 6."

Another highly successful cross for Hill—that of Showdown on a mare named Buttons Sewell—produced three more of the stallion's early champion get.

"Buttons Sewell was a granddaughter of the King Ranch-bred stallion, King George," Hill says. "I bought her in 1955 from R.H. Sewell of Folsom, New Mexico. In 1956 she produced a sorrel colt by Showdown I named Showdown Wimpy. He earned a Superior at halter in 1960 and his AQHA Championship in 1962.

"In 1957, I got a sorrel filly from the same cross. Her name was Wimpy Hazel Hill and she qualified for her AQHA Championship in 1967. In 1958 Showdown Mitzy, a bay full-sister to Wimpy and Hazel, hit the ground. She earned a Superior in cutting in 1966.

"Taking everything into consideration,

This good-looking mare is Showdown Eloise, a 1964 daughter of Showdown who was out of Brenda Lee, by General Lee. Yet another of her sire's AQHA Champions, she earned 40 halter and 34 performance points.

Photo Courtesy of *The Quarter Horse Journal*

Showpond's dam was Pondora, one of the breed's all-time greats.

the Showdown-Buttons Sewell cross turned out to be one of the better ones I ever made."

Showpond, a 1959 sorrel stallion, was the next of Showdown's get to add to his sire's growing reputation as an AQHA Champion sire. His dam was Pondora, one of the breed's all-time greats.

"Ed Heller of Dundee, Tex., bred Pondora," Hill says. "She was sired by Pondie and out of Ellen H, by Little Black Joe, by Joe Hancock. Charles King of Wichita Falls, Tex., showed Pondora for years. She was a great halter and performance mare who was equally adept at cutting, calf roping, and reining. She was also one of the very first AQHA Champions ever named.

"When Charles decided to disperse his Quarter Horses in 1958, I went up to Wichita Falls and bought them all. Among the other top horses I got in the deal were Poco Bay and Poco Chata, by Poco Bueno, and Poco Pondora, a nice young mare by Poco Bay and out of Pondora."

Showpond, the first son of Showdown and Pondora, proved that the old adage of "like to like begets like" was a sound one when he followed his dam into the AQHA Championship ranks in 1963.

Two of Showdown's get earned their

Alibi Hill was Show-down's first registered get and show champion.

Photo by Stewart's

AQHA Championships in 1965. They were Showdown Jr., a 1959 bay stallion out of Panzarita Daugherty, and Showdown Rick, a 1961 sorrel stallion out of Miss Fizz by Humdinger.

Show Maid, a 1957 bay mare out of Miss Circle H III by Brown Ceaser, and Showdown Eloise, a 1964 sorrel mare out of Brenda Lee by General Lee, became Showdown's ninth and tenth AQHA Champions when they finished their requirements for the award in 1966.

Showdown's most productive year as an AQHA Champion sire came in 1967, with five of his get, including the already-mentioned Wimpy Hazel Hill, earning the award.

Show Tip, a 1960 sorrel stallion by Showdown and out of Darky Jo Spark by Scooter Powers, became his sire's top point-earner en route to his championship. He earned a total of 15 halter and 473.5 performance points in a show career in which he was named the 1968 AQHA High-Point Western Riding Stallion, and the 1969 High-Point Western Riding Horse and High-Point Reining Stallion.

Rounding out Showdown's list of AQHA Champion get were Showdown Linda, a 1960 sorrel mare out of L'Allegro Linn, by L'Allegro; Ho Down Dio, a 1961 bay mare out of Shorty's Janie, by Shortcut;

This is Pandarita Hill after she was named grand champion mare at a Quarter Horse show in Uvalde, Tex., in June 1959. Owner B.A. Skipper Jr. is her handler.

Photo by Swofford's Studio

and Caliente Hill, a 1962 sorrel stallion out of Brenda Lee.

Caliente Hill, the last AQHA Champion sired by Showdown, was also the stallion O.G. Hill chose to keep as a replacement for his famous sire.

"Caliente was a lot like his daddy," the Texas rancher says. "He was a little taller, maybe, but a lot like Showdown nevertheless. I turned him over to Billy Allen to break and show and Billy did a real good job with him. In addition to his AQHA Championship, Caliente stood grand at the 1967 Denver National Western Stock Show.

"And like his daddy, he went on to make a pretty good sire for me. I even leased him to the CS Ranch of Cimarron, N.M., for a couple of years."

By the late 1960s and early 1970s, O.G. Hill had scaled back his horse-show activities. He continued to breed top middle-of-the-road Quarter Horses, however, and Showdown continued to be popular as a sire.

"In 1969, I leased Showdown to a breeding combine up in Wisconsin," Hill says, "but other than that, he lived out his life right here on the ranch. I always expected him to pull his own weight around here as a ranch horse, and he held up his end of the bargain. He was always a nice horse to be around. He didn't have a mean hair on his body."

Showdown remained healthy and was a sound breeder into his 20s. In the spring of 1974 he bred and settled half a dozen mares. He died that fall—August 2 to be exact—at the age of 23.

6 ROYAL KING

By Jim Goodhue

He combined the gentle disposition and willingness of the King-bred horses with a gritty determination that gave him a style of his own.

EARL ALBIN liked the sorrel. As it turned out, he liked the 17-month-old colt so much that he was willing to buy him twice.

A knowledgeable horseman, Albin ranched at Comanche, Tex., on a piece of land near the place settled by his great-grandparents before the Civil War. The family had always made horses a major part of their livestock operations. Albin's father, C.M. Albin, had purchased horses for the U. S. Army during the early part of the century.

This father and son were among the earliest breeders to register their horses with the AQHA. The expertise of the younger Albin was recognized by Helen Michaelis, one of the organizers and early secretaries of the organization. For her and the association, Albin made

Royal King, by King P-234 and out of Rocket Laning, was an immensely useful horse; first as a top flight show horse for over a dozen years and then as a sire of champion offspring. Evidently he had a wonderful disposition or he wouldn't have been trusted with the safety of these three children. There is no identification on this photo, but presumably they are related to the Albin family, owners of Royal King.

Courtesy of *The Quarter Horse Journal*

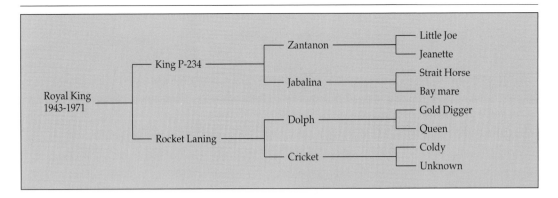

```
                                          ┌─── Little Joe
                            ┌─ Zantanon ──┤
                            │             └─── Jeanette
              ┌─ King P-234 ┤
              │             │             ┌─── Strait Horse
              │             └─ Jabalina ──┤
Royal King ───┤                           └─── Bay mare
1943-1971     │
              │             ┌─ Dolph ─────┬─── Gold Digger
              │             │             └─── Queen
              └─ Rocket Laning ┤
                            │             ┌─── Coldy
                            └─ Cricket ───┤
                                          └─── Unknown
```

many trips throughout his part of the country to check on bloodlines of the horses being used to form the foundation of the breed.

In September of 1944, Albin heard that Felton Smathers of Llano, Tex., was having some health problems and wanted to cut back on his herd. One member of that group was a 1943 son of King P-234, a stallion who rapidly was gaining a reputation as a sire of using horses.

Smathers also owned a very good mare he called Rocket (later registered as Rocket Laning). She obviously was a mare of top quality, although her pedigree did not show her to be close up to horses who were well-known and popular in the early days of the AQHA.

Rocket Laning was sired by Dolph, a son of Gold Digger. This particular Gold Digger was sired by Folsom. A palomino stallion of unknown breeding, Folsom was good enough as a mature horse to have been bought and used in the breeding program of W.T. Waggoner. He is noticeable in the pedigrees of many good horses produced on the Waggoner ranches.

Dolph was out a mare called Queen, who was sired by the famous Yellow Jacket. This son of Little Rondo was bred by Waggoner and also used as a sire by the Burnett Ranches with much success. Out of a mare called Cricket, by Coldy, Rocket Laning is believed to have Yellow Jacket blood on this side too.

Smathers knew that Rocket Laning had the quality to warrant being bred to

Halter and Performance Record: Performance Register of Merit; Superior Cuttting; 1953 NCHA Reserve World Champion Cutting Horse; NCHA Bronze and Silver Awards.

Progeny Record:

Foal Crops: 27	Performance Point-Earners: 160
Foals Registered: 590	Performance Points Earned: 3,545.5
AQHA Champions: 10	Performance Registers of Merit: 88
World Champions: 1	Superior Performance Awards: 15
Registers of Merit: 88	Race Starters: 2
Halter Point-Earners: 62	Race Money Earned: $67
Halter Points Earned: 426	
Leading Race Money-Earner: Royal Band, ($47)	

King P-234. The result of this mating was the sorrel colt appropriately named Royal King.

Aware that sons of King P-234 were beginning to bring substantial prices, Albin persuaded his friend Jack Whiteside to look at the Smathers horses with him and to partner with him in buying Royal King. They paid $250 for the yearling, who wasn't halter broke and was still running at the side of his dam.

Early the next year, they took Royal King to a Quarter Horse show at San Angelo, Tex., where he attracted considerable attention. One admirer was so impressed that he

In this mid-1950s photo, Royal King won a get-of-sire class with (from left) Major King, Kitten, and Maggie.

Photo by Neal Lyons, Courtesy of *The Quarter Horse Journal*

offered to buy the youngster for $1,500.

Whiteside thought this was a good price for the colt and a good return on their investment. He wanted to take the offer, but Albin liked the colt more than he liked the money. Without hesitation, Albin gave Whiteside $750 for his half and became the sole owner of Royal King.

Since he had so much money invested in the colt, Albin decided to start breeding Royal King as a 2-year-old. The resulting first crop of foals was remarkable.

At 2, Royal King was bred to 17 mares belonging to Whiteside and the two Albins. They dropped 16 foals, from which 13 lived to maturity. Of those 13, an unusual percentage qualified for the Register of Merit in performance events. Miss Nancy Bailey and Major King—destined

to become his best-known daughter and son—were both from that first crop.

That, of course, was just the beginning. He was bred to 51 mares as a 3-year-old and continued to cover a large number of mares each year throughout his career. He normally covered between 80 and 100 mares each year. It is of interest to note that he started his breeding career with a fee of $25. When his foals began to show their worth, his fee was advanced gradually to $250. After breeding season, he was returned to competition in cutting arenas.

At 5, Royal King was taken to Bob Burton for serious cutting training. Though he was still green the following year, Royal King began his cutting career. James Boucher was the trainer and rider when Royal King won his first cutting at the 1949 Dublin, Tex., show.

As an 8-year-old in 1951, Royal King became a top contender. Milt Bennett rode him during the summer months and

James Boucher returned in the fall. Throughout his career, Royal King demonstrated that he didn't care who was riding; he performed well for any competent rider. He appears to have had as many as 19 riders and was consistently good with all of them.

Stanley Bush was up during the early part of 1952. This duo placed second at the prestigious National Western Livestock Show in Denver, among other good showings.

Kirby Walters took over the reins after that breeding season and Royal King was campaigned from California and Oregon to Minnesota, and back to Texas. He won or placed in most of his contests during that busy season.

By this time, Albin was riding a horse named Rocky Red, who had carried him to seventh place in the 1952 NCHA top 10. A younger full brother to Royal King, Rocky Red became lame in the summer of 1952, so Albin switched to Royal King and headed east. In quick order, this pair won the cuttings at the state fairs in Illinois, Minnesota, and Missouri.

Among other things, this proved that the gritty little stallion could turn in top performances under considerable weight and handle the disadvantage of being passed from rider to rider. A large man, Albin weighed 225 pounds in trim shape. Royal King stood 14.1 or 14.2 and weighed about 1,040 pounds.

When ranch duties called Albin back to Comanche, Royal King's reins were handed to Andy Hensley. The successful cutting campaign that fall included a win at San Francisco's Cow Palace. To gain that notch in his belt, Royal King defeated Little Tom W, that year's NCHA world champion cutting horse. (Little Tom W was registered with the AQHA as Little Tom Wing.)

Royal King gathered more wins in the remainder of that year's competition, but nothing seemed as spectacular as the Cow

Miss Nancy Bailey, a 1946 daughter of Royal King out of Nancy Bailey, was an AQHA high-point cutting horse, who also ended up being in the NCHA Hall of Fame. In this photo, the mare is being shown in Tucson by owner Bob Burton, Arlington, Texas.

Photo by Matt Culley

Royal Jazzy, owned and ridden by Bubba Cascio, was a 1955 daughter of Royal King out of Jazmau. Cascio said she was so intense in front of a cow she would tremble all over.

Photo by Las Vegas News Bureau, Courtesy of *The Quarter Horse Journal*

Palace triumph. At the end of the year, NCHA files showed that Royal King stood third among the top 10 cutting horses.

Royal King began a 1953 campaign at Denver's National Western. Again, he had to settle for second money, but a lot of very good horses placed behind him.

Royal King was back on top in his next show, winning the cutting at Fort Worth's Southwestern Livestock Exposition and Fat Stock Show. As usual at Fort Worth, Royal King met many of the very best cutting horses in competition at the time.

Hensley made it a particularly memorable occasion when he commuted by plane back and forth between Fort Worth and Houston so that he could take part in both shows at the same time. In Houston, he competed on Royal King's daughter, Miss Nancy Bailey. They had to settle for

second at Houston, but it was over well-known cutters and was a major victory for the family.

After Fort Worth, Hensley and Royal King found time to register a win at San Antonio. Then it was time for the usual return to the ranch for breeding season, followed by Albin showing the tough little stallion at a few shows in the area.

A Duel at the Cow Palace

Later that year, Royal King and Milt Bennett made another trip to California. At the Cow Palace, they took part in a duel that has long been remembered by those lucky enough to see it. At that show, Royal King's major competition was Skeeter (sometimes called Chigger), a horse who had reigned supreme as the 1950 and 1951 NCHA World Champion Cutting Horse. He was by no means beyond his prime in 1953.

Skeeter, a tall rangy horse ridden by the equally tall and rangy Phil Williams, and the diminutive Royal King looked like

Like Miss Nancy Bailey, Major King was in Royal King's first foal crop and was destined to be one of his best offspring. Major King, out of Moon Harris, won grand championships at halter as a weanling. Later, in the breeding shed, he was a leading sire of halter and performance horses.

Courtesy of *The Quarter Horse Journal*

Both were armed with determination and ability, though, so the performances they gave had the crowds roaring.

Mutt and Jeff in size and differing styles. Both were armed with determination and ability, though, so the performances they gave had the crowds roaring. When the dust had cleared, the judges' score cards tallied up to a tie between the game pair.

At the end of the year, Royal King was the NCHA Reserve World Champion Cutting Horse. The only horse ahead of him in earnings was the brilliant gelding Snipper W. In an interview many years later, Albin's wife, Charlie Mae, accurately pointed out that Royal King undoubtedly would have been the 1953 world champion if he hadn't been taken out of competition and returned to the ranch for the breeding season.

Returning to Denver's National Western early in 1954, Royal King again was packing Albin. For the third time, Royal King bested all contenders but one.

A new rider, Buck Williams, campaigned Royal King after that year's

breeding season. Their partnership was crowned by a win at Omaha's Ak-Sar-Ben.

For 1954, Royal King was still among the NCHA top 10 money-earners, finishing in sixth place. Royal King stayed among the top 10 during 1955. By now a 12-year-old, he finished in a strong ninth place.

After 1955, Royal King competed on a much lighter schedule. He went to enough shows to prove he still knew his way around a feisty critter. And he continued to win or place enough to make his presence felt.

NCHA records credit Royal King with winning $23,976 in contests sanctioned by that organization. He was given the NCHA Bronze Award when he passed the $10,000 mark and the NCHA Silver Award

Major Thunder, a son of Major King, could halter as well as perform. He was an AQHA Champion and a high-point roping horse. In this 1960 photo, Dwight Stewart accepts the ribbon for grand champion stallion from show manager Chet Todd.

Photo by Ruth Rutledge, Courtesy of *The Quarter Horse Journal*

when he exceeded $20,000 in earnings. Those dollar amounts were more impressive during the 1950s than in later years when opportunities were so much greater.

It has been noted that Royal King was a distinctive horse in many ways. He combined the gentle disposition and willingness of the King-bred horses with a gritty determination that gave him a style of his own. Most cutting horses drop their front ends when engaged in head-to-head competition with a cow, but Royal King's entire body hunkered lower. The stallion's unusual style was consistently passed along to his offspring.

In her book *Cutting—A Guide for the Non Pro Competitor*, Sally Harrison quotes Bubba Cascio, who owned and rode Royal Jazzy. About this top daughter of Royal King, Cascio said, "When she'd stop a

cow, she'd get lower and lower, pounding her feet, and just kind of trembling all over." Members of the Royal King family made intensely aggressive cutting horses.

Miss Nancy Bailey

Long before Royal King gave up being at the top of the heap, his daughter Miss Nancy Bailey showed signs of aiming for that same distinction. Bred by Mrs. E.A. Whiteside, Miss Nancy Bailey recorded her first official NCHA win as a 3-year-old. At that time, she was owned by Mike and Millie Leonard. In 1950, her winning ways gained her the NCHA Certificate of Ability.

The next year, Miss Nancy Bailey passed into the ownership of Herbert and Dorothy Frizzell. They sold her that same year to Bob Burton. Since Burton had helped start Royal King on his cutting career, he obviously knew what he might expect.

Burton exhibited the young mare to standings in the NCHA top 10 for 4 consecutive years—1952 through 1955. In both 1952 and 1953, she placed immediately behind her illustrious sire in the

NCHA rankings. She had lifetime earnings of $38,084 in NCHA contests. This qualified her for the NCHA Hall of Fame.

Miss Nancy Bailey also was the AQHA high-point cutting horse in 1952 and 1953, and she earned the title of AQHA Superior cutting horse.

Major King

Mr. and Mrs. Leonard also owned Major King, the other top star from Royal King's first crop. Starting his halter career at 2 months of age, Major King won four grand championships as a weanling, according to Mrs. Leonard. She added that he was never lower than sixth at halter, despite always being the youngest in the class.

Although he showed considerable potential at cutting and qualified for the AQHA ROM in working events, Major King was restricted primarily to a breeding career.

Annual AQHA lists published during Major King's prime showed him among the leading sires of halter horses as well as the leading sire of performance horses for several years. Along with 10 AQHA Champions, Major King sired 43 ROM performers in working events and 1 racing ROM.

Major's Maco, a son of Major King, finished ninth in the 1964 NCHA World Championship competition, earned the NCHA Bronze Award, and an AQHA Superior in cutting.

Another prominent son of Major King was Major Thunder, the AQHA high-point calf roping stallion in 1958 and 1959. Major Thunder and Major's Marquay, both AQHA Champions, were the two foals by Major King who were also Superior halter horses.

Major Thunder's offspring included numerous ROM arena performers and three AQHA Champions: Somebody, Sunny Thunderette, and Thunder's Sally.

Major King's daughters and granddaughters also made important contributions as broodmares. One granddaughter, Manana's Rosa, produced the multitalented Major Bonanza. Officially credited with Superiors in halter and western pleasure, Major Bonanza also was an AQHA high-point working cow horse stallion.

At stud, Major Bonanza was equally successful. His offspring include The Major Leaguer, an AQHA world champion cutting horse, and Major Investment, the 1981

Major Bonanza, who died in June 1997 and who traced to Royal King through his dam, Manana's Rosa, proved that good looks and performance can go together. He was a Superior halter and western pleasure horse and high-point working cow horse. In turn, he sired a line of good-looking performance horses.
Photo by Don Shugart, Courtesy of *The Quarter Horse Journal*

AQHA World Champion Junior Cutting Horse and the AQHA Reserve World Champion Junior Reining Horse.

Leading Sire

For several years beginning with 1951, Royal King figured prominently among the AQHA annual lists of leading sires of performance contest winners. In fact, between

Button's King, a 1950 son of Royal King out of Lady Gore, was one of five Royal King foals to earn a Superior rating in cutting.

Courtesy of *The Quarter Horse Journal*

One of the top cutting contenders in the early 1960s was Royal King's daughter Royal Jazzy.

1959 and 1964, he was either first, second, or third on the list. His competition included two other sons of King: King's Joe Boy and Poco Bueno. His son, Major King, joined the ranks in 1963, placing third.

Royal King sired 10 AQHA Champions, 88 working ROM horses, 12 Superior cutting horses, and 2 Superior reining horses. His one Superior western pleasure horse, Royal Lightning, was the 1963 AQHA High-Point Western Pleasure Stallion.

Cutting Royalty

Royal Chess, by Royal King, joined Miss Nancy Bailey in the NCHA Hall of Fame. Royal Chess stayed in the NCHA top 10 for 4 years, placing as high as second in

1969. He was the NCHA world champion gelding for 4 years.

Although Royal Chess was usually piloted by Stanley Bush, who had started him in cutting as a 2-year-old, he also won when ridden by other members of the family. Bush's wife, Wanda, rode him to championships in the Girls Rodeo Association (later renamed the Women's Professional Rodeo Association). Daughter Shanna showed him successfully in cutting and western pleasure at youth shows. In 1972, Royal Chess was named the AJQHA World Champion Cutting Horse.

One of the top cutting contenders in the early 1960s was Royal King's daughter Royal Jazzy. In AQHA events, she earned a Superior award. In NCHA standings, she in the top 10 in both 1961 and 1962. Her untimely death prevented her from passing her talents down to later generations.

Fortunately, Royal Jazzy's full sister,

Royal Jazabell, carried on the family traditions. She qualified for the AQHA performance ROM, but did not reach the heights attained by the older sibling. Instead, she settled for creating a dynasty. She produced Bill's Jazabell, third in both the 1973 NCHA Futurity and Non-Pro Futurity, and she was the NCHA world champion mare in 1976.

Bill's Jazabell produced Jazabelli Quixote, the 1982 NCHA Non-Pro Futurity Champion. This mare, in turn, produced the 1988 NCHA Non-Pro Futurity winner Jazalena, the 1989 NCHA Open Futurity Champion July Jazz, and the 1990 NCHA Futurity Non-Pro Reserve Champion All That Jazz.

Royal King's Jazzy Socks earned a second-place finish in the 1969 NCHA Non-Pro Futurity. Jazzy Socks, from the same female family as Royal Jazzy and Jazabell Quixote, produced Doc Wilson and Son Ofa Doc. Doc Wilson was third in the 1983 NCHA world championship race and earned his place in the NCHA Hall of Fame with earnings of more than $121,000. Son Ofa Doc was the 1982 AQHA Reserve World Champion Senior Cutting Horse.

Both of these stallions became leading sires of NCHA money-earners. Son Ofa Doc sired the 1991 NCHA World Champion Cutting Horse Bob Acre Doc and the 1991 NCHA Reserve World Champion Son Ofa Senior. He also sired All That Jazz, a double-bred member of the Royal King family mentioned earlier as a son of Jazabell Quixote. So, All That Jazz is linebred to both Royal King and Jazmau (dam of Royal Jazzy and Royal Jazabell).

Jazzy Socks' full brother, Royal King Tony, sired the very capable cutter Jazzotte. In 1984 and 1985, Jazzotte was the NCHA World Champion Non-Pro Cutting Horse. Then in 1986, Jazzotte moved up to become the NCHA Open World champion.

Royal Royale, a son of Royal King, tied for sixth in the 1973 NCHA Futurity. The next year, Royal Royale came back to score high in AQHA junior cutting ranks.

Marilyn Twist, by Royal King, proved to be a top cutter for both junior and adult riders. In 1974, she placed 10th at the AQHA World Championship Show. The next year at the AJQHA World Championship Show, she carried a junior pilot to

The description on the back of this photo says that Royal Tate, owned and ridden by Dick Martin, of Arcadia, Calif., won the registered cutting in Norco. Royal Tate was a 1951 son of Royal King who earned an ROM in performance.

Photo by Ruth Rutledge, Courtesy of *The Quarter Horse Journal*

Royal Santana, one of the greatest cutting horses of his day, won in open, youth, and amateur events, in both AQHA and NCHA competition. Here, he's being ridden by Sonny Rice in the 1974 NCHA Futurity. The gelding was by Peppy San and out of Royal Smart, by Royal King.

Photo by Dalco, Courtesy of *The Quarter Horse Journal*

third place. Marilyn Twist's daughter Gay Bar Twist upheld the family honor by placing eighth in the 1977 AQHA World Championship Show junior cutting.

In addition to all of these high-ranking Royal King foals, five other sons and daughters earned AQHA Superiors in cutting: Royal Morris, Bunner, Royal Dandy, Buttons King, and Chocker.

The athletic abilities of the Royal King offspring were not limited to cutting. Both Miss Royal Dandy and Royal Angel were named AQHA Superior reining horses.

Maternal Grandsire

Despite Major King's excellent record, it would appear that Royal King's influence on later generations has come primarily through his daughters. For example, Royal King is the maternal grandsire of both the sire and dam of Mis Royal Mahogany, the 1980 NCHA Futurity champion.

The Royal King daughters produced 88

halter point-earners and more than 250 performance point-earners. These included 21 AQHA Champions and 6 AQHA Youth Champions. In addition, this honor roll included 113 ROM performers in open events, 13 amateur ROM, and 25 youth ROM qualifiers.

Royal King's 1948 daughter White Sox Lady, for instance, has to be mentioned as one of the breed's outstanding producers. Although she herself earned just 2 points in halter and none in working events, her foals placed her on the list of leading dams of AQHA Champions. These outstanding individuals were Lady Barbie Sox, Vaquero King, Bill Royal, and Time Royal. Her other performance ROM representatives were Tacos Royal, Lady Nifty Sox, and Hygro Royal.

Dalpha Billy, a son of Royal King's daughter Kitsie A, displayed another kind of talent in adding to the family legend. In 1973, he was the AQHA high-point jumping gelding and the AJQHA reserve world champion jumper.

Another unusual producer among Royal King's daughters was Miss Nix. She produced two AAA sprinters, Cajon

Dimples and Cajon Bar Queen. Each of these two fillies also produced ROM race foals.

Royal Rita was a versatile daughter of Royal King—earning 2 working points and placing third in one of her two starts. Then she produced the very capable Royal Agget. He was champion senior cutting horse at the 1974 AQHA World Show and in the same year was seventh among AQHA cutting horse point- earners. In 1979, he was the AJQHA Reserve World Champion Cutting Horse.

Royal's Jeep, by Royal King, produced two ROM performance horses. The best-known was Denim Dude, by Padre's Dude. Between 1987 and 1990, Denim Dude was three times the AQHA high-point amateur reining horse and once the youth high-point reiner.

Another daughter, Royal Ida May, produced the outstanding Cutter's Rocket, a dun gelding who was the AJQHA world champion working cow horse in 1983 and 1985. In 1983, he also placed seventh in reining.

Royal King's daughter Miss Holly Royal produced three ROM performance horses. Of these, Sport Model Holly placed second in the 1975 NCHA Non-Pro Futurity. Another, Honey Something, was fifth in the 1971 NCHA Non-Pro Futurity. The third was Sport Model Royal. Miss Holly Royal's son, Dox Royal Hickory, placed ninth in the 1985 NCHA Cutting Horse Futurity. In 1989, he was the amateur reserve champion cutting horse at the World Show and third among amateur cutting horse point-earners. He placed fifth at the 1990 world show in amateur cutting.

Queen Royal, by Royal King, produced two ROM performers, Royal De King and King's Maple Leaf. Royal De King was the AQHA Reserve World Champion Junior Reining Horse of 1974.

Call Me Royal was a persistent campaigner out of Royal King's Miss Royal Fleet. This AQHA Champion was the 1978 World Champion Senior Reining Horse. He also was Superior in halter and western pleasure.

Royal Angel, a 1956 mare by Royal King and out of Ida Red, was an AQHA Champion with a Superior rating in reining, proving that the get of Royal King excelled at more than cutting.

Photo by Budd, Courtesy of *The Quarter Horse Journal*

In youth events, Call Me Royal was among the top 10 point-earners for 2 years in reining, for 2 years in western horsemanship, and for 1 year among halter geldings. In addition, he twice finished in the top 10 in the youth world show reining. He was both an AQHA Youth Champion and an AQHA Youth Performance Champion.

Royal King's daughter Lady Ruffles produced two open ROM performance

Tony Manning, a Royal King gelding out of a mare named Penny, was successful enough in the show ring to earn an AQHA Championship.

Courtesy of *The Quarter Horse Journal*

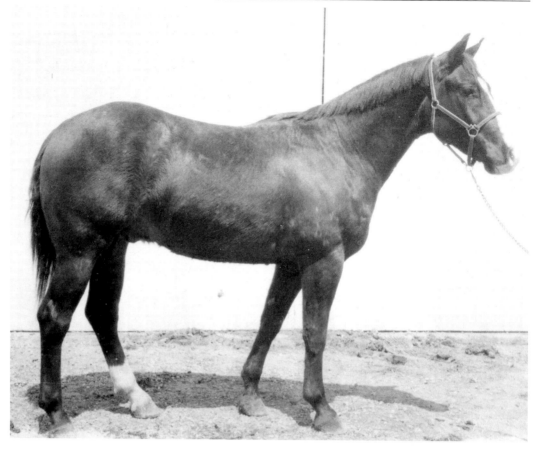

horses. One of these, Mi Royal Remedy, also earned a ROM in youth arena events. In 1988, Mi Royal Remedy placed eighth in AQHA world show reining. Returning to the world show in 1992, he was 10th in both reining and heeling.

Royal Panky Doll was one of Royal King's many daughters who qualified for the performance ROM. Retired from the arena, she produced the excellent youth horse Licensed To Slide, a chestnut gelding who was the AJQHA World Champion Reining Horse of 1983 and then came back the next year to be reserve champion. In 1984 he also placed eighth in the youth world show working cow horse.

Royal Tex Top, by Royal King, added three more high-caliber horses to the family. One of them was the AQHA Champion Shesa Royal Nugget, who earned third place in the 1983 world show

in junior trail and was a Superior western pleasure horse. Another foal, Playboys Tamara, was sixth for 1993 high-point amateur cutting horses, and the third foal, Sir Royal Lynx, was sixth in the 1984 NCHA Non-Pro Derby.

Royal King's Royal Hen added two more good campaigners to the family by producing two working ROM horses—Miss Royal Dry Doc and Wimpys Royal Misty. Specializing in a relatively new event, team penning, Miss Royal Dry Doc earned amateur and youth ROMs.

The Most Influential

Possibly the most influential daughter in performance events is Royal Smart. Not a successful performer herself, she once sold for $850 at a time when big prices were the norm. Once she became a broodmare, however, she was to outshine those whose records and price tags had gotten all of the attention.

In the show ring, her most outstanding foal was her gelded son Royal Santana, who was successful in NCHA and AQHA open, youth, and amateur events. He finished both 1977 and 1979 in the NCHA top 10. Then in 1980, he was second in the NCHA Non-Pro Futurity finals and second in the NCHA non-pro world championship race. He was in the NCHA non-pro top 10 in 1978, 1979, and 1981.

Royal Santana was the 1986 AQHA High-Point Amateur Cutting Horse and was sixth in the AQHA World Championship Show cutting. In 1988, he was the fourth highest point-earner in youth cutting and placed sixth in the youth world show.

Winner of the title of 1991 World Champion Amateur Cutting Horse, Royal Santana was seventh highest point-earner in amateur cutting and ninth in youth standings for the year. In 1993, he had moved up to fifth place among youth cutting horse point-earners.

Prior to foaling Royal Santana, Royal Smart had produced two full sisters to him. All three were sired by Peppy San. The fillies were the ROM arena performer Pepard and Smart Peppy. The latter did not qualify for ROM, but did gather 7 working points in open shows and 2 in youth.

Smart Peppy then gave her dam a run for honors in the broodmare field. She did this by producing two spectacular sons— both sired by Doc O'Lena. One of these is Smart Peppy Doc, who has earned more than $120,000 in NCHA contests. The other is the legendary cutting horse and sire of cutting horses, Smart Little Lena.

After winning the 1982 NCHA Futurity, Smart Little Lena returned to be co-champion (with Peppymint Twist) of the 1983 NCHA Derby and was the sole winner of both the 1983 Super Stakes and the 1984 Masters Championship. These major events make up the NCHA Triple Crown. Smart Little Lena was the first to win this prestigious trio. (The only other horse to achieve it was Docs Okie Quixote the following year.)

Retired to stud, Smart Little Lena quickly became one of the leading sires of NCHA money-winners. He is the only winner of the NCHA Futurity who was sired by a NCHA Futurity winner and who also sired a NCHA Futurity winner. He topped this by siring two more NCHA Futurity winners—Smart Date and Smart Little Senor. Smart Little Lena added even more luster to this record by siring two NCHA Futurity reserve champions— Smart Play and Commandicate.

These and other winners mean that the partnership forged by Earl Albin and Royal King has left a legacy that shows no signs of fading away.

Earl Albin's son Billy was a teenager in the later years of Royal King's heyday. Billy competed primarily in American Junior Rodeo Association events in those days. He earned the titles of 1964 AJRA World Champion Optional Roper and 1965 AJRA World Champion Steer Wrestler. He also was the champion calf roper in 1964 and 1965 in the southern region. He showed further versatility by riding a son of Royal King to a successful career in cutting. One of his roping horses was also sired by Royal King.

Today, Billy is a rancher whose operation includes part of the land previously owned by his father. He says, however, that Royal King was buried on a different part of the ranch. He remembers that the old horse was active and vigorous almost until the time of his death.

A stone marker over Royal King's grave records the fact that the 28-year-old stallion died in May of 1971. The greatest memorial to this 1997 inductee into the AQHA Hall Of Fame, though, is the reputation of the many fine horses of today and yesteryear who count him among their ancestors.

7 JACKSTRAW (TB)

By Frank Holmes

He was known for his lightning-fast starts and blazing early speed.

ALTHOUGH NOT as well-known a sire of racing Quarter Horses as some of his Thoroughbred contemporaries—most notably Three Bars, Depth Charge, and Piggin String—Jackstraw left his mark on the breed. An iron horse on the Thoroughbred tracks during the 1940s, Jackstraw put a host of impressive

Quarter runners on the ground in the 1950s and 1960s.

They were easily identifiable in two ways. Most were good-looking chestnut horses with blazes and stockings, and most were sprinters at their best from 400 to 870 yards.

Jackstraw was bred by J.O. Keene,

Jackstraw was 20 years old when this picture was taken in January 1962, but his attractive head and stock-horse conformation are still apparent.

Photo Courtesy of A.B. Munsey

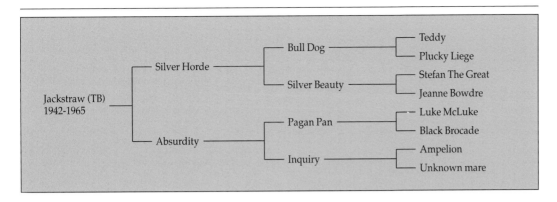

C.E. Buckley, and H. Maybriar and was foaled on March 7, 1942. Sired by Silver Horde and out of Absurdity, he traced on both sides of his pedigree to Luke McLuke, the maternal grandsire of Three Bars (TB). Given that fact, it was only logical that Jackstraw should someday show promise as a sire of Quarter race horses.

After being sold to Four Oaks Stables of Toronto, Canada, as a yearling, Jackstraw was put into race training. His first start as a 2-year-old was at Oaklawn in Hot Springs, Arkansas. In a 3/8-mile race, he covered the distance in 35 seconds flat and bested the field by 2½ lengths.

During the next 8 years, under several owners, Jackstraw went to the post an incredible 111 times, and racked up 33 firsts, 22 seconds, 14 thirds, and $52,288 in earnings.

The big chestnut did most of his running during the World War II era, when travel in the United States was restricted. As a result, he made numerous unofficial starts at the Hipodromo de las Americas in Mexico City. One of his most impressive victories occurred there on April 5, 1947.

The occasion was the 5/8-mile Mexico City Allowance. Jackstraw was pitted against Big Racket (TB), the local favorite and a world and track record-holder. Jackstraw went to the post saddled with 115 pounds, while Big Racket carried 107. At the finish, it was Jackstraw by 10

Halter and Performance Record: Won 33 Thoroughbred races, with 22 seconds, and 14 thirds, $52,288 in earnings.

Progeny Record:

Foal Crops: 13	Performance Registers of Merit: 3
Foals Registered: 157	Race Starters: 101
Halter Point-Earners: 3	Race Money Earned: $531,440
Halter Points Earned: 72	Race Registers of Merit: 50
Superior Halter Awards: 1	Superior Race Awards: 5
Performance Point-Earners: 7	Race World Champions: 2
Performance Points Earned: 62.5	
Leading Race Money-Earner: Sea Nymph ($166,410)	

lengths over Big Racket, with Fast Message (TB), the third-place horse, another length and a half back.

In 1946, Jackstraw set a track record in Mexico City for 5½ furlongs that held up for more than 20 years, when it was finally broken by Beduino (TB). In 1948, Jackstraw won the George Wolfe Handicap at Del Mar in southern California. Throughout his career, Jackstraw was known for his lightning-fast starts and blazing early

Jackstraw was nearing the end of his long racing career in this photo taken after winning a 6-furlong race at Del Mar in southern California. Hall of Fame jockey Johnny Longden guided the 8-year-old stallion to victory in the race.

Photo Courtesy of A.B. Munsey

* JACKSTRAW *   JOCKEY JOHN LONGDEN UP.
WINNING THE FOURTH RACE, SEPTEMBER 9, 1950 AT DEL MAR, CALIFORNIA.
  Meadowvale Boy (2nd)   (6 furlongs-1:10.2) Drake Mallard (3rd)
NELSON & PHILLIPS, OWNERS.   R.H. McDANIEL, TRAINER.

speed. It was not uncommon for him to be 5 lengths in front of the field within the first 50 yards of a race.

Jackstraw was also known as a horse who would go wherever the money and competition were. In 1946, while under the ownership of the popular Mexican movie star Emilio Tuero, he became the first horse to ship out of Mexico City by air. He was sent to compete at Arlington Race Track in Chicago.

Finally, Jackstraw was known as a horse who would always run with a great deal of determination over any kind of surface. Soft, hard, or muddy, it made no difference to him. As the wizened old railbirds were apt to point out, he "didn't have to carry his racetrack with him."

Jackstraw raced for eight full seasons—

78

Kaystorm, a 1956 sorrel mare out of Kaybu, was one of the first of Jackstraw's get to make a name for herself on the Quarter tracks. A Superior race horse, she earned $27,256 in an era of small purses.

Photo Courtesy of *Speedhorse* **Magazine**

from 1944 through 1951—and was then retired. In 1952, he was purchased by A.W. Howard, a Memphis, Tex., horseman who had been searching for several years for a sprinting Thoroughbred to cross on his Quarter Horse mares. Shortly after returning to the Lone Star state with his new stallion, Howard passed away. His abrupt death left the Howard estate unsettled, and Jackstraw was forgotten.

Eventually though, the estate was settled, and Jackstraw was sold. After changing hands at least one more time, he was purchased for $750 in 1955 by A.B. Munsey, a New Mexico horseman who owned him for the rest of his life.

"I'd been interested in Jackstraw for quite some time, and had done a fair amount of asking around about him," Munsey said in explaining his decision to purchase the relatively unknown stallion.

"I knew he'd outrun everybody in Mexico like he was breaking sticks. And

he was inbred to Luke McLuke, and thus to Domino. To my way of thinking, Domino was the greatest speed horse we ever had in the United States.

"Jackstraw was a breedy-looking horse who stood around 15.3 and weighed about 1,100 pounds. He had a lot of conformation. They also said he was a killer," Munsey continued. "He killed his groom while he was in training in Mexico City. From what I was told, the groom was going after Jackstraw with a pitchfork,

79

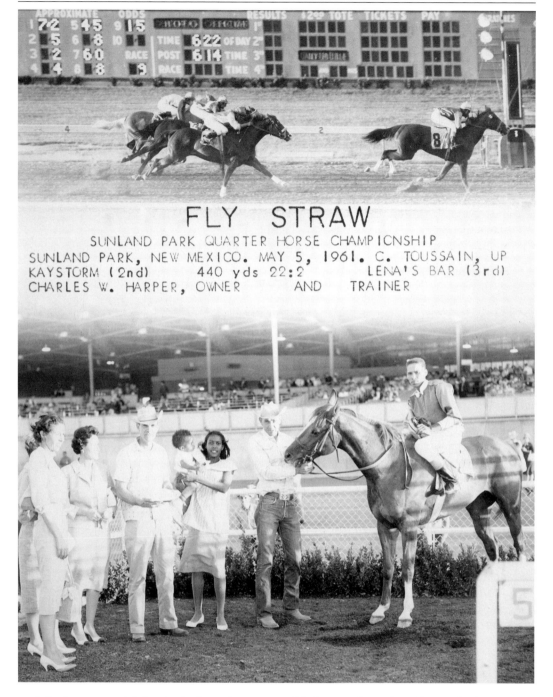

FLY STRAW
SUNLAND PARK QUARTER HORSE CHAMPICNSHIP
SUNLAND PARK, NEW MEXICO. MAY 5, 1961. C. TOUSSAIN, UP
KAYSTORM (2nd)   440 yds 22:2   LENA'S BAR (3rd)
CHARLES W. HARPER, OWNER   AND   TRAINER

In this historic photo, Jackstraw's first world champion runner, Fly Straw, races to victory in the 1961 Sunland Park Quarter Horse Championship over her half-sister Kaystorm and Lena's Bar (TB), who later produced Easy Jet. The information on the photo gives the winning time as 22.2 for the 440-yard race, the jockey as C. Toussain, and the owner-trainer as Charles W. Harper.

Photo Courtesy of *Speedhorse* **Magazine**

and the horse wouldn't take it. I used to ride him with nothing but a halter."

After purchasing Jackstraw, Munsey hit tough going.

"I tried to stand Jackstraw for $50 when I first got him," he says. "No one was interested. I tried to give away breedings to people who had good mares, but they didn't care about breeding to Jackstraw." Munsey did manage to get, by his count, eight mares bred to Jackstraw in 1955. From that first small foal crop came two legitimate stars. Nosey Josey (TB) won the 1958 New Mexico Thoroughbred Futurity at Ruidoso Downs by 17 lengths. Kaystorm, her Quarter Horse half-sister, did likewise in the New Mexico-Bred Futurity at Albuquerque.

At one point during her career, Nosey Josey won nine straight races. During her

STRAW FLIGHT   JOCKEY RONALD BANKS, UP.
                THE CHICADO V. STAKES
Winner Eighth Race April 27,1963 Purse $5000. Los Alamitos Race Course
   Moolah Bar (2nd)   400 yds.- 20.   89'er Lassie (3rd)

OWNER: RED BEE RANCH, INC.   TRAINER: DALLAS CLARK

Straw Flight, the only multiple world champion by Jackstraw, won the 1963 Chicado V. Stakes at Los Alamitos over Moolah Bar and 89'er Lassie. It was one of seven stakes wins for the fleet full sister to Fly Straw. She was ridden by jockey Ronald Banks, trained by Dallas Clark, and owned by Red Bee Ranch Inc.

Photo Courtesy of *Speedhorse* **Magazine**

4-year career, Kaystorm won 21 races from 350 to 870 yards. "With those two fillies working for him," Munsey said, "I thought people would jump at the chance to breed to Jackstraw. I was wrong again. They still weren't interested.

"I talked and pleaded. I kept his stud fee low and gave away a lot of breedings. He just wasn't doing well on the east side of New Mexico, so I moved him to Farmington."

In 1957, the first year he stood Jackstraw in Farmington, Munsey ran into W.O. Nelson, a local horseman. Nelson co-owned a mare named Flying Bobette, and Munsey talked him into breeding the mare to Jackstraw for free.

A streamlined chestnut filly by the name of Fly Straw resulted, and when she hit the Quarter tracks, she saw to it that

Double L Straw, a 1965 son of Jackstraw Jr out of Margie Burke, was a top performer on the track and in the show ring, as this ad in the February 1972 issue of The Quarter Horse Journal *shows.*

Photo by Orren Mixer

DOUBLE L STRAW

445,400
AAA • AQHA CHAMPION

Fly Straw saw to it that nobody ever overlooked Jackstraw again as a sire of speed.

1972 FEE
$500
$2.00 PER DAY
MARE CARE

GODDARD RANCH

RT. #1, HWY. 177
(405) 294-3631

ARDMORE, OKLAHOMA 73401
(214) 368-3161

nobody ever overlooked Jackstraw again as a sire of speed.

In her race career from 1961 through 1963, Fly Straw went to the post 53 times and earned a Top AAA rating. She recorded 19 firsts, 9 seconds, 9 thirds, and won just short of $40,000. Six of her victories were in stakes races, and she at one time co-held the mare record at 400 yards. In 1961 she was named as the Champion Quarter Running 3-Year-Old Filly.

In March of 1962, Fly Straw was pitted against a highly regarded Thoroughbred named Sea Raider (TB) in a $4,500, winner-take-all match race at Sunland Park. Legendary jockey Willie Shoemaker

Miss Straw, a 1961 sorrel mare by Jackstraw and out of Lula Hair, won both the New Mexico State Fair Futurity and the Sunland Park Fall Derby. Owned by A.B. Munsey, she also held the 440-yard track record at Sunland Park.

Photo Courtesy of A.B. Munsey

Although a registered Thoroughbred, Jackstraw Jr. sported excellent stock-horse conformation. Rated AAA, he founded his own family of good-looking sprinters. The information on the back of this photo gives the owner as Garner Mattingly, De Witt, Iowa.

Photo by Orren Mixer, Courtesy of *The Quarter Horse Journal*

As shown by this three-quarter front conformation study, Jet Straw, a 1964 chestnut stallion out of Miss 89'er, possessed the classic Jackstraw look.

Photo by Orren Mixer

was aboard Sea Raider, but even he was not enough to offset the blazing speed of Fly Straw as she won the 870-yard race in the world record time of :44.8.

Straw Flight, a full sister to Fly Straw, was the runaway star of Jackstraw's 1959 foal crop. From 66 starts, spread over a 4-year race career, Straw Flight, rated AAAT, amassed 19 firsts, 17 seconds, 4 thirds, and $46,202. In stakes competition, she placed first seven times, second seven times, and third four times.

She set three track records during her career and was the 1962 Champion Quarter Running 3-Year-Old Filly and the 1963 Champion Quarter Running Aged Mare.

Due to the fact that neither Fly Straw nor Straw Flight had yet made their appearances on the tracks, Jackstraw's 1960 and 1961 foal crops continued to be on the small side. Nevertheless, they made their presence felt.

On August 26, 1962, at Ruidoso Downs, the first race was a 5½-furlong event for New Mexico-bred horses. The top four finishers in the race—Nester, Truckin Straw, Sweet Straw, and Miss Straw—were all sired by Jackstraw.

Pep Straw, a 1960 chestnut stallion out of Pepper Olla, achieved a speed index of 100 and was the stakes-placed winner of $10,352. He was also voted the top 2-year-old at Sunland Park.

Jack Pere (TB) was also foaled in 1960, and by 1963 was considered one of the toughest 870-yard horses in the country.

M. Straw (TB), a 1960 bay daughter of Jackstraw, typified the durability of the line. On September 8, 1963, she won a stakes race at Ruidoso Downs. Twelve days later, she won a 6-furlong race at Albuquerque. She was then hauled more than 900 miles to New Braunfels, Tex., where, on September 28, she ran the fastest 3/8-mile recorded in that state.

Jackstraw Jr. (TB), a 1961 chestnut stallion out of Sweet Treat, achieved a high speed index of 95. It should be noted that a number of New Mexico Quarter Horse tracks allowed Thoroughbreds to compete in their sprinting futurities during the

With 53 points to his credit, Lucky Pierre, a 1964 chestnut stallion by Jackstraw and out of Winsum Miss, was his sire's top halter point-earner.

Photo by Marge Spence, Courtesy of *The Quarter Horse Journal*

Lucky Straw, a 1971 sorrel tobiano Paint stallion by Lucky Pierre, by Jackstraw, and out of Bon Bon, was an American Paint Horse Association Supreme Champion. He also sired eight APHA Champions.

Photo by Judy Schehen, Courtesy of *Paint Horse Journal*

1950s and 1960s. This enabled several Thoroughbreds such as Jackstraw Jr. and the famous Lena's Bar (TB) to receive official AQHA race ratings.

Generally acknowledged as one of the most perfectly conformed Thoroughbreds of all time from a stock-horse standpoint, Jackstraw Jr. went on to found a great line of halter and performance Quarter Horses of his own. Among his top sons was the AAA-rated AQHA Champion Double L Straw.

Other noteworthy champions from Jackstraw's 1961 foal crop included Miss Straw, speed index 100, winner of the 1963 New Mexico State Fair Futurity and 1964 Sunland Park Fall Derby, and Skip Straw, speed index 100, a Superior race horse.

Looking Up

By 1962 and 1963, things were beginning to look up for A.B. Munsey and his Thoroughbred stallion. Far from being in the position where his breeding services had to be doled out free, Jackstraw had risen in stature to the point where he could command a $1,000 stud fee.

Led by Maggie Straw, speed index 100, a multiple stakes winner and halter and performance winner, a host of Jackstraw's sons and daughters were race and show

winners in 1962 and 1963. Included were Straw's Socks, speed index 95; Cha Cha Dial, speed index 95; and Miss Straw Hat, sixth-place AQHA high-point working hunter in 1968.

1964 proved to be another banner year, with such speedsters as Broom Straw, Cindy Straw, Jacaranda, Straw Doll, Straw Lil, Jet Straw, and Lucky Pierre all achieving speed indexes of 95 or higher.

Although the Jackstraws were known as a good-looking family of horses, Jet Straw and Lucky Pierre were especially noteworthy during the late 1960s for their success as halter champions.

Jackstraw's 1965 foal crop produced Sea Nymph, his all-time leading money-earner. This chestnut mare, who was out of Dream Baby, earned $166,420 and a Superior race award during her 2-year career. She won the 1967 Blue Ribbon and Sunland Park fall futurities, the 1968 Oklahoma Derby, and placed second in the 1967 All American Futurity.

Three Jackstraw sons—Aft Of Me, Cork's Strawboss, and Jac A Muffin—were foaled in 1964, and each achieved a speed index of 95 or higher.

From Jackstraw's abbreviated last foal crop, which hit the ground in 1966, there were 11 race starters. Led by The Last Straw, speed index 100, and Troubles Straw, speed index 99, five achieved their racing Register of Merits.

In the spring of 1965, Jackstraw passed away at the age of 23.

"I'd become tremendously attached to him, and his death was really hard on me," A.B. Munsey said. "He'd reached the point where his ol' legs would swell up really bad. They'd taken a lot of punishment in all of those starts.

"It was a wonderful feeling, developing a horse like Jackstraw. I went along for several years feeding him out of my

Sea Nymph, a 1965 chestnut mare out of Dream Baby, was Jackstraw's leading race money-earner. Largely due to her second-place finish in the 1967 All American Futurity, she earned $166,410 in two seasons on the track.

**Photo by
Darol Dickinson**

pocket, using money from a small salary for hay and oats; money that should have been spent for other things.

"I talked to people and tried to make them believe in my horse. They listened and grinned, and then let me know in a roundabout way that everyone who has a horse thinks that horse is the best. They also let me know they were not about to bring their mares to my horse until he'd proven his worth.

"When did I know that Jackstraw had finally arrived?

"I suppose it was when such great breeders as Art Pollard (of Lightning Bar fame) started booking mares like Miss Wonder Bar to ol' Jackstraw. I knew then that we'd finally made it."

8 PIGGIN STRING (TB)

By Diane Ciarloni

Piggin String, like his sire, was a perfect example of a Quarter Horse-type Thoroughbred.

EVERY SUMMER, one of the most prestigious Thoroughbred yearling sales in the nation is held at Keeneland in Lexington, Kentucky. Back in 1943, among the crowd at the sale were Rukin and Frances Jelks of Arizona. They, like everyone else, were interested in the Thoroughbreds scheduled to be sold, but they wanted a special kind of Thoroughbred who would cross on Quarter mares. They found him in a yearling colt they later named Piggin String.

"Rukin was a Quarter Horse man," says Frances, "but he went to Kentucky that year searching for a Thoroughbred stallion who looked like a Quarter Horse. He knew he had found him when he saw Piggin String."

No one could doubt Jelks' Quarter Horse loyalties. During the early years, Arizona was the heartbeat of Quarter Horse racing as well as the headquarters for the American Quarter Racing Association. Jelks, whose farm was on River Road in Tucson, was a director of the Southern Arizona Horse Breeders Association, (which later became the AQRA).

Piggin String was a Thoroughbred with near-perfect Quarter Horse conformation.

Photo by Sam Levitz of the Tucson *Arizona Daily Star*, Courtesy of the American Quarter Horse Heritage Center & Museum, Amarillo, Texas.

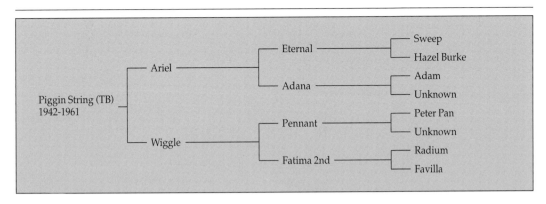

In the early 1930s, Jelks was among the pioneers who leveled out a stretch of dirt on his ranch, called it a racetrack, and set up match races. His ideas regarding breeding did much to lay the groundwork and shape the contemporary sport of Quarter Horse racing. He was among the first Quarter Horse people who decided the running segment of the breed needed an infusion of Thoroughbred blood—provided it was the right kind of Thoroughbred blood.

In 1949, 6 years after Jelks bought Piggin String at Keeneland, he told Willard Porter about his trip to Kentucky. According to that story, Jelks left his hotel room the day before the sale and took a careful look at the 400 yearlings scheduled to go into the ring. He hadn't looked beyond the cover of his sale catalog and, before he went for his inspection tour, he left the catalog with Frances. The objective was to find the "right look" without being influenced by breeding. There were 397 horses who didn't fit his mental picture. There were three who did.

The three yearlings Jelks liked were Tiger Call (who later defeated the Quarter Horse Joe Palooka in 1947), Free For All (who later won all but one of his seven starts and earned nearly $112,000), and Piggin String.

Piggin String appealed to Jelks more than the other two yearlings. Bred by Mereworth Farm in Lexington, he was a

Halter and Performance Record: Race Register of Merit; 1943-44 AQRA Co-Champion Quarter Running Stallion; 1945-46 AQRA Champion Quarter Running Stallion.

Progeny Record:

Foal Crops: 19	Performance Points Earned: 29
Foals Registered: 142	Performance Registers of Merit: 3
World Champions: 1	Race Starters: 93
Halter Point-Earners: 4	Race Money Earned: $177,907
Halter Points Earned: 10	Race Registers of Merit: 56
Performance Point-Earners: 6	Superior Race Awards: 4
Leading Race Money-Earner: Rukin String ($21,894)	

bay with a white star. Foaled in 1942, he was by Ariel, by Eternal, by Sweep.

As a 2-year-old, Ariel was hailed as a speedball, and won five of his nine starts. He returned to the track as a 3-year-old, but had only one start. He was retired to stud.

"We saw Ariel when we bought Piggin String," said Frances Jelks. "He was black and looked just like a Quarter Horse. He was a leading sprinter, and was extremely fast. He was dimpled all over with mus-

Piggin String was twice a world champion and held two track records. Jockey Frankie Figueroa, who rode the stallion throughout his career, said he was easy to ride and handle.

J. Leinenkugel Photo, Courtesy of *The Quarter Horse Journal*

Ariel (TB), the sire of Piggin String. According to Frances Jelks, "Ariel looked just like a Quarter Horse."

Piggin String shown with Frankie Figuerora in the irons after winning a race at Rillito in December 1945.

Photo Courtesy of J. Rukin Jelks Jr.

Rukin String was one of Piggin String's most successful sons, both as a race horse and as a sire. He was a three-time world champion who set multiple track records and sired 44 ROM race horses and 4 ROM performance horses. He was out of the multiple world champion runner Queenie, by Flying Bob. Queenie was also a leading dam of race ROM-earners.

Karl Johnson Photo, Tucson, Courtesy of *The Quarter Horse Journal*

Sahuaro, by Piggin String and out of Cholla Blossom, earned a race ROM as did his full sister, Silhouette. The information on the back of this photo identifies the couple as J.D. and Nora Walker, presumably owners of Sahuaro.

Buehman Studios, Courtesy of *The Quarter Horse Journal*

cles. His disposition was wonderful, and so was Piggin String's."

Piggin String wrote most of his history in the racing books of the Quarter Horse industry, but there's an account of the stallion given by Willard Porter in the November 1949 issue of *The Quarter Horse Journal* that shouldn't be ignored. Porter wrote, "His conformation closely resembles ideal Quarter Horse conformation—the working-type horse—and in the 2 years he was entered in the Tucson live-stock show in 1945 and 1946, he won the stallion cow horse classes.

"Combined with this nearly ideal working horse build, Piggin String shows great running power in his heavily muscled frame, a muscling that runs evenly throughout his body and which is put together on him for utilization of extreme early speed. He possesses tremendous driving power in the hind legs. He has good bone. His thigh is wide and heavy, and a thick layer of muscling makes for a powerful gaskin. . . . In racing condition as a 3-year-old, he weighed 1,160 pounds. His height is 15 hands and ½-inch, and today, retired to stud, he weighs close to 1,260 pounds."

Although Piggin String was a registered Thoroughbred, he was raced at Quarter Horse distances, which was allowed under the rules of the AQRA.

In the 1940s the AQRA was conducting all recognized racing (before being amalgamated with the AQHA). The only requirement for running in a recognized race was to be listed with the AQRA. To be listed required paying a small fee and recording all of the horse's known breeding as accurately as possible. This made it possible to race any horse the owner thought could run short—including Thoroughbreds.

Piggin String not only raced at short distances, but did well enough to be named AQRA Co-Champion Quarter Running Stallion in 1943-44, sharing the title with

Bit, a Superior race horse, was another one of Piggin String's good runners out of a Flying Bob mare. Bit's dam was Effie B.

Courtesy of *The Quarter Horse Journal*

Wiggy Bar, a maternal grandson of Piggin String through his dam Piggy Wiggy, was an AQHA Champion with ROMs in performance and racing.

Ralph Morgan Photo, Courtesy of *The Quarter Horse Journal*

Piggin String was the maternal grandsire of Bambi Bar Miss, who earned both a AAA rating on the track and an arena ROM. Her sire was Three Bars (TB) and her dam was the great broodmare, Piggy Wiggy, who was out of Effie B, by Flying Bob. When bred to Three Bars, Piggy Wiggy also produced Wiggy Bar, Niggy Bar, Jiggy Bar, and Ziggy Bar, all horses with race and/or show records.

Darol Dickinson Photo, Courtesy of *The Quarter Horse Journal*

Texas Lad. In 1945-46, as a 3-year-old, he was the sole earner of the same title.

Frankie Figueroa broke Piggin String to saddle, and rode the stallion throughout his racing career.

"He was easy to ride, and we could do anything with him," said Figueroa. "We decided to run him short because Rukin wanted to prove a Thoroughbred could compete with Quarter Horses.

"He was a dark bay with a roan kind of tail. I don't think his head was the best in the world, but other than that, he had good conformation. Overall, he was a good-looking horse.

"He was extremely fast and he could come out of a gate like crazy. Really, the gate was where he won all his races."

Piggin String showed tremendous promise from the first time Figueroa broke him out of the gates at Rillito Track in Tucson. Unlike a lot of Ariel's offspring, though, he was somewhat slow to develop as a 2-year-old. Still, Melville Haskell devoted significant space to the bay colt in the 1944 *AQRA Yearbook*. Haskell noted that Piggin String had started only twice ". . . and it wasn't the time, so much as the impressive way he won his races, that earned him the right to consideration. . . . Piggin String, like his sire, is a perfect example of a Quarter Horse-type Thoroughbred. On conformation alone, he could beat most Quarter Horses in the show ring."

In 1945, as a 3-year-old, Piggin String again made only two starts. He won the first one and lost the second. The next year, he was sent postward 12 times. He finished first seven times, was second twice, and failed to hit the board three times. He set a track record when he was clocked at :22.7 over 440 yards at Rillito, and the fastest time of the year when he logged :28.8 for 550 yards. No one could take exception when he received the champion Quarter running stallion title.

Piggin String had accomplished just

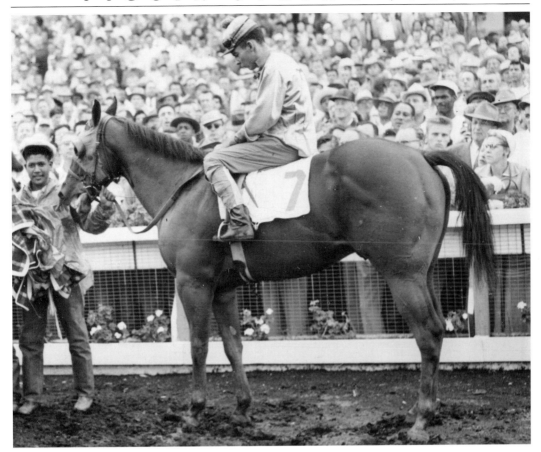

Gunny Sack, a full brother to Rukin String, was yet another successful race horse by Piggin String out of the Flying Bob daughter Queenie. This photo shows Gunny Sack winning the 1954 Rocky Mountain Quarter Horse Association Derby.

Ralph Morgan Photo, Courtesy of *The Quarter Horse Journal*

His ability as a sire was the final accomplishment left for Piggin String, and once again, he proved Jelks was correct.

about everything Jelks wanted to prove in the Quarter Horse world. So, in the spring of 1947, the Arizona horseman decided to load up the bay stallion and take him to California for some Thoroughbred competition. But, fate intervened.

"I was giving Piggin String a work at Rillito," recalled Figueroa. "We were going along fine when, all of a sudden, he stepped in a hole and went down. That was it for him. He didn't race again."

Piggin String had fractured both sesamoids and torn his suspensory ligaments. He was put in a cast for a prolonged period, but was permanently crippled. Fortunately, he was sound for breeding and could exercise comfortably in his pasture.

His ability as a sire was the final accomplishment left for Piggin String, and once again, he proved Jelks was correct. Until other Thoroughbreds, such as Three Bars and Top Deck, made their reputations as sires of running Quarter Horses, he was the dominant Thoroughbred sire of Quarter Horse runners.

"We broke the first bunch of his colts

Royal Bar, who was out of Piggin String's daughter Queen O' Clubs J, earned a AAA rating and race ROM on the track and points in the show ring. Here, he demonstrates his talent in front of a cow. The rider is unidentified.

Courtesy of *The Quarter Horse Journal*

and went to the track with them," recalled Figueroa. "They started winning right away. After that, they started selling like hotcakes."

Cholla String, Silhouette, and Sahuaro were three of Piggin String's first successful runners. All three were out of the Rukin Jelks-bred mare, Cholla Blossom, by Ben Hur, and all three earned their AAA rating on the track.

From Piggin String's 1949 crop of foals, Bit, Marrano Hilo, and Running Iron all earned AAA ratings. Running Iron, out of

Wampus Kitty, by Red Man, went to the post 128 times, winning 26, placing second 9 times, and third 18 times.

One of Piggin String's most outstanding sons was Rukin String. This bay stallion was foaled in 1950 and was out of the great 1945-46 World Champion Quarter Running Horse, Queenie, by Flying Bob. Rukin String was the 1952 Champion Quarter Running 2-Year-Old Colt, the 1953 Champion Quarter Running 3-Year-Old Colt, and the 1952 Champion Quarter Running Stallion. In 1952 he set a world record of :20.4 for 400 yards at Rillito, over the likes of Stella Moore, Brigand, and Tonto Bars Gill.

Among the other notable race horses

sired by Piggin String were Tucson Gangway, Black Mikette, Can't Catch It, Cochina (TB), Gannador, Gunny Sack, Dear Bonny (TB), Comical Sue, and Three Strings. All achieved race ratings of AAA or higher.

As a broodmare sire, Piggin String continued to transmit his speed and siring ability.

In all, the daughters of Piggin String produced 188 starters who earned $385,260 and 93 racing Register of Merits. Among his more accomplished producing daughters were Queen O'Clubs J, Piggy Wiggy, Can't Catch It, and My String.

Cord String, by Piggin String, was a producer of note in a slightly different arena, as she was the dam of Hu Zat Riker, by Kid Five. Hu Zat Riker earned 237 performance points and was the 1973 AQHA high-point horse in junior jumping and junior working hunter, and the overall high-point horse in working hunter.

The Jelks sold their property in Arizona when Piggin String was in his late teens. They had no place to keep the bay stallion, so they sold him to Rowland Stanfield of Broken Arrow, Okla., who promised to take good care of him. The horse died in 1961 at the age of 19.

"He did exactly what Rukin thought he'd do," mused Frances. "He was fast on the track, and successful in the stud. He had a lot of outstanding offspring, with Rukin String being one of the best.

"Nothing upset him. I used to feed him lumps of sugar, and he loved them. You don't forget horses like Piggin String, no matter how long ago it all happened. He did a lot for us. He was a gentle horse who gave us nothing but pleasure."

9 POCO LENA

By Kim Guenther

Today, several decades later, she is still considered by many to have been the epitome of perfection.

Even today, Poco Lena is considered one of the greatest performance mares in Quarter Horse history. She was described as having "a head like a princess and a rump like a washerwoman."

Photo Courtesy of *The Quarter Horse Journal*

THE BIRTH of bay foals at either of E. Paul Waggoner's sprawling Texas ranches, the famed Waggoner Ranch in Vernon or the Three D's Ranch near Arlington, wasn't all that unusual in the late 1940s. In fact, it was to be expected. Poco Bueno, the ranch's premier young bay stallion, was not known for passing on many other colors to his progeny.

Thus, when a bay Poco Bueno filly was born to an unproven Waggoner brood-mare on April 29, 1949, she was given no more attention than any of the other foals

already romping through the lush green pastures of the Three D's. Sporting a tiny star on her forehead and a smidgen of white on her left hind foot, Poco Lena, as the filly was later named, was just another foal. Just one of fourteen sired that year by the AQHA Champion who had yet to prove himself in the breeding barn. Had it been possible for Waggoner or his then-ranch managers, Pine Johnson and Glenn Turpin, to have foreseen the impact this little filly would have on the cutting and Quarter Horse worlds, they might have

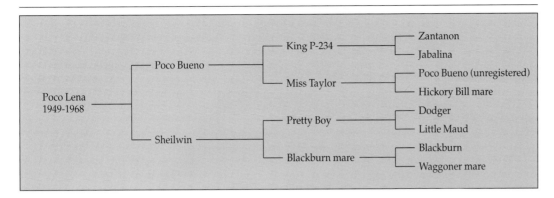

```
                                              ┌─ Zantanon
                            ┌─ King P-234 ─────┤
                            │                  └─ Jabalina
            ┌─ Poco Bueno ──┤
            │               │                  ┌─ Poco Bueno (unregistered)
            │               └─ Miss Taylor ────┤
Poco Lena ──┤                                  └─ Hickory Bill mare
1949-1968   │
            │                                  ┌─ Dodger
            │               ┌─ Pretty Boy ─────┤
            │               │                  └─ Little Maud
            └─ Sheilwin ────┤
                            │                  ┌─ Blackburn
                            └─ Blackburn mare ─┤
                                               └─ Waggoner mare
```

heralded her arrival with more fanfare.

Born to Sheilwin, a dun daughter of the Quarter Horse stallion Pretty Boy, Poco Lena was the third foal of a gentle, athletic mare who had been broke to ride, but was never shown. At the time of Poco Lena's birth, Sheilwin had produced two other foals sired by Poco Bueno: a dun yearling stallion, Pretty Pokey, who would be the AQHA's Honor Roll working cow horse in 1960, and the solid bay 2-year-old stallion Poco Tivio, one of Poco Bueno's first foals, who in the 1950s earned an AQHA Champion award, and went on to sire 10 AQHA Champions himself. ("Poco Tivio," *Legends*).

The solidly built Poco Lena was, like her sire, endowed with award-winning conformation. "This mare," wrote *The Quarter Horse Journal* Editor Willard H. Porter in his article "Poco Lena, A Mare of Distinction," "is one of the sweetest-looking equines ever to peer through a leather halter in a conformation class.

"Her dark, rich bay coat, a color inherited from her sire, is smooth and glossy. She has a beautiful head with the faintest trace of a star in the middle of her forehead. She has a good, strong shoulder, sturdy legs, powerful quarters, and she cinches up large around the middle. She's a beauty to look at. . . ."

An observation AQHA judges agreed with. At her first show, when she was barely 14 months old, Poco Lena set a precedent of what the competition could expect by winning her halter class at the Olney, Tex., show. A few months later, at

Halter and Performance Record: Performance Register of Merit; AQHA Champion; Superior Halter, 174 points; Superior Cutting, 671 points; AQHA Hall of Fame; 1959, 1960, 1961 AQHA High-Point Cutting Horse; NCHA Hall of Fame (first horse inducted); 1959, 1960, 1961 NCHA World Champion Cutting Mare; 1954, 1955, 1959, 1960,1961 NCHA Reserve World Champion; NCHA Earnings, $99,782; NCHA Silver Award; NCHA Bronze Award.

Progeny Record:

Foal Crops: 2	Performance Points Earned: 98
Foals Registered: 2	Performance Registers of Merit: 1
Performance Point-Earners: 2	Superior Performance Awards: 1

the prestigious Dallas State Fair Quarter Horse show, she again took the blue ribbon in halter.

Poco Lena could obviously hold her own in a halter class. Now, it was time to find out if she could do the same with a cow. Like so many other Waggoner horses of the era, Poco Lena was broke to ride by Andy Hensley, who always made it a point to saddle up the filly a little before noon each day.

"When it came time for lunch," recalled legendary horseman Don Dodge, who would later purchase Poco Lena, "Andy used to ride Lena to his house there on the

Barbara Worth Oakford, married at the time to Don Dodge, winning the Red Bluff Round-up on Poco Lena, beating Dodge on Snipper W.

Photo Courtesy of Deborah A. O'Brien

"Poco Lena, I believe, is the most outstanding get of Poco Bueno up to this time..."

ranch. He'd tie her up while he ate, and that mare would paw a hole in the ground big enough to bury an elephant in."

An impatient filly who quickly matured both physically and mentally, Poco Lena was soon put on cattle. Her trainer was Pine Johnson, who had ridden Poco Lena's sire, Poco Bueno, to fame.

"Poco Lena was like a mischievous child," Johnson once recalled of the mare who inherited her sire's cow savvy, but added her own pizazz. "She couldn't stand still. She wasn't nervous, but ambitious. She wanted to move. She had to move. The mare seemed to be saying, 'Just let me get into the center of that herd, and I'll show you what I can do'" ("An All-Time Money Winning Cutting Horse," *Western Horseman, February, 1962*).

In 1951, at an AQHA show held in Stamford, Tex., Poco Lena got her chance to show the cutting public her talent. In her first official outing, the 26-month-old youngster placed second in the junior cutting. With the passing of each show, Poco Lena became even more tenacious at holding a cow.

"When she went to turn, she'd drop straight down, seemed to me like 6 or 8 inches from the ground, and then glide away," said Johnson in a book authored by Sally Harrison, *Cutting, A Guide For The Non-Pro Competitor.* "She never did turn standing up."

With Johnson aboard, Poco Lena started off the 1952 season with an impressive win in the AQHA junior cutting at the Fort Worth Stock Show. Later that year, at the State Fair of Texas, the now 3-year-old cutter set what would be the first of many records she would establish by winning both the junior registered cutting and the 33-entry NCHA-approved open cutting.

As Poco Lena began making her presence felt in the cutting pens of Texas, noted California horseman Don Dodge had started thinking that his saddle might look pretty good on the back of this promising young performer. In 1951 and 1952, Dodge had ridden Poco Lena's full brother, Poco Tivio, to the NCHA Top 10. Poco Lena, Dodge accurately thought, might prove even more talented.

"Even though I won quite a little bit on Poco Tivio," said Dodge, who also at one time or another rode NCHA Hall of Fame cutters Fizzabar, Peponita, Peppy San, and Snipper W, "there was only one kind of cow that he would work—one that really ate his lunch. He was a horse who did a lot, but he couldn't compare to Poco Lena. She was the best one of them all."

During the 1953 National Western Stock Show in Denver, Dodge—with Pine Johnson acting as the go-between—negotiated with Glenn Turpin to purchase Poco Lena. When she was a young filly, Poco Lena had been given to Turpin by his employer and long-time friend, Paul Waggoner. Turpin was now willing to sell the mare—for a price.

Just exactly when, during the 10-day show, Dodge and Turpin came to an agreement regarding the value of Poco Lena is uncertain. However, when Dodge drove away from the Mile-high City, he was one horse richer, and his bank account $10,000 lighter.

In a February 19, 1953, letter Turpin wrote to Willard Porter shortly after the National Western Stock Show, he had this to say about the mare he had just recently sold: "Poco Lena, I believe, is the most outstanding get of Poco Bueno up to this time, and she is, in my opinion, the best living Quarter Horse mare today, taken from every standpoint and in all-around requirements of a good Quarter Horse mare."

Dodge didn't disagree. However, rather than taking Poco Lena with him from Denver, he asked Johnson to haul her back to the Three D's. Dodge was campaigning Snipper W for the NCHA world championship at the time, and there were shows he wanted to haul the dun gelding to before heading back to the West Coast. Dodge had missed winning the 1952 title on Snipper W by a mere $98.76. He did not want to be denied the top spot in '53. Poco Lena would have to wait a while before she made her debut with Dodge in the saddle.

When Poco Lena did arrive in Califor-

Don Dodge owned and rode Poco Lena to the peak of her success in the show ring. The fender on the saddle reads "Pacific Coast Cutting Horse Champion 1954."

Photo Courtesy of Don Dodge

nia, about a month or so after the Denver Stock Show, Dodge was eager to show off his pride and joy.

"We rode horses outside in the open country back then," Dodge recalled in Gala Nettles' book *Doc Bar*. "So I'm out there walking her around and I'm so proud of her. Everything's fine until I kick her into a lope and when I did, that mare took off like a raving idiot, and boy could she run!

"Back in those days I used to smoke cigarettes," Dodge continued, "and I

Showing her famous style, Poco Lena holds a cow. Don Dodge is in the saddle in this 1954 photo.

Photo by Ernie Mack.

smoked plenty of them because of her. I'd get so mad at her because I couldn't lope her. Day after day it was the same thing. You'd think that after a while she'd change, but not her! This mare had heart! You'd get to fighting her and that was worse, so I'd get off of her, sit under a tree and just stare at her while smoking a cigarette and cussin' her."

At the same time Dodge was trying to figure out a way to get Poco Lena to slow down and lope, he was also showing her at a few jackpot cuttings, as well as at some smaller AQHA shows in both cutting and halter. However, when one of California's premier events rolled around, the Red Bluff Round-up, Dodge was in a dilemma.

"I promoted a lot of shows in those early days," said Dodge, who at the time was serving as an NCHA vice president. "At Red Bluff, they told me they would put up $1,000 if I would guarantee them 10 horses in the cutting. Well, we only had seven or so in California, so to make up the numbers, I put Barbara Worth, whom I was married to at that time, on Poco Lena. Now Lena was a very strong mare, and of course in those days, we had to work a lot of rerun cattle and we only had one turn-back rider.

"Back then, you had to get the cattle yourself and your horse had to run more. Well, at Red Bluff, Poco Lena had to run so hard to head a cow that she ran into the fence with Barbara. They ended up winning the cutting, though, and after that, Barbara said she'd never get on her again!"

Not only did Barbara Worth, a respected horsewoman herself, win Red Bluff on Poco Lena, but she did so handily. Judge Charles G. Araujo awarded the pair a two-round total score of 144 points, 3 more than he gave Dodge on the veteran Snipper W.

As the 1953 season progressed, Dodge entered Poco Lena in more shows, occasionally letting his friend Chester Cook

At the American Royal in October 1955, Poco Lena was named reserve grand champion mare and won the open cutting.

ride Snipper W. At year's end, Snipper W had clinched the NCHA world championship with $12,250 in winnings from 37 shows. Poco Lena finished fourth in the standings with earnings of $5,354 in 21 NCHA shows. In AQHA competition that year, the talented 4-year-old Poco Lena earned the prestigious title of AQHA Champion, accumulating Superior awards in both halter and cutting.

Although Dodge had focused his efforts on Snipper W in 1953, the next 5 years he devoted to Poco Lena. An easy task, according to Dodge, because "Lena would instill a lot of confidence in you. There was seldom any doubt in her mind about what she was doing. All I'd have to do was show her the cow, move her up a little, and then let her take care of the rest. One year I kept track and I think she lost a cow only one time during the entire year. Her confidence was remarkable."

A Natural Talent

Poco Lena's natural ability to control a cow was described more vividly by Willard Porter in Bruce Beckmann's article "Poco Lena, The Princess," which appeared in the November 1990 issue of *The Quarter Horse Journal*.

"Into a crowd of cattle she would go— eager, ready, expectant. And when she got after them, eyeball to eyeball, the clods would fly and, more often than not, the critters would be the first to weaken. She simply was too much for livestock. She may well have been the most-watched cutting horse of all time. Everybody loved her because she had a head like a princess and a rump like a washerwoman."

She also had a mind of her own. During the 6 years Dodge owned Poco Lena he

> She may well have been the most-watched cutting horse of all time.

103

Don Dodge and Poco Lena back in the days when cutters didn't hold onto the saddle horn.

never did convince her to lope just the way he wanted her to.

"She always liked to run," Dodge recalled. "So, I would let her. When I would get her ready to show, it was the same every time. We'd be jiggin' along for a while and then I'd stand up and let her run. She'd go flying around the arena just as fast as she could for about two or three laps, then she would just stop, give a big puff, and walk off. When she did that, I knew she was going to be ready.

"Me getting Poco Lena ready entertained a lot of people," Dodge continued. "Back then, we showed at a lot of rodeos and because there was only one arena, we'd have to wait for the rodeo to get over before we could get in the arena and exercise our horses. That would end up being

about 3 in the morning. I think a lot of those boys back then would get up early and come down to the arena just to watch me get Poco Lena ready."

Despite the fact that she was always ready, willing, and quite capable of winning an NCHA world championship horse title, that honor was not among the many that Poco Lena would claim during her brilliant career, although she did earn the champion mare title several times. In 1954, she was the NCHA's reserve world champion cutting horse, behind Marion's Girl, owned by Marion Flynt of Midland, Tex., and ridden by Buster Welch.

In 1955, the race for the cutting title proved to be a close one between 6-year-old Poco Lena and Milt Bennett's 7-year-old palomino mare Snooky. Going into the final show of the season, the prestigious Cow Palace cutting in San Francisco, Poco Lena had a $27 lead.

In the first go-round in San Francisco Poco Lena earned $300 for posting the round's top score. A solid second-round performance put her in a good position

B.A. Skipper Jr. rode Poco Lena to a reserve championship in the NCHA Finals at the 1960 Fort Worth Stock Show.

Photo by L.H. Launspach

to win the Cow Palace and the world championship. Then, misfortune struck. One day before the finals, Poco Lena colicked from eating the straw bedding in her stall. So severe was her condition that she was rushed to the University of California-Davis.

"She showed a lot of guts," Dodge recalled of that near-tragic day. "We wheeled the trailer up to her stall and as sick as she was, she went right in. A couple of the boys, Stanley Bush and Dick Carlisle, rode in the trailer with her to Davis to keep her from going down."

Once at Davis, Poco Lena was immediately operated on. Doctors John Wheat and Bill Linfoot were not sure that their patient would survive. They did not know, however, the grit Poco Lena possessed.

"She was a poor risk," Wheat told Dodge after the operation proved to be a success. "I didn't think we could save her. But your mare certainly has a lot of heart."

A heart that would, according to Porter, enable Poco Lena to "give her very all every time out." After Poco Lena won her second NCHA reserve world championship in 1955 and after she fully recovered from her operation, Dodge hauled her to only a few select shows during the next 3 years. With limited showing, she still managed to stay in the NCHA's Top 10, finishing in the No. 4 position in 1956, and as the No. 5 horse in both 1957 and 1958. She also continued to wow the judges in halter.

"Lena was a good-looking mare to a performance man's standards," said Dodge of the solid 15.1, 1,250-pound per-

> **"I didn't think we could save her. But your mare certainly has a lot of heart."**

Shorty Freeman and Doc O' Lena showing the style that helped them win the 1970 NCHA Futurity.

Photo by Frank Conrad, Courtesy of NCHA

former he led to numerous grand championships. "I think she won every big stock show at one time or another at halter. And she probably won the cutting at all of them too. Back then, there was a big joke about Poco Lena because she usually didn't win them both at the same time. One show it would be halter and the next one it would be cutting. When she won at halter, the other boys figured they had a better chance of winning the cutting."

Dodge showed Poco Lena from 1953 to 1959, winning close to $50,000 in NCHA money during an era when the average worker's take-home pay was significantly less than that. He also saw her inducted as the first horse into the NCHA Hall of Fame.

"One of the better Quarter Horse mares in competition today is Poco Lena," wrote Porter in an article that appeared in the August 1957 issue of *The Quarter Horse Journal*, "a cattle carver who separates steers and heifers like a butcher chopping choice cuts off a side of beef.

"Some horses have to be 'picked up,' pushed, or cued. Not Poco Lena. She likes the way she earns her hay and oats. She gives her very all every time out. She has the fantastic ability to go to the head of a cow and, when the cow turns, to turn herself—belly to the ground, ears back, looking the cow-critter straight in the face.

"If she happens to make a small mistake—the best ones do occasionally—she has the action and speed to 'get out of it' far faster than most horses. And the wilder the cattle, the more 'coyote' she becomes, challenging them, anticipating their moves, blocking them at every turn."

B.A. Skipper Jr.

Ironically, during the 6 years that Dodge showed his famed Poco Lena, no one ever asked him to put a price on her.

"Nearly everybody showing in the early days was a cowboy," Dodge noted. "There were no non-pros and anyone who

Poco Lena's first foal by Doc Bar, Doc O' Lena, created his own dynasty of cutting horses, who have earned in excess of $13 million. He died in 1993. Shorty Freeman is the handler.

Photo Courtesy of *The Quarter Horse Journal*

was of a non-pro type had to show right in there with the rest of us. So consequently, there wasn't a big demand for cutting horses. The people who were willing to pay a big price for a horse were few and far between."

Wealthy Texas businessman Barney A. Skipper Jr. was one of those few. A non-pro type with the desire and the bank account to take on the cowboys, Skipper, who was described in an early issue of the *Cuttin' Hoss Chatter* as a "master of showmanship with an encyclopedic knowledge of cattle," made his first showing in the NCHA standings aboard Poco Mona, a mare who he, Bubba Cascio, and Shorty Freeman rode to a 1955 third-place finish behind Snooky and Poco Lena.

Skipper eventually sold Poco Mona to the Pinehurst Stables of Houston for a price reported to be in "the neighborhood of $25,000." Late in 1958 he began looking for a horse to replace her. Not just any cutter would do, however; Skipper wanted 9-year-old Poco Lena. And, he

was willing to pay for her. His offer of $18,000, however, was much less than what he received for Poco Mona.

When Dodge told his good friend Milt Bennett that Skipper had offered him $18,000 for Poco Lena, Bennett had only one thing to say. "You'll just be sorry once, Don, and that will be from now on."

"And, it turned out that way," acknowledges Dodge, who decided to sell Poco Lena to Skipper in the spring of 1959.

A busy new chapter in the life of Poco Lena began. The mare that Porter described as a horse who "liked the way she earns her hay and oats" would have ample opportunity to put in overtime working under her new owner. In 1959 in his first year of showing her, Skipper hauled Poco Lena to 42 AQHA shows and competed in 55 NCHA-approved cuttings

Randy (left) and M.L. Chartier with Dry Doc at Fairhaven Farms in Michigan in the 1970s. Dry Doc was Poco Lena's last foal. He died in 1997.

Photo Courtesy of *The Quarter Horse Journal*

throughout the United States and Canada.

That year, with Skipper held securely in the saddle with a seat belt, the ever-consistent Poco Lena performed valiantly, earning her third NCHA reserve world championship and for the first time the title of world champion cutting mare. Although her half-brother, Poco Stampede, shown by Jack Newton, denied her the NCHA title, Poco Lena was, for the first time in her career, named the AQHA's high-point cutting horse. Also in 1959, she and Poco Mona shared the title of co-champions of the six go-round NCHA Tournament of Champions.

In 1960 and again in 1961 Poco Lena earned the titles of NCHA reserve world champion, world champion cutting mare, and the AQHA's high-point cutting horse. However, an extensive show schedule was beginning to take its toll. Late in 1961 Poco Lena foundered.

Tragedy Strikes

Down for a little while, but certainly not out, Poco Lena was back on the road halfway through the 1962 season. She was again racking up wins in both cutting and in halter when tragedy struck.

After his win on Poco Lena at a show in Douglas, Ariz., Skipper flew himself home in his private plane. Poco Lena—who was closing in on a then-unheard-of $100,000 in NCHA earnings—would be hauled back to Texas by a hired driver. Unfortunately, however, sometime after 3 o'clock the morning of October 1, 1962, Dallas radar lost contact with Skipper. Four days later the wreckage of his plane was found. Skipper did not survive the crash.

In the confusion that followed, Poco Lena was left in the trailer, parked somewhere between Arizona and Texas without food and water. When she was finally

M.L. Chartier cutting on Dry Doc. Chartier and two partners bought the bay stallion after his full brother, Doc O'Lena, won the 1970 NCHA Futurity. Dry Doc followed in his footsteps and won the 1971 event, ridden by Buster Welch.

Photo by Dalco

located on October 5, her founder was much worse, and she would never cut again.

A few months after that ordeal, at the B.A. Skipper Jr. Estate Dispersal Sale held in Gladewater, Tex., Poco Lena was one of 84 horses to sell.

"It seemed like every Quarter Horse man in the country was there at the sale," said Ike Hamiliton (now deceased), who presided over that sale. "Several of them even brought their vets to look at her because everybody knew about her condition. . . .

"When the bidding started, quite a few bid on her at first. D.C. Johnston . . . was a heavy bidder and bid on her up to $14,000, but Grady Madden stepped in then, bid $14,200 and bought her." . . . "(*Doc Bar*, Gala Nettles)

Madden, of Minden, La., may have been the successful bidder, but Poco Lena was never transferred into his name. A few days after the sale, Madden, for unknown reasons, decided that Poco Lena was not the horse for him. While the details of all of this were being worked out between Madden and trustees of the Skipper Estate, Poco Lena was held at a cattle rest at the Texas-Louisiana border for several days. While there, the champion's crippled feet, as well as her overall physical condition continued to deteriorate.

News traveled fast in the Quarter Horse world, and when California dentist Stephen Jensen and his wife, Jasmine— relative newcomers to the equine industry—heard that the March 20, 1963, sale of Poco Lena never went through, they were eager to buy her. They thought she might cross well with their 7-year-old halter champion, Doc Bar, a stallion they had purchased the year before for $30,000.

Smart Little Lena, who is Poco Lena's grandson through his sire Doc O' Lena, won the NCHA Futurity, Derby, and Super Stakes. Smart Little Lena traces to Royal King, also featured in this book, through his dam, Smart Peppy, who is out of the Royal King daughter Royal Smart.

Photo Courtesy of *The Quarter Horse Journal*

With the help of Bob Elliot, who was a good friend of B.A. Skipper Jr., the Jensens purchased the badly crippled Poco Lena for $12,500.

"They took a chance buying Poco Lena," noted Stephenie Ward, the Jensens' daughter. "Some might even say that they were crazy. But, they thought that if they could get even just one colt out Poco Lena, it would be worth it."

Wanting their new mare to be as comfortable as possible while making the long trip from Texas to California, the Jensens arranged a trailer with special foam rubber on the floor to carry her west. Her destination was the veterinarian clinic of Doctors Gary Deter and Frank Wayland in Salinas. There, Poco Lena's crippled feet would receive the attention they so desperately needed.

On the day she would arrive in Salinas, the Jensens eagerly waited at the clinic. Elation, however, turned to heartbreak as the couple watched the malnourished Poco Lena painfully make her way off the trailer.

"They were just horrified at her appearance," Stephenie sadly recalled. "She could barely stand and her physical condition was appalling. They considered putting her to sleep right then because she looked like she was in so much pain."

Doctors Wayland and Deter had another idea. Utilizing breakthrough technology for the time, the doctors resectioned Poco Lena's hoofs, removing the outer shell and replacing it with acrylic. Although the procedure did not heal her, it did help ease her pain. Poco Lena had been saved.

While Poco Lena spent time recovering in the irrigated pastures that surrounded Wayland and Deter's clinic in Salinas, her doctors were faced with yet another challenge—getting Poco Lena in foal to Doc Bar. Month after month the Jensens, the doctors, and their assistants eagerly waited for Poco Lena to show some sign of ovulatory activity. Month after month they were disappointed.

During her years in the show ring, Poco Lena had been given injections to control her heat cycle. This and the fact that she was 14 years old and had never had a foal were daunting obstacles the doctors seemed unable to overcome.

However after 2 years and much effort, the doctors finally got the mare to conceive in 1966.

"You couldn't describe our excitement," said Stephenie. "Dr. Wayland, who was in the hospital when he heard the news, couldn't wait to get out and palpate Poco Lena. He wanted to feel for himself that she was in foal."

At their Double J Ranch in Paicines, Calif., the Jensens were adamant that Poco Lena would not be turned out with the other broodmares, where she might run the risk of being kicked. Nor would she be confined to a stall or dusty paddock. No, Poco Lena, queen of the cutting pen for so many years, would receive the royal treatment she so richly deserved. Her domain would be the plush lawn that surrounded the Jensens' home. There, she could rest as she pleased on the soft, cool turf, or nibble at will on the buffet of choice greenery and tasty flowers that surrounded the yard.

"Sometimes when Poco Lena would lie down, we would go over and rub her legs," Stephenie recalled, "and she would just lie there like it felt so good. There were even times when my mother would put blankets down so it would be easier for her to walk across the driveway."

It was on the Jensens' lawn that Poco Lena's first foal, Doc O' Lena, was born. The following year she gave birth to another bay colt sired by Doc Bar, Dry Doc. Although both Doc O' Lena and Dry Doc enjoyed the luxury of lawn-living, they were never denied the opportunity to socialize with the other foals.

"When Doc O' Lena was born," Stephenie recalled, "we took off the lower two boards of the fence that separated the yard and the pasture so that he could go underneath the fence and play with the other colts. When he got hungry he came back and nursed, slept for a while, and then played some more. I guess he and Dry Doc kind of had the best of both worlds."

Like their mother, both Doc O' Lena and Dry Doc took the cutting world by storm. In 1970—while Poco Lena was still the NCHA's lifetime leading money-earner— Doc O' Lena was the horse to beat at the NCHA Futurity. With Shorty Freeman aboard, the 3-year-old stallion rewrote the record books as the first horse to sweep the event, winning the go-rounds, the semifinals and the finals for then-owner Adrian Berryhill of Scottsdale.

As a sire, Doc O' Lena (now deceased) was equally as impressive. His get— including such notable performers as Smart Little Lena, Tap O Lena, Lenas Dynamite, and Scarlett O Lena—have earned more than $13 million in the cutting pen. Doc O' Lena also sired horses who earned a total of 4,335 halter and performance points in AQHA competition.

Doc O' Lena's sibling, Dry Doc, followed hot on the heels of his full brother as both a champion performer and a sire. At the 1971 NCHA Futurity, Dry Doc, ridden by Buster Welch, was all the rage. The stallion bested a record 245 entries to win the futurity crown and $17,246 in prize money for then-owners M.L. Chartier, Frank Ward, and Stanley Petitpren, all from Michigan. Chartier later bought out his partners and became the sole owner of Dry Doc.

As a sire, Dry Doc also excelled. Get such as Dry Clean, Dry Oil, Dry Dot and Dry Doc's Dottie helped push the total earnings of Dry Doc's progeny to almost $4 million. Dry Doc, now deceased, also sired one AQHA Champion. His offspring have earned a total of 2,596.5 halter and performance points in open, amateur, and youth classes.

Dry Doc was the last foal the legendary Poco Lena would produce. On December 16, 1968, a few months after the colt was weaned, Poco Lena was put to sleep. Poco Lena's legacy, however, continues to be carried on through the many champion performers whose pedigrees boast her name.

In her heyday Poco Lena was often described as "near-perfect." Today, several decades later, she is still considered by many to have been the epitome of perfection.

10 POCO PINE

By Frank Holmes

Poco Pine grew up from a shaggy little bay colt to win 50 halter championships and become a leading sire.

WHEN PAUL Curtner decided to attend E. Paul Waggoner's Quarter Horse sale in Vernon, Tex., May 17, 1954, he did so with an exact purpose in mind. The Jacksboro, Tex., resident had already been in the Quarter Horse business for several years, and owned a promising young stallion by the name of Town Crier. Curtner decided that it was time to begin assembling some quality mares.

"I went to the Waggoner sale determined to buy a daughter of Blackburn," Curtner recalls. "They were renowned as producers, no matter what you bred them to. Furthermore, I wanted whichever Blackburn mare that I wound up with to have a Poco Bueno filly at her side, and to be bred back to Poco Bueno." What Curtner wound up with was a buckskin daughter of Pretty Boy, with a Poco Bueno colt at her side.

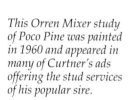

This Orren Mixer study of Poco Pine was painted in 1960 and appeared in many of Curtner's ads offering the stud services of his popular sire.

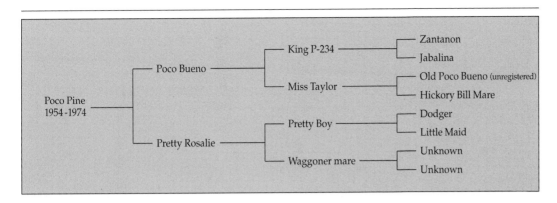

```
                                              ┌── Zantanon
                                  ┌── King P-234 ──┤
                                  │               └── Jabalina
                  ┌── Poco Bueno ──┤
                  │               │               ┌── Old Poco Bueno (unregistered)
                  │               └── Miss Taylor ─┤
Poco Pine ────────┤                               └── Hickory Bill Mare
1954-1974         │
                  │                               ┌── Dodger
                  │               ┌── Pretty Boy ──┤
                  └── Pretty Rosalie ─┤            └── Little Maid
                                  │               ┌── Unknown
                                  └── Waggoner mare ─┤
                                                  └── Unknown
```

"I looked at a pen full of Blackburn mares before the sale," Curtner says, "and found a couple I sure wouldn't have minded owning. There was also a nice buckskin, Pretty Rosalie, I kind of liked. She stood around 15 hands and would weigh in the neighborhood of 1,100 pounds. She had a good head, nice long neck, a big hip, and a lot of hind leg. But she had a shaggy little bay colt at her side who didn't impress me, so I put her out of my mind.

"It turned out that she was a daughter of Pretty Boy, another well-known Waggoner broodmare sire. She was the dam of Poco Stampede, who was just beginning to make a name for himself as a cutting horse, and she and her colt were one of the first lots in the sale.

"My wife was at the sale with me and, when Pretty Rosalie came into the sale ring, she casually said, 'If you're going to buy a mare, you might as well buy this one.' They had a bid of $1,500 on the pair at the time, and were asking for $1,550. Without really thinking about it, I stuck my hand up. The auctioneer recognized my bid, asked for $1,600 around twice, and then knocked them off as sold to me.

"I was a little stunned. That was a lot of money to give for a mare and colt in 1954. I got up out of my seat and headed to the pens to see what I had bought.

"I hadn't gotten very far," Curtner continues, "when Bob Burton, who had trained horses for the Waggoners, stopped me and said, 'Paul, you bought the best mare in the sale. I broke her to

Halter and Performance Record: Halter Points, 135; Performance Points, 17; AQHA Champion; Superior Halter; Performance Register of Merit.

Progeny Record:

Foal Crops: 19

Foals Registered: 464

AQHA Champions: 37

Youth Champions: 4

Halter Point-Earners: 163

Halter Points Earned: 3,312.5

Superior Halter Awards: 15

Performance Point-Earners: 180

Performance Points Earned: 7,637

Performance Registers of Merit: 105

Superior Performance Awards: 39

Race Starters: 1

ride as a 5-year-old. She threw me off pretty regular, but in between times she sure had a lot of cow.'"

Reaching the pen that held Pretty Rosalie and her foal, Curtner ran into Pine Johnson, another well-known Waggoner Ranch trainer. "Pine said the same thing to me about Pretty Rosalie that Bob had," Curtner says. "So I asked him what he thought about her colt. 'I think he's the best Poco Bueno colt I've ever seen,' Pine replied.

"To be completely truthful, I just wasn't that keen on the colt to begin with, but I got to thinking about what Pine had said while I was driving home that evening, and I decided that, if he was that high on

Curtner and Poco Pine, when the stallion stood grand at a Quarter Horse show in Fairfield, Texas.

Photo by Glenn Hippel, Courtesy of *The Quarter Horse Journal*

In this winner's circle shot, Curtner receives the championship trophy from B. F. Phillips for Poco Pine's win at the 1959 American Royal in Kansas City, Mo., while ringmaster Ralph Morrison looks on.

Photo Courtesy of *The Quarter Horse Journal*

With 239 points to her credit, Poco Margaret was the top open halter point-earner sired by Poco Pine. The 1962 AQHA Honor Roll Halter Horse, she also produced Gold Margarita, the 1971 AQHA High-Point Halter Horse.

Photo by Bert Bollinger, Courtesy of *The Quarter Horse Journal*

him, I'd just name the colt after him. So I registered him as Poco Pine."

Once Curtner got his new purchases home and began to work with the colt, he found that he liked him enough to take him to some shows. Exhibited four or five times as a weanling, Poco Pine won each time. Finding that the youngster was somewhat of a slow developer, Curtner chose not to show him to any great extent as a yearling or 2-year-old.

As the fall of 1957 rolled around, however, Curtner deemed the then-3-year-old-stallion ready.

"Poco Pine had not been shown in quite a while," he says. "They were having a show in Fort Worth, and I decided to take him to it. On the morning of the show, I went down to his stall and started to clean him up. It was hot, and he was dirty, and about the time I got one side done, I got discouraged, quit, and went back to the house.

"The more I thought about it, the more I wanted to take him, so I went back to the barn and finished what I'd started.

"When I got to the show," Curtner continues, "the first thing I saw was Loyd Jinkins unloading a trailerful of good-looking King Ranch horses. I thought to myself, 'I don't stand a chance here,' and I almost quit again. But I went ahead and led him into the 3-year-old stallion class, and we won it.

"While I was waiting to go back in for grand and reserve, I was talking to a few of the boys who were sitting on the fence near the in-gate. B.F. Phillips was there, and Billy Bush, the cutting horse trainer, and another fella whose name I can't recall. I said to them, 'There's not much

Poco Mon Cherrie, a full sister to Poco Margaret, earned both an AQHA Championship and Superior halter award while owned by Lloyd Geweke of Ord, Nebraska.

Photo by Roger Wilson, Courtesy of *The Quarter Horse Journal*

"Poco Pine had won his first grand championship, and I had lost $3 because of it. But I was proud I had."

sense in me going back in. I don't stand a chance of standing grand or reserve.' B.F. replied, 'I'll bet you a dollar you win grand.'

"'You're on,' I replied. Bill made the same offer, and so did the other guy. I wound up betting $3 that my horse wouldn't win the championship.

"George Tyler, from Gainesville, Tex., was the judge that day and, after he'd looked 'em all over, he said, 'Paul, just bring your horse right up here to the front.' Poco Pine had won his first grand championship, and I had lost $3 because of it. But I was proud I had."

Curtner had let it be known from the beginning of Poco Pine's halter career that his goal was for the stallion to win 50 grand championships at halter. During his 3-year-old year, the bay stallion garnered four grands. The following year he earned three more. In 1959, Poco Pine was shown 29 times and stood grand 21 times. By October of 1960, he had added 21 additional grands to his record. His total now stood at 49.

On October 27, 1960, Curtner took the then-6-year-old stallion to a show in Beaumont, Texas. George Tyler was the judge and, as he had 3 years earlier, he made Poco Pine the grand champion stallion. "I went up to George after the show," Curtner recalls, "and said to him, 'I wanted to win 50 grands with Poco Pine. You gave him his first, and you gave him his last.' And then I retired him from halter competition."

Even while he had him fitted for halter competition, Curtner had started Poco Pine under saddle.

"I broke Poco Pine myself, in the fall of his 2-year-old year," he says. "There really wasn't any 'break' to it. After I'd saddled

Poco Coed, a 1959 bay mare out of Do Way, was another of Poco Pine's top show offspring. An AQHA Champion and Superior halter horse, she also went on to become a solid producer.

Photo Courtesy of *The Quarter Horse Journal*

Texas Pine, a 1960 black stallion, was one of several top horses produced when Poco Pine was bred to the Bill Cody daughter Codalena.

Photo Courtesy of *The Quarter Horse Journal*

Pine Bo was a gelded full brother to Texas Pine, who went on to become one of Poco Pine's most accomplished show performers. He amassed 1,122 points in open, amateur, and youth competition.

Photo by Darol Dickinson, Courtesy of The Quarter Horse Journal

Another highly successful cross was Poco Pine on the Hobo daughter Hobo Sue. Mr. Poco Pride, a 1967 gelding, was one of the resulting foals. As a show horse, he earned 954 points in open, amateur, and youth competition.

Photo by LeRoy Weathers, Courtesy of The Quarter Horse Journal

him a few times, I just stepped on, and he walked off like he'd been ridden every day of his life.

"After I'd ridden him for a while, I took him to Bill Ihler of Roanoke, Tex., for cutting training. Bill showed him in the junior cutting at the Southwestern Livestock Exposition in Fort Worth the following January. He placed fifth in a class of 36, as

I recall. At the same show the following year, with Milt Bennett riding him, he placed first."

Although Poco Pine gave every indication that he possessed NCHA-caliber cutting horse skills, Curtner found it hard during the late 1950s to juggle his popular stallion's multifaceted career as a halter horse, cutting horse, and breeding stallion. In 1958 alone, Poco Pine was bred to 80 outside mares at a $500 fee. As a result, the stallion's performance career was pushed to the background until the summer of 1960. At that time, it was decided to go after the remaining performance points needed for an AQHA Championship. On

Dollie Pine, a 1960 sorrel mare, was another of the Poco Pine-Hobo Sue off-spring. An AQHA Champion herself, she went on to produce, among others, the leading AQHA pleasure sire Zippo Pine Bar.

Photo Courtesy of *The Quarter Horse Journal*

In 1959, a second offer to buy Poco Pine was fielded by Curtner. This one was even harder to turn down.

August 23, 1960, the last of these points were accumulated and Poco Pine was retired from the show ring.

In looking back on his stallion's stellar show career, Curtner recalls two of the many opportunities that he had to sell him. "E. Paul came up to me at a show when Pine was a 3- or 4-year-old," he says. "He told me that Barney Skipper, who owned Poco Mona and later Poco Lena, sure wanted to own Poco Pine. He said he thought he could get me $40,000 for Poco Pine. I told him that I really didn't care to sell him.

"This was around the time that Thoroughbred stallions such as Three Bars, Depth Charge, and Piggin String were becoming popular as sires, and E. Paul wasn't too happy about it.

"'You might as well sell Poco Pine,' he told me. 'Those Thoroughbred boys are going to put us all out of the business before they're through.'

"'No they're not,' I replied. 'We just have to pick a few of these good performance-bred mares and breed them.' And I

proved that I was right about that a few years later when I took a daughter of Leo by the name of Leo Pat, bred her to Three Bars (TB), and got Zippo Pat Bars." In 1959, a second offer to buy Poco Pine was fielded by Curtner. This one was even harder to turn down.

"I was at a show in Vernon in 1959 when a fellow from west Texas asked me to price Poco Pine," he recalls. "I said, 'Well, if I was going to sell him, it would take $100,000 to buy him.' I figured that would put a stop to his interest.

"'I'd just give that for him,' he replied. It was early in the day, and I hadn't had anything to eat yet. My ol' stomach was

Poco Pecho, a 1960 sorrel stallion by Poco Pine and out of Bird Flowers, earned his AQHA Championship in 1964.

Photo Courtesy of *The Quarter Horse Journal*

"George Tyler was standing right there, taking it all in. He whispered, 'Take the money, take the money!'"

churning something fierce. One hundred thousand dollars was sure a lot of money.

"George Tyler was standing right there, taking it all in. He whispered, 'Take the money, take the money!' Then Matlock Rose walked by, with a bridle looped over his arm, and he said, 'Paul, you've got a good horse there. If you plan to stay in the business, you might as well keep him.'

"That was just the kind of support that I needed right at that moment. I thanked Matlock, turned the man's offer down, and went and got some breakfast."

So Poco Pine remained with Curtner and, in very short order, developed into one of the top young show sires of the breed.

Bred to a limited number of mares as a 2-year-old in 1956, Poco Pine sired two AQHA Champions and one Superior halter horse from his first foal crop. By the time his last foal crop hit the ground 19 years later, he had put 464 get into the AQHA registry. An impressive 230 of these, or just under 50 percent, were performers, and they earned a total of 3,312.5 halter and 7,637 performance points in open, youth, and amateur competition. And it should be pointed out that the AQHA's youth and amateur programs were in their infancy during the period

120

that the bulk of Poco Pine's get were being shown. Prior to Poco Pine's arrival as a breeding horse, the names that dominated the AQHA's yearly top sires lists were those of his sire and grandsire, Poco Bueno and King P-234. By the time he was through, Curtner's shaggy bay colt changed all of that.

Thirty-seven of the Poco Pines went on to earn AQHA Championships and that was enough to place Poco Pine No. 1 in that category for years. As of 1997, he was still the No. 2 most-prolific AQHA Champion sire.

Like their sire, the Poco Pines proved to be versatile two-way champions, adept in both the halter ring and performance arena. Poco Margaret, a 1958 sorrel mare out of Charlotte Ann, was Poco Pine's top open halter point-earner. The 1962 AQHA High-Point Halter Horse, she earned a total of 239 points.

Pine Chock Lily, a 1966 bay mare by Poco Pine and out of Lil Cody, earned 176 halter points during her show career, and Poco Sniggle, a 1963 sorrel Poco Pine daughter out of Showdown Cupie, amassed 146.

Among the other top halter point-earners sired by Curtner's bay were Poco Coed (139), Annie Lee Pine (107), and Pine's Annie (102).

With 294 points to his credit, Pine Osage, a 1968 sorrel gelding out of Lil Cody, was Poco Pine's top point-earner in open performance competition. He was closely followed by the top show mare Pine's Bar Lady, a 1963 sorrel out of Bar Feathers. The 1970 AQHA Open High-Point Trail Horse Mare, Pine's Bar Lady, earned 252.5 points.

Other top Poco Pine arena performers included Karla Jet Pine (215.5), Barney's Lori (191), Mr. Poco Pride (150.5), and Pine Bo (136). In addition, Pine's Holly Boy, a 1964 black stallion out of Holly Five, was the 1967 AQHA Open High-Point Western Pleasure Stallion; and Paisano Pine, a 1964 chestnut stallion out of Juana Jay, was the 1971 AQHA Open High-Point Reining Stallion.

As was alluded to earlier, the AQHA youth program was just getting under

Among the top show horses that Poco Pecho, a son of Poco Pine, sired was Pecho Dexter, who earned 2,568.5 points in halter, western pleasure, trail, and hunter under saddle. The 1964 sorrel gelding is shown here as a 2-year-old with John Cratty of Marion, Ohio, in the saddle.

Photo by Roger Wilson, Courtesy of The Quarter Horse Journal

With the likes of Poco Stampede (left) and Poco Pine, it was easy to see why Pretty Rosalie could win produce-of-dam classes.

Photo by Swofford's Studio

way when the majority of the Poco Pines were being shown. Despite this, several of the bay stallion's get enjoyed stellar careers as youth show mounts.

In addition to the 1,245 open and amateur points that Pine Bo amassed, he also earned 877 youth points to secure the position of being Poco Pine's top point-earner in that division. The 1985 AQHA World Championship Show All-Around Amateur Horse and 1988 AQHA Youth High-Point Reining Horse, Pine Bo also earned an open AQHA

Championship, youth performance championship, youth versatility award, and seven open and youth Superiors.

Mr. Poco Pride, a 1967 gelded full brother to Poco Margaret, was another top youth mount. To go along with his 275 open and amateur points, he also accumulated 613 youth points.

Pine Osage (395), Mister Big Pine (321), Barney's Lori (207), and Lady Bar Pine (190) were more of the Poco Pines who proved to be achievers as mounts for youth competitors.

All told, the sons and daughters of Poco Pine earned 10,949.5 points in open, amateur, and youth competition. They amassed 105 ROMs, 15 halter Superiors, and 39 performance Superiors.

Although he proved over the years that he could sire competitive show horses out of virtually any kind of mare, there were several bloodlines that Poco Pine crossed especially well with. Tops on the list would have to be the Bill Cody line.

"Watt Hardin was a close personal friend of mine," Curtner says, "and he was the man who brought Bill Cody into this area from the King Ranch. Over the years, and even after he sold him, Watt helped me locate good Bill Cody mares to put in my broodmare band."

Among the Bill Cody-bred mares that Curtner acquired were such outstanding producers as Codalena, Lil Cody, and Annie Lee Cody. Codalena, a 1952 sorrel mare out of Watt's Niki, and thus a full sister to Town Crier, produced six horses by Poco Pine who went on to become AQHA Champions. They were Texas Pine, Pine Pancho, Pine Chock, Pine's Codalena, Pine's Leana, and Barry Pine.

Lil Cody, a 1951 sorrel mare out of Short Stuff Foster, produced three top show horses when crossed on Poco Pine. Two of them—Pine Bullet and Pine Chock Lily—became AQHA Champions. The third—Pine Osage—earned a Superior in western pleasure. Annie Lee Cody, a 1956 sorrel mare by Lee Cody and out of Annie Lee S., was the dam of AQHA Champion Pine Wampy and the Superior halter horses Annie Lee Pine and Pine's Annie.

But probably the greatest cross Curtner ever made to establish the Poco Pine bloodline as one that would endure came about when he bred the Joe Moore granddaughter Hobo Sue to the popular sire. A 1951 bay mare sired by Hobo and out of Home Gal, Hobo Sue produced several top show horses by Poco Pine, including the already referenced top youth mounts Mister Big Pine and Pine Bo. She also produced two full sisters to the geldings who would go on to become AQHA Champions. One was a mare named Pine's Penny, the other a mare called Dollie Pine.

Dollie Pine, when retired to the broodmare band and bred to Curtner's Three Bars (TB) son, Zippo Pat Bars, produced the legendary pleasure horse sire Zippo Pine Bar and his full sister, Scarborough Fair. The latter mare, after a fantastic show career in which she earned an AQHA Championship and 178 halter and performance points, went on to produce the world champion halter horse and leading sire Zip To Impress.

And Dollie Pine was not the only Poco Pine daughter who proved she could pull her own weight as a producer. To date, the Poco Pine daughters have produced the earners of 19,228.5 halter and performance points, 256 ROMs, 101 Superiors, and 28 AQHA Championships.

Not to be outdone by their sisters, a number of Poco Pine's sons went on to become noteworthy sires. Included are such horses as Poco Pecho, Texas Pine, Pine Wampy, Pine Chock, Paisano Pine, Barry Pine, and Heart Bar Feathers.

Poco Pecho, in particular, did his part to further the family's reputation as the sire of the all-time leading AQHA point-earning show horse, Pecho Dexter.

As for the head of the clan, Poco Pine lived a full and productive life, all in the ownership of Paul Curtner, and passed away quietly in his sleep in 1974, at the age of 20.

History has proven that Poco Pine is, as a couple of top Waggoner cowboys maintained he would be, one of the very best sons of Poco Bueno.

11 POCO DELL

By Jim Goodhue

"My first impression when I saw him was that this was going to be the horse I had to have."

Poco Dell, a 1952 bay stallion, was an outstanding sire for Jimmie Randals of Montoya, New Mexico.

Photo by Harvey Caplin, Courtesy of *The Quarter Horse Journal*

IN 1952, 26-year-old New Mexico rancher Jimmie Randals had a bad case of cutting horse fever. He had ridden his home-trained ranch gelding, Jessie Lee, to a third-place ribbon in a New Mexico cutting while competing with such top-caliber horses as Chickasha

Mike, ridden by Buster Welch. Chickasha Mike won the class, and Randals decided he needed an even better cutting horse.

Randals echoes the popular sentiment of that era by remarking, "When I got interested in cutting, naturally I

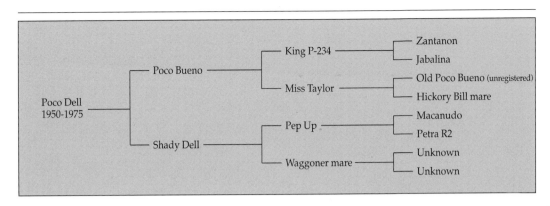

| | | | King P-234 | Zantanon |
| | | | | Jabalina |

Poco Dell
1950-1975

Poco Bueno
— King P-234
— Zantanon
— Jabalina
— Miss Taylor
— Old Poco Bueno (unregistered)
— Hickory Bill mare

Shady Dell
— Pep Up
— Macanudo
— Petra R2
— Waggoner mare
— Unknown
— Unknown

thought of Poco Bueno. At that time, Poco Bueno was the top of the heap when it came to cutting horses, and I wanted one of his sons. You couldn't have sold me another horse."

Poco Bueno was owned by E. Paul Waggoner, and it just happened that Waggoner's 3D Stock Farm was having an auction that summer, featuring the get of Poco Bueno.

Two weeks before the sale, Randals went to Texas to study carefully the horses being offered. "I just didn't want to come in there cold turkey," he explains. "I wanted to be prepared." He didn't want to make any quick, last-minute decisions in a matter so important, and he knew he would be bidding against some of the most experienced horsemen in the country.

Randals is a strong believer in the value of first impressions. He acknowledges that he was not a proven judge of horses at the time, but he had been around horses all his life and says, "I had my own idea what I wanted." Among the horses being fitted for the sale was a striking 2-year-old. "My first impression when I saw him," he says, "was that this was going to be the horse I had to have."

Randals' choice was a bay colt by Poco Bueno and out of a red dun Pep Up mare named Shady Dell. The colt, named Poco Dell, was her first foal and so the would-be buyer was not influenced by the fact that she was to become one of the most famous broodmares of the breed. As he had always done with his cattle operation,

Halter and Performance Record: Halter Points, 35; Performance Points, 15; Performance Register of Merit; AQHA Champion.

Progeny Record:

Foal Crops: 24
Foals Registered: 474
AQHA Champions: 18
Halter Point-Earners: 126
Halter Points Earned: 2,308
Superior Halter Awards: 11

Performance Point-Earners: 123
Performance Points Earned: 1,927.5
Performance Registers of Merit: 52
Superior Performance Awards: 4
Race Starters: 2

Randals made his decision solely on the conformation and obvious quality of the individual.

Shady Dell was sired by Pep Up, a stallion the famous Waggoner Ranch had acquired from his breeder, the equally famous King Ranch. Pep Up went to the Waggoner Ranch at an early age and proved to be an excellent cross with the home-bred Waggoner mares, such as the dam of Shady Dell.

Other than the sire, Poco Dell's breeding may have not been the primary factor in making the selection, but naturally it

Poco Dell in pasture with some mares. According to Randals, "Poco Dell never liked to be in a stall."

Photo Courtesy of *The Quarter Horse Journal*

This picture of Poco Dell was taken when he stood reserve grand champion stallion at an Amarillo Quarter Horse show in the late 1950s. The handler is Stanley Glover.

Poco Ra Dell, one of Poco Dell's 18 AQHA Champions, was a 1959 foal of Racine McCue, by Dell Monte. The handler is Keith Slover.

contributed to his superior conformation, disposition, willingness to learn, and ability to perform.

Poco Bueno's sire, King P-234, was well-known as a sire of performance horses. He was a son of the legendary Zantanon, by Little Joe. Miss Taylor, the dam of Poco Bueno, was a daughter of Old Poco Bueno, another son of Little Joe.

"I don't know why I wanted a stud," Randals says now. "I didn't even own one mare." On his ranch at Montoya, N.M., there was, however, a large box canyon just south of the ranch house, which could be made into a practical pasture simply by fencing across its entrance. He reminisces about a vague idea he had that when Poco Dell's cutting days were over, a group of about five mares could be found to put in the box canyon with the stallion so that he might raise some good foals under natural conditions in the rough canyon. The fence never got built.

Knowing that it was the smart way to go to an auction, Randals set a limit of $2,000 on the amount he would bid for Poco Dell. As a top feature of the sale, the colt was the second individual to come

into the sale ring and when it became obvious that Poco Dell was a crowd-pleaser, Randals got rather anxious. True to his decision, he quit bidding at $2,000. Then when the bid got several hundred dollars higher, he took another good look at the colt and got back in. His final bid of $2,800 bought the colt. "I paid a premium price," Randals recalls, "but I lucked out."

On the way home to the ranch, the proud owner and his new stallion stopped at Snyder, Tex., where Randals' father could have a look. "I really believe that my dad thought I had completely lost my mind by giving that much money for a horse," Randals says. "I'll never forget that."

The price seems an obvious bargain now, but it was definitely an attention-

> **"I really believe that my dad thought I had completely lost my mind by giving that much money for a horse,"** Randals says.

Dell Tommy, a 1958 son of Poco Dell and Bonnie Benear, was an AQHA Champion and the 1961 and 1962 Honor Roll Western Pleasure Horse.

Photo by J.E. Colby, Courtesy of *The Quarter Horse Journal*

Shady Dell proved her worth by producing five AQHA Champions.

grabber at that time. It was more than $500 over the average of the other good sons of Poco Bueno in the sale. Several of those young stallions eventually earned show records that make their names well-known even today. Other sons catalogued in the sale included Poco Deuce, Poco Turp, and Poco Bill.

The yearling sons of Poco Bueno in the sale averaged $800. They included Poco Speedy, Poco Line, and Poco Mike. Poco Shade, a full brother to Poco Dell, sold for $400.

Another indication of the top price commanded by Poco Dell is a comparison with prices brought by outstanding mares in the sale. The noted Patsy Daugherty went for $660. Poco Doll brought $775, and Poco Red Ant went for $300. Shady Dell, only a 6-year-old at the time and

bred to Poco Bueno, sold for $310. Poco Tiny, a weanling full sister to Poco Dell, went under the hammer for $280.

Shady Dell proved her worth by producing five AQHA Champions: Poco Dell, Poco Willy (also by Poco Bueno), Poco Deuce Jr (by Poco Deuce), Snipper Reed (by Logan's Bobby Reed), and Poco Pep Up (by Poco Deuce). Poco Willy and Snipper Reed gained further renown for the family by becoming noted sires. Shady Dell's Poco Shade and Shady Reed (by Logan's Bobby Reed) were Register of Merit performers. Her two other halter point-earners were Shady Chic and Shady Van. She produced a total of 17 foals.

Poco Dell won his halter class at the New Mexico State Fair a few weeks after he was purchased by Randals. The next year, he went back to that show to win grand champion honors. This got the attention of some long-time Quarter Horse breeders in the state who were using other bloodlines long famous in New Mexico. "I thought they were going to wear out their boots," Randals laughs. "They would walk over to his stall and frown. Then they would walk off for a while and then come back for another look."

That big win turned out to be a preview of the many grand and reserve championships he would win at other prominent shows of the day. Randals laughs when he points out in winner's photos that many

Shady Fawn, by Poco Dell and out of Scar Face Fawn, was a top horse in youth events. At the 1973 All American Quarter Horse Congress, Debbie Jones rode the mare to win the youth all-around trophy.

Photo Courtesy of *The Quarter Horse Journal*

Poco Dana, by Poco Dell and out of Dutchie Chub, by Chubby, was foaled in 1956. A Superior halter horse with 93 points, she was also an AQHA Champion.

Photo by Bill Mobley, Courtesy of *The Quarter Horse Journal*

Jimmie Randals with Poco Dondi, by Poco Dell and out of Miss Lady, by King P-234. Says Randals, "Of all the horses I ever raised, Poco Dondi was the most wasted horse I ever had. . . ." because he had to compete for mares with his more famous sire.

Alexander Photo

Nunes' Cameo was a 1957 chestnut mare bred by the Nunes brothers of Clovis, California. By Poco Dell, this mare was out of Dana Wilson by Wilson's Smokey Joe. Later owned by E. Paul Waggoneer of Vernon, Tex., Nunes' Cameo earned an AQHA Championship. This picture was taken at the 1961 San Antonio Livestock Exposition where the mare stood grand champion. The handler is Jimmie Randals.

Judy Dell, by Poco Dell and out of Quit That, by Billy Maddon, had more white than most of Poco Dell's get. Foaled in 1959, she was bred by Randals and later owned by Carol Harris of Reddick, Florida. Judy Dell was a top halter mare.

Photo Courtesy of *The Quarter Horse Journal*

"I think one of the things that kept him popular was the fact that he bred the type of horses who were becoming more popular."

of the wins came while Poco Dell was being shown in a Johnson halter, which was typical of that era.

Phil Williams, the famous old-time cutting horse trainer and exhibitor from Tokio, Tex., took Poco Dell for 30 days of training and showed him one time. Then Randals took over and rode the horse throughout the rest of his career. At the end of 90 days, Poco Dell was showing some of the moves that were to make him successful in cutting competition.

He soon qualified for the AQHA's Register of Merit ranking. Combined with his many wins at halter, his cutting abilities also earned him the title of AQHA Champion. Besides breed competition, he won in National Cutting Horse Association events, but they were scarcer at that time than AQHA cuttings. It seemed that the only field left for him to conquer was the competition among breeding sires.

Poco Dell matured to a height of about 14.2, which was more or less the average height at the time he was being shown.

Somewhat surprisingly, his foals often were taller then he—even as tall as 16 hands. "I think one of the things that kept him popular was the fact that he bred the type of horses who were becoming more popular." Randals explains, "He kept up with the times; let's put it that way."

Although an aggressive horse in a stall, he was an easy horse to handle when at halter or under saddle. "He never did kick or bite anybody, but he had a lot of bluff about him. He was always on the move, and when put in a stall, he would run at you and bite the heavy wire on the front of his stall and make it sing. He just did not like to be in a stall." Randals emphasizes, "In a bridle, he was a completely different

Randals says that Madonna Dell was one of the two most outstanding daughters of Poco Dell. A 1960 mare, she was out of Quo Vadis and earned a total of 202 halter points. The information on the back of this old photo says the handler is Judy Seely.

horse. He was no problem to handle and was no trouble when you got him away from the ranch."

Randals didn't fence off the box canyon, but he did put together a band of top-quality mares. "I can honestly say that I never did go out and pay any big money for mares. I just picked mares I could afford and who were good enough individuals to do the job. I went with just the conformation of the mare and bloodlines, although I never set out to buy certain bloodlines."

For instance, Randals bought what was to be one of his top producers from Guy Troutman, who was already known as one of the foundation Quarter Horse breeders of New Mexico. Speaking of this, Randals says "I gave him a hundred dollars for Nestora; and Nestora wasn't even halter-broke. She was a wild ol' mare. She was also a plain-looking mare, but she was an

own daughter of Billy Clegg and I knew the family he came from."

Quo Vadis was possibly the best producer to grace the Randals Ranch and is buried beside Poco Dell in the ranch cemetery. For her, Randals gave $500 and a breeding to Poco Dell. The breeding was to be used for Miss Circle H III, a daughter of Brown Ceaser and the dam of Quo Vadis. (The result was a winning halter and performance filly named Poco Circle.)

"Quo Vadis wasn't directly off the King Ranch, but she had King Ranch breeding. She came from down at San Jon (New Mexico). Ross Roberts, in San Jon, had that mare and that's where she came from."

In addition to Randals' growing broodmare band, good outside mares began to show up at the court of Poco Dell, brought by Quarter Horse and cutting horse enthusiasts from almost all of the western states. "The West Coast was a real good market for us," Randals recollects. "The Nunes brothers of California usually brought at least five good mares a year. Oklahoma was good for us, too, and such states as Idaho. We had a lot of return customers."

Those outside mares included such well-known individuals as Mayflower Daugherty, Susette Clapper, Panzarita Daugherty, and Navie Girl.

Poco Dell did his part to uphold the prestige of his bloodlines. He sired 474

Poco Jeff was one of three Poco Dell sons whom Randals considered particularly outstanding. Foaled in 1956, Poco Jeff was out of Nestora by Billy Clegg. Poco Jeff was an AQHA Champion. We believe the handler shown here is Bill Stockstill, who owned Poco Jeff.

AQHA-registered foals. From these, there were 126 halter point-earners and 123 point-earners in performance events.

As might be expected with foals who could work as well as win halter classes, 18 became AQHA Champions. Dell Tommy, Poco Della, Poco Ra Dell, Poco Dondi, Poco Jeff, Poco Dana, Poco Mickey, Nunes' Poco Joe, Hooky Dell, Poco Honcho, and Dell Jiggs were among the well-known horses who earned this title. This established a firm position for Poco Dell on the list of leading sires of AQHA Champions.

It was not a fluke that Poco Dell was siring the kind of horses who could win top honors. His daughters later produced enough AQHA Champions to also put him on the roll of leading maternal grand-sires of AQHA Champions.

One Poco Dell son, Dell Tommy, earned a Superior title in western pleasure and trail. Impressive Dell also earned a Superior in western pleasure.

Dell Tommy, a 1958 brown son of Bonnie Benear, who was another mare of Troutman breeding, was the AQHA Honor Roll western pleasure horse in both 1961 and 1962. In 1970, he was the AQHA high-point trail horse stallion and was fourth among individuals of all sexes. The next year, he came back to top all competition as the Honor Roll trail horse.

A colt out of Casey's Golden Sandie, named Poco Mickey, was the high-point western pleasure stallion of 1960. He was a bay, foaled in 1955, from Poco Dell's first crop. After his show career, Poco Mickey was ridden in cowboy polo contests. Later, his disposition made it possible to use him in a horseback riding program for physically challenged children.

Nunes' Bubblgal ranked fifth in trail standings in 1968. She was a Poco Dell daughter out of Betty Wilson.

A foal named Shady Fawn, out of Scar Face Fawn, proved it didn't always take an adult to win on a Poco Dell foal. In addition to becoming a performance ROM qualifier in open shows, Shady Fawn was a ROM qualifier in youth events. She also was a Superior western pleasure horse in youth classes.

At the AJQHA World Show in 1972, Shady Fawn placed in the top 10 in reining, western riding, and western horsemanship. The next year, she was among

Dell Jiggs, by Poco Dell and out of Nestora, by Billy Clegg, was foaled in 1960 and earned an AQHA Championship. **Photo Courtesy of** *The Quarter Horse Journal*

the top 10 point-earners in reining, western riding, and trail horse, and placed seventh at the youth world show in western riding.

Eleven Poco Dell foals earned credit as Superior halter horses. These were Madonna Dell (202 halter points), Poco Dondi (135 points), Judy Dell (102 points), Nunes' Cameo (96 points), Poco Dana (93 points), Poco Ra Dell, Hooky Dell, Poco Jeff, Dell Jiggs, Wise Poco, and Nunes' Debonair.

One year during this period, Randals took his show string of Poco Dell offspring to the Southwestern Livestock Horse Show at Fort Worth. After winning "practically everything in sight," Randals was approached by Fagan Miller, who worked for E. Paul Waggoner. As a result, the Waggoner Ranch bought all the horses in the group except Poco Dondi, who had been the grand champion stallion. The amount of money involved was considerably more than the "premium" price Randals had paid Waggoner for Poco Dell.

Randals recalls with pleasure three sons of Poco Dell he considered particularly outstanding. They were Poco Jeff, Poco Dondi, and Poco Ra Dell.

Bill Stockstill of Pampa, Tex., owned Poco Jeff. "Bill did a real good job of exhibiting Poco Jeff," Randals remembers. "He was a bay horse out of Nestora. Poco Jeff was a good winner at both halter and cutting.

"Poco Dondi was out of an own daughter of King P-234 whom I bought from Earl Albin," Randals notes. "Her name was Miss Lady. Of all the horses I ever raised, Poco Dondi was the most wasted horse I ever had."

Like Poco Jeff, Poco Dondi was a foal of 1956, Poco Dell's second crop. Because he spent much of his life as a mature stallion on the Randals Ranch, Poco Dondi had to compete for mares with his more famous sire. "It was hard for me to pull mares away from Poco Dell whom I knew had been successful with him." Despite that, Poco Dondi proved to be a consistent sire of winners such as Lady Dondi and Jimmie Dondi, both grand champions at major shows.

Poco Ra Dell was not only a good winner at both halter and under saddle, he also demonstrated his breeding ability at the Pitzer Ranch in Nebraska. That ranch, of course, is known as one of the country's best producers of using horses.

Poco Ra Dell was out of Racine McCue, who was owned by J.D. and Elsie Kitchens of Fort Sumner, New Mexico. Although admirers of Poco Dell, the Kitchens, who were schoolteachers, compared stud fees and bred Racine McCue to Poco Dondi. Randals recalls that "she was a kinda squirrely ol' mare, but a good-looking palomino, and Poco Dondi was a funny horse to breed. He would not breed that mare." So, Racine McCue was bred to Poco Dell and the result was Poco Ra Dell. The Kitchens further demonstrated their knowledge of horses by winning the 1976 All American Futurity with a homebred youngster named Real Wind.

Randals bought Poco Ra Dell as a youngster and immediately started win-

Hooky Dell, owned by Jack Givens of Nampa, Ida., was another Poco Dell son who earned a Superior in halter and an AQHA Championship. A 1963 foal, Hooky Dell was out of Cookie Mount by Music Mount.

Photo Courtesy of *The Quarter Horse Journal*

ning halter classes with him. After being named the grand champion stallion at the National Western Stock Show in Denver, he was purchased by Howard Pitzer. At the same time, Pitzer bought the excellent show mare Lady Dondi, by Poco Dondi, for his broodmare band.

When asked to name some of the most outstanding daughters of Poco Dell, Randals hesitated and then came up with the names of Poco Dana (pronounced Dan-uh) and Madonna Dell.

Poco Dana, too, was from the crop of 1956. Bred by O.G. Hill Jr. of Hereford, Tex., Poco Dana was out of Dutchie Chub, a daughter of the famed sire Chubby. Although Poco Dana won 18.5 points under saddle, she is best remembered for her outstanding halter career. Among her wins was a grand championship at the Texas State Fair in Dallas when she was only 2 years old.

Madonna Dell, a striking black mare, was out of Quo Vadis. Madonna Dell won a total of 202 halter points (amazing for those years) at such big events as the Houston Livestock Show, where she was the grand champion mare.

After a long career in which he showed that he was at the top of the heap, Poco Dell died in 1975. He was 25. "Thank goodness," Randals says strongly, "I was not here. The horse died while I was in Albuquerque at the state fair." Other than being badly crippled with arthritis, the horse had been in good health.

The death of this grand old horse, however, did not end the popularity of his line. People who knew of him still value his blood. "You'd be surprised how many people today still write me or call me or look me up to ask me if I still have any daughters of Poco Dell," Randals remarks.

12 QUO VADIS

By Larry Thornton

"Quo Vadis was one of those horses who was before her time."

QUO VADIS was one of those mares every breeder dreams of for the brood-mare band. An outstanding performer, she became an AQHA Champion, earning 29 performance points in cutting, reining, working cow horse, and western riding.

Also an outstanding halter mare, she earned 40 points with 5 grand championships and a reserve grand championship in 13 shows. Quo Vadis completed her legacy as an outstanding broodmare by producing 12 registered foals with 11 performers. They earned 637.5 points in 6 events with 4 AQHA

Championships, 7 ROMs, and 3 Superior halter awards. All of her foals could halter as well as perform.

It all started when Jimmie Randals first saw Quo Vadis. Randals, a breeder of outstanding horses on his Montoya, N. M., ranch, has owned and/or bred such noted horses as Poco Dell and Poco Dondi. Quo Vadis was a much-valued asset to his breeding program.

"That was a long time ago," related Randals while discussing Quo Vadis and how she came to his ranch. "She was owned by Ross Roberts of San Jon, N.M., over east of Tucumcari. I had seen the mare, I think it

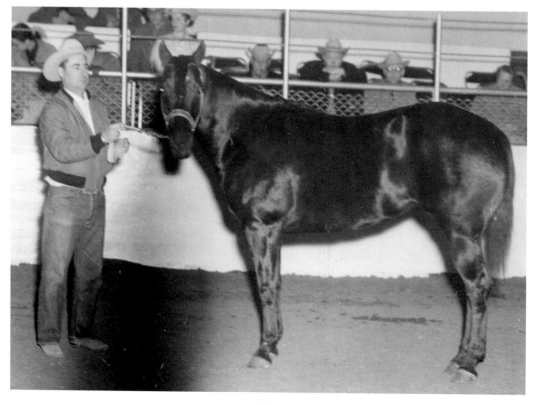

At Fort Worth in 1957, Jimmie Randals showed Quo Vadis to the reserve champion mare title.

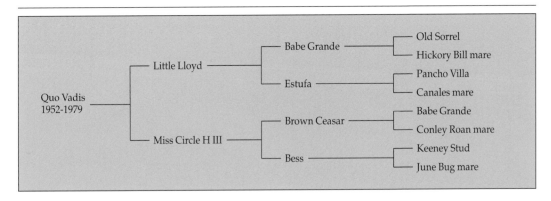

```
                                           ┌─── Old Sorrel
                           ┌── Babe Grande ─┤
                           │                └─── Hickory Bill mare
            ┌── Little Lloyd┤
            │              │                ┌─── Pancho Villa
            │              └── Estufa ──────┤
Quo Vadis ──┤                               └─── Canales mare
1952-1979   │
            │                               ┌─── Babe Grande
            │              ┌── Brown Ceasar ─┤
            │              │                └─── Conley Roan mare
            └── Miss Circle H III┤
                           │                ┌─── Keeney Stud
                           └── Bess ────────┤
                                            └─── June Bug mare
```

was at the state fair in Albuquerque. I liked her and I worked out a deal with Ross. I guess it was my lucky day. Anyway we made an agreement and I ended up with the mare. Actually I traded to get her for my sister Marianne." Marianne Randals became the owner of Quo Vadis for $500 and a breeding to Poco Dell.

Randals, who trained and showed Quo Vadis for his sister, found her to be a very powerful mare who was a natural to train. She was the kind of mare who would do anything she was asked to do. He described her natural ability and her conformation this way:

"Quo Vadis was one of those horses who was before her time. She was all by herself in conformation. She was a nice big mare. Of course, what I called a nice big mare at that time and what we see now are not the same. She would have stood 15, maybe 15.1 hands. She was a nice mare and anytime you stopped her, she would be correct (stand square on all legs). You didn't have to back her. You just stopped her and she was there . . . just as straight as a string and no problem to show."

Quo Vadis was foaled in 1952 and was bred by Ross Roberts. Her sire was Little Lloyd, a King Ranch-bred stallion by Babe Grande. Babe Grande was by the legendary Old Sorrel, foundation sire of the King Ranch Quarter Horses. The dam of Babe Grande was a mare by Hickory Bill, who

Halter and Performance Record: Halter Points, 40; Performance Points, 29; Performance Register of Merit; AQHA Champion.

Progeny Record:

Foal Crops: 12
Foals Registered: 12
AQHA Champions: 4
Halter Point-Earners: 11
Halter Points Earned: 504

Superior Halter Awards: 3
Performance Point-Earners: 9
Performance Points Earned: 133.5
Performance Registers of Merit: 7

also was the sire of Old Sorrel, making Babe Grande inbred to Hickory Bill.

Estufa, the dam of Little Lloyd, was a King Ranch outcross mare sired by a horse known as Pancho Villa, who was sired by Little Joe. The dam of Pancho Villa was Jeanette, by Billy, by Big Jim. This makes Pancho Villa a full brother to the famous stallion Zantanon, the sire of King P-234. The dam of Estufa was known as a Canales mare. Her breeding was unknown.

Little Lloyd sired two ROM show horses, Little Punkin Garret and Quo Vadis. Little

This picture of Quo Vadis was taken at the 1954 New Mexico State Fair when she was a 2-year-old. We believe the handler is her breeder, Ross Roberts.

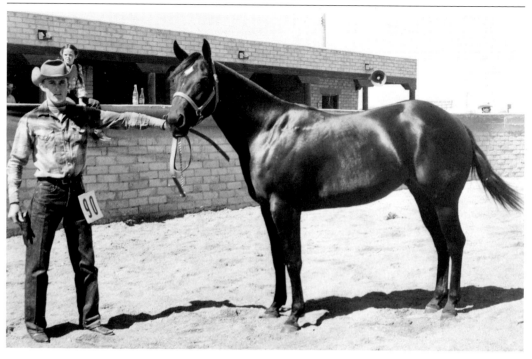

In addition to being a good halter mare, Quo Vadis was a natural athlete under saddle, in the show ring, and on the ranch.

Lloyd was also the paternal grandsire of Mister Boss, an AQHA Champion and sire of 38 ROM and 14 Superior award earners and 3 AQHA Champions.

The dam of Quo Vadis was Miss Circle H III, by Brown Ceasar. Brown Ceasar sired the noted broodmare Lassie Caesar. Lassie Caesar produced Blonde Joan, 1957 Champion Quarter Running 3-Year-Old Filly; and Lassie's Dream, 1955 Champion Quarter Running 2-Year-Old Filly. Lassie's Dream was the dam of Magnolia Bar, an AAA-AQHA Champion.

Brown Ceasar was sired by Babe Grande. This makes Quo Vadis inbred to Babe Grande, a major sire for the King Ranch. Bob Denhardt, in his book *The King Ranch Quarter Horses*, wrote that Babe Grande "was a natural-born cow horse" who was "noted for the excellence of his broodmares." He was used on the King Ranch from 1931 to 1951. His influence on the King Ranch came through the use of his daughters in the broodmare band. Babe Grande was the paternal grandsire of such noted horses as Babe Mac C, one of the first AQHA Champions. Babe Grande also sired Rey Del Rancho, an important stallion in the King Ranch breeding program, and Saltillo, the sire of the good cutting mare Alice Star.

The dam of Brown Ceasar was the

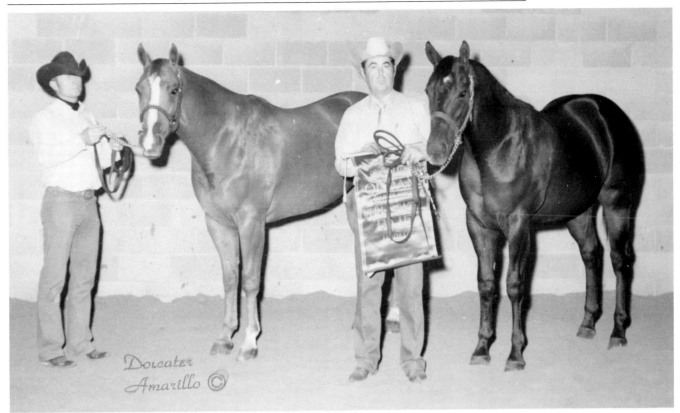

Dolcater
Amarillo ©

Conley Roan mare by Little Hickory, sired by Hickory Bill, by Peter McCue. This gives Quo Vadis at least five crosses to Hickory Bill.

The dam of the Conley Roan mare was the Garcia mare by Graig Roan, who was sired by a horse listed in the *AQHA Stud Book* as O'Connor Blue.

Miss Circle H III was out of a mare named Bess. Bess was sired by a horse called Keeney Stud, by Yellow Wolf. The dam of Bess was the June Bug Mare, by Windy City (TB).

Randals believes that Miss Circle H III and Quo Vadis were a lot alike. As he put it, "Miss Circle H III was one of those needle-in-a-haystack kind of mares, a lot like Quo Vadis. They're the kind of mares who are hard to find, but when you find them, they are outstanding."

Miss Circle H III reinforces Randals' statement as she was the dam of three AQHA Champions. In addition to Quo Vadis, she produced the AQHA Champions Show Maid and Set Up.

Poco Circle was the foal sired by Poco Dell and out of Miss Circle H III . . . part of the deal that Randals worked out with Ross Roberts. This show mare earned 11 halter points and 3 performance points.

Many mares will make great show horses and then end up not being producers in the breeding shed. This was not the case with Quo Vadis. Randals explained:

"If I ever had a mare I felt I was stepping up to the plate with, it was Quo Vadis. With most mares you think you've

At the 1970 Tri-State Fair in Amarillo, Miss Impressive (left) and Mr Perfection won the produce-of-dam class for Quo Vadis. The handlers are Stanley Glover (left) and Jimmie Randals.

Photo by H.D. Dolcater

Madonna Dell, by Poco Dell and out of Quo Vadis, earned a Superior in halter with 202 points and an arena Register of Merit. Says Randals, "She has to be the top horse I showed."

Photo by H.D. Dolcater, Courtesy of *The Quarter Horse Journal*

Dell's Hombre, by Poco Dell and out of Quo Vadis, earned 9 halter points and 3 western pleasure points before his untimely death. This picture was taken at the 1969 New Mexico State Fair, where he won the 2-year-old stallion class.

Photo Courtesy of *The Quarter Horse Journal*

Miss Impressive was a 1966 foal by Two Eyed Jack and out of Quo Vadis. She earned 14 halter and 7 performance points and "was a really sweet mare," says Randals. She is handled here by Wayne Pooley.

Of all Quo Vadis' foals, Madonna Dell was special to Randals.

got just another colt out of them. With Quo Vadis, you just didn't have another colt, you had an exceptional colt."

He added, "I think as time went on, regardless of who we bred her to, the colts seemed to be more refined, and more classy. They were showy colts who were more athletic then she was."

The produce record of Quo Vadis indicates that her versatility in the show arena wasn't an accident, since her foals earned points in six performance events. She had another attribute that breeders like to see and that was the ability to produce good foals by different stallions.

Quo Vadis produced six foals by Poco Dell. The first was Poco Becky, an AQHA Champion with 14 halter points and 16 performance points in working cow horse, reining, western pleasure, and western riding.

Laura Dell came along next and earned 10 halter points.

Madonna Dell followed in 1960 and she was a Superior halter mare with a performance Register of Merit.

Dino Dell was her first colt. He earned 15.5 western pleasure points and 5 halter points.

Dellfene, foaled in 1965, earned 36 halter points, 10.5 open performance points, 16 youth halter points, and 6 youth performance points. All of her performance points were earned in western pleasure.

Dell's Hombre was foaled in 1967 and would be the last Poco Dell-Quo Vadis foal. This good-looking colt earned 9 halter points and 3 western pleasure points before his untimely death.

Of all Quo Vadis' foals, Madonna Dell was special to Randals. "Madonna Dell had to be the top horse I showed. You

Doctor Montoya was a grandson of Quo Vadis, sired by Doc Bar and out of Miss Impressive. Foaled in 1977, he sold for a record $150,000 at the 1979 NCHA Futurity Sale in Fort Worth to Joe Ayers (left) and Terry Riddle (far right). Jimmie Randals is at the lead and his son, Richard, is next to him.

Photo by *The Quarter Horse Journal*

couldn't draw a more perfect horse," stated Randals as he talked about this great show mare.

He later added, "She was a little bit more refined than her mother. She was refined all over and that was the biggest thing about her."

Madonna Dell earned Randals' admiration and respect by winning 202 halter points as a Superior halter horse. She was grand champion mare at such shows as the Houston Livestock Show, Chicago International, and the New Mexico State Fair. Madonna Dell also earned 7.5 AQHA

performance points in cutting and western pleasure.

Bonita Dondi, foaled in 1963, was the first Quo Vadis foal sired by a horse other than Poco Dell. Her sire was Poco Dell's great son Poco Dondi, the second AQHA Champion out of Quo Vadis. Bonita Dondi earned 31 halter points and 16 performance points in reining, western riding, and western pleasure.

Randals took Quo Vadis to Nebraska in 1965 to be bred to Two Eyed Jack. The result of this mating, Miss Impressive, earned 14 halter points and 7 performance points, all in cutting.

"Miss Impressive was a really sweet mare, as nice a mare as you'd want to have. She had some cow to her, and you don't always see a halter mare who is an

Majestic Dell, a 1973 black stallion by Eternal Dell and out of Quo Vadis, earned 49 halter points. Bred by Randals, he was later owned by Carol Harris of Ocala, Florida. The handler here is Jerry Wells.

Photo Courtesy of *The Quarter Horse Journal*

athlete, at least not as far as cutting goes," stated Randals.

Miss Impressive's produce record showcases the versatility of the Quo Vadis family. She produced Impressive Dell by Poco Dell and Doctor Montoya by Doc Bar. Impressive Dell earned a Superior in western pleasure with 75 points, in addition to 17 points in halter.

"I took three mares out to Doc Bar—Quo Vadis, Miss Impressive, and Peppy Della. That was the year Doc Bar went sterile, and Miss Impressive was the only mare who got in foal. The resulting foal was Doctor Montoya. I believe he still holds the record as the high-selling horse in the NCHA Futurity Sale. Joe Ayers and Terry Riddle bought him for $150,000," states Randals.

Doctor Montoya went on to be the champion of the Oklahoma Cutting Futurity as well as a finalist at the 1982 NCHA Classic/Challenge. He earned eight

AQHA cutting points and was in the top 10 at the 1981 AQHA World Championship Show in junior cutting.

Mr Perfection came along in 1969. This son of Quo Vadis was sired by Three Chicks. He was an AQHA Champion with a Superior in halter, earning 68 points, with 15 grand championships and 18 reserve grand championships. He won his class at the Fort Worth Stock Show 3 years in a row. His 18 performance points came in reining, working cow horse, and western pleasure.

"Mr Perfection had all of his dam's characteristics as far as conformation and

Miss Impressive's produce record showcases the versatility of the Quo Vadis family.

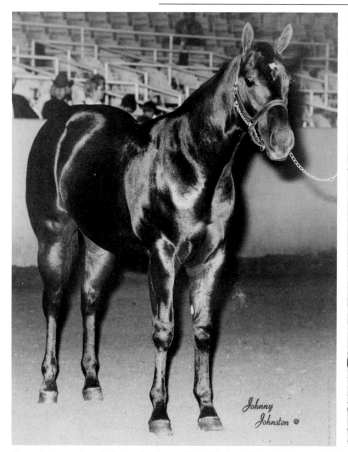

Two photographs of Mr Perfection, a 1969 black stallion by Three Chicks and out of Quo Vadis. An AQHA Champion, "He was an outstanding individual," says Randals.

Photo by Johnny Johnston

Photo by H.D. Dolcater

disposition go. You'd think he was a gelding. He was an outstanding individual, a big horse with a lot of bone. A very sensible horse. He got his claim to fame with Billy Allen showing him," stated Randals.

He added, "After Billy had all that success showing him, we fooled around here with him, and he had a lot of cow."

Mr Perfection became a good sire, with foals like Perfection Plus, who earned 429 AQHA points; Perfection's Smoke, who earned 617 AQHA points; and Lady Perfectionist, who earned 260 AQHA points.

Miss Pocket Money was the only foal not be shown. She was sired by Triple Money, by Triple Chick. Triple Money was a stallion Randals stood at one time.

Miss Pocket Money was not shown, but her two foals proved that she was valuable as a broodmare. She produced Vester Vision and Safety Deposit, both sired by The Invester. These two pleasure horses were the only foals produced by Miss Pocket Money, but both became Superior western pleasure horses and AQHA Champions.

The last two foals out of Quo Vadis

144

Kali Amanda was a terrific reining horse and a daughter of Kaliman, who was out of Quo Vadis. The mare is shown here with owner Jim Robin, winning the 1987 NRHA Non-Pro Futurity.

Photo by Waltenberry, Courtesy of *The Quarter Horse Journal*

were both stallions. The first was Majestic Dell, by Eternal Dell. Then came Kaliman, by Dell Milagro, by Poco Dell.

Majestic Dell was a good halter stallion, earning 49 points. He was shown 33 times earning 29 class wins with 19 grand championships and 9 reserve grand championships. Majestic Dell proved to be a good sire with foals like Majestic Rascal, a youth world champion and high-point junior horse in hunter under saddle in 1988; and Swakara, a youth performance champion in 1988, with Superiors in six events.

Kaliman was an AQHA Superior halter horse and AQHA Champion with points in three events: reining, trail, and western pleasure. He earned 30 performance points and 50 halter points with 12 grand champion-

ships and 6 reserve grand championships. He is a noted reining horse sire with foals like Kali Amanda, the 1987 NRHA Non-Pro Futurity Champion, and Kaliflower, another NRHA non-pro champion.

Quo Vadis went to Kansas to be bred in 1979. But another foal was not in the cards for this great mare. She died while in Kansas, and Randals sent a trailer to bring her home. She is buried in the backyard of the Randals' home along with Poco Dell. Randals has placed a large marker on the burial site with the names of these two Quarter Horse legends.

13 QUESTION MARK

By Jim Goodhue

He was a popular sire of both racing and performance horses.

MANY HORSES are named for one or more of their physical characteristics, but few horses have a distinguishing feature as unique as the blaze the colt bred by Oklahoma oilman Waite Phillips had. It was strikingly similar to a question mark and so this became his name. Question Mark was foaled on Phillips' Philmont

Ranch near Cimarron, N.M., in the spring of 1937.

There never was a question, even at an early age, about his attributes. He was endowed with a conformation and a clear golden color that were to make him an important contributing factor in the development of both the Palomino Horse Breeders of America and the American Quarter Horse Association. The two organizations were formed during his early years and he sired foals who were notable in both areas.

As the youngster grew up, he was broke and used to work cattle on the ranch. His athletic ability and exceptional disposition, combined with an obvious cow savvy, showed that Question Mark could have been successful if he had been confined to that career. He later proved, however, to have enough speed to put him among the tops in the racing field. His ability to pass along both traits makes his history even more special. Nelson C. Nye, in his book *Speed and The Quarter Horse*, wrote favorably about "the truly great Question Mark, who did about all his track work before the advent of organized Quarter Horse racing."

The sire of Question Mark was the Philmont Ranch's premier stallion Plaudit. Also a golden palomino, Plaudit was sired by King Plaudit, a brown Thoroughbred stallion who had been placed in western Colorado by the Army Remount program. When bred to Colorado Queen, a granddaughter of Old Fred, King Plaudit went down in history as a progenitor of one of the most famous

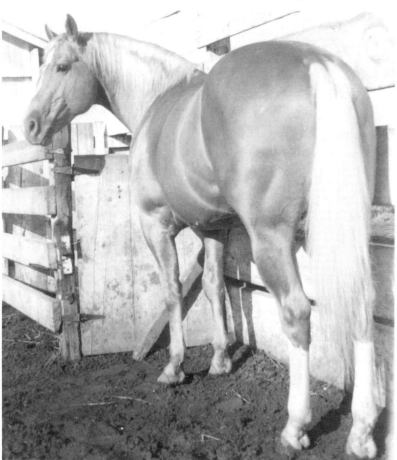

Question Mark, a hard-knocking race horse during the early 1940s, went on to become a foundation sire in both the Palomino and Quarter Horse registries.

Courtesy of *The Quarter Horse Journal*

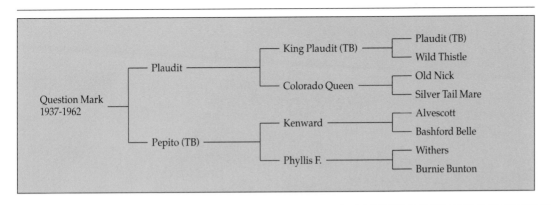

			Plaudit (TB)
		King Plaudit (TB)	
			Wild Thistle
	Plaudit		
			Old Nick
		Colorado Queen	
Question Mark			Silver Tail Mare
1937-1962			
			Alvescott
		Kenward	
			Bashford Belle
	Pepito (TB)		
			Withers
		Phyllis F.	
			Burnie Bunton

bloodlines in Quarter Horse history. (See a more complete story of Plaudit in the first volume of *Legends*.)

King Plaudit, out of Wild Thistle, was a 1916 son of the 1898 Kentucky Derby winner also named Plaudit. This Thoroughbred Plaudit was conceived in England by the great stallion Himyar and was carried to the United States by the imported mare Cinderella. Himyar also sired another progenitor of brilliant speed, Domino.

Question Mark's dam, Pepito, did not have 100-percent Thoroughbred blood, but she had enough to be listed with The Jockey Club for racing purposes under the rules then in existence. She had a very successful racing career before she was retired as a broodmare. Nelson Nye has reported that, at one time, Pepito held the track record for three-eighths of a mile at Tanforan, a popular California track for speedsters.

For the two seasons before she foaled Question Mark, Pepito was leased by Ed Springer, who also ranched at Cimarron. For Springer, Pepito produced Little Joe III and Don Jose. Both were sired by the Springer Ranches' famous stallion known in AQHA records as both Little Joe II and Old Joe, but only as Little Joe at the ranch. Both of these sons of Pepito became well-regarded sires, and the blood of Little Joe III was used exten-

Halter and Performance Record: None.

Progeny Record:

Foal Crops: 24
Foals Registered: 246
Halter Point-Earners: 12
Halter Points Earned: 22
Performance Point-Earners: 12
Performance Points Earned: 36
Leading Race Money-Earner: Aero Mark ($12,050)

Performance Registers of Merit: 6
Race Starters: 63
Race Money Earned: $113,303
Race Registers of Merit: 26
Superior Race Awards: 3

sively by the Springers in their production of all-around using horses.

Pepito was sired by the Thoroughbred Kenward, a son of the imported Alvescott. Her dam was Phyllis F by the Thoroughbred stallion Withers.

There were scoffers when it was suggested that Question Mark, a cowpony with the pretty color, might also be a race horse. Under the capable supervision of Frankie Burns, however, Question Mark picked up the training he needed for a straightaway career. Running with a distinctive low-to-the-ground, head-straight-out stance, Question Mark made himself

In addition to being a highly successful sprinter, Question Mark also fared well in the halter ring. Here he is, circa 1946-47, after competing in the Palomino show at the Denver National Western Stock Show.

Photo by Morris Engle, Courtesy of the Palomino Horse Breeders of America

The cross of Question Mark on the Zandy daughter Lorane resulted in several noteworthy horses, including Grey Question, a gray stallion foaled in 1947. A multiple stakes-winner of 11 races, Grey Question went on to enjoy moderate success as a sire.

Photo by Eugene Wilson, Courtesy of *The Quarter Horse Journal*

My Question, a 1943 palomino mare out of Annapoise (TB), was one of Question Mark's first get to achieve success on the track. A Register of Merit winner of six races, she went on to produce two AAA-rated sprinters.

Courtesy of *The Quarter Horse Journal*

Osage Red, a 1945 sorrel stallion by Question Mark and out of Levis Maid, was a AAA-rated sprinter. In 1948, he won eight straight races and set three track records in the process.

Courtesy of *The Quarter Horse Journal*

Denver was a hotbed of Palomino activity in the late 1940s and early 1950s, and Question Mark and his get were often the horses to beat in the halter competition there. In this rare photo taken at the Denver National Western Stock Show in 1946, Question Mark (left) is shown after being named grand champion stock-type Palomino stallion. Two of his daughters were named as the show's champion stock- and pleasure-type Palomino mares.

Photo by John Stryker

known as a capable contender in a series of races across New Mexico and Colorado. He came to be known as a horse who raced with great heart and gave completely of himself in every race.

No better proof of this could be given than a description of his final race. In this half-mile contest at Trinidad, Colo., Question Mark was matched against the notable Joe Lewis and the legendary mare, Shue Fly, who was owned by the Hepler brothers. Those two horses were at the peak of their careers and their numerous wins had established them in the top ranks of sprinters.

After the first eighth, Question Mark's golden hide was conspicuously in the lead. Then, before reaching the quarter-mile pole, the courageous palomino seemed to stagger. He faltered momentarily and then continued his drive. He not only lasted for the full half-mile, but man-

aged to pull back ahead of the Hepler flier before reaching the finish line.

When it was announced after the race that he had completed the race on a mighty heart and a broken pastern bone, it became even more evident that Question Mark was an unusual horse. Unfortunately, the announcement also had to be made that he would not race again.

A Succession of Owners

Question Mark then passed into the ownership of William Walker of Lamar, Colo., who used him as a breeding horse for the first time. Walker sold Question Mark to Mike Levis, of Pueblo, Colo., who later sold him at Denver's 1945 National Western Stock Show. He was purchased by Tom Gray, a Tulsa automobile dealer and president of the Oklahoma Palomino Exhibitors Association, for $6,000—a breathtaking price at the time.

During December of 1947, Question Mark became the property of another Tulsan, J. R. Cates, who had already bred

The streamlined Question's Gold was yet another of Question Mark's durable racing get. From 89 official starts, she recorded 9 firsts, 16 seconds, and 13 thirds.

Courtesy of *The Quarter Horse Journal*

some outstanding foals from this golden sire. During this ownership, Question Mark was leased for the 1954 breeding season to Spencer Childers of Fresno, California. At the time of his death in December of 1962, the 25-year-old Question Mark was owned by Roland L. Pelt of Las Vegas, N.M., very near to where he began his life. Pelt reported that he had 15 mares safely in foal to the great horse when he died.

Although recognized races were scarce and purses were low when Question Mark was used for breeding, 63 of his 246 registered foals made 1,324 starts in recognized races. Of these, 34 were winners and 26 qualified for the race Register of Merit. They earned a respectable $113,303 in purse money. His foals repeatedly put him on the annual lists of top money-earning sires up through 1956. At the end of 1965, Question Mark still remained on the list of all-time leading sires of racing money-earners.

During the same time, Question Mark showed his inherent versatility by siring 12 point-earners in performance events and 12 point-earners at halter. Six of his offspring qualified for the working Register of Merit.

One of the earliest performers sired by Question Mark was the elegant palomino mare My Question, queen of the 660-yard races. Although her best distances were longer than the races then recognized for the Register of Merit, she did qualify by winning 440-yard races at such tracks as Del Rio in Texas and at the New Mexico State Fairgrounds in Albuquerque. In another good race at that distance, she was a very close second to the top mare Leota W at Bay Meadows.

She further demonstrated her versatility by running at distances up to 6 fur-

One of the earliest performers sired by Question Mark was the elegant palomino mare My Question.

*Golden Flight, a 1942
gelding by Question
Mark, was bred by J. W.
Shoemaker of Watrous,
New Mexico. He sold in
the late 1940s for $7,500
and went on to become a
top show horse on the
West Coast.*

Photo by Tallant

Golden Flight, a 1942 gelding by Question Mark, was bred by J. W. Shoemaker of Watrous, New Mexico. He sold in the late 1940s for $7,500 and went on to become a top show horse on the West Coast.

Photo by Tallant

Question Mark's biggest money-earner was Aero Mark.

longs. Foaled in 1943, My Question was out of a Thoroughbred mare named Annapoise by Proctor Hug.

Another demonstration of the value of the cross between Pepito and the CS Ranches bloodlines was made by the very handsome stallion Osage Red, bred by Mike Levis. He was by Question Mark and out of Levis Maid, a CS-bred mare. Along with other victories, he capped his career by winning eight straight races in his 1948 campaign "more or less as he pleased" as stated in the *AQRA Running Horse Yearbook.*

In the first of those (his initial recognized start), Osage Red toted 133 pounds over a muddy 440 yards at Sacramento and won handily. As a 3-year-old that year, he set new track records at Hanford, Calif. (330 yards); Las Vegas, Nev. (400 yards); and Salinas, Calif. (440 yards). In 1950, Osage Red won the Stallion Stakes at Rillito in Tucson and placed second in the Rillito World Championship.

In 1946, a gray Question Mark filly was produced by Rainy Hancock, a mare sired by Rainy Day. Bred by the Tom L. Burnett Estate, Rainy Hancock was a granddaughter of both Midnight and Joe Hancock. This filly, named Savannah Gray, made her mark both as a runner and as a great broodmare. Racing under the name of Savannah G, she qualified for the race Register of Merit at 2 and by the end of her track career had earned enough points to be named a Superior race horse.

Meanwhile, she had set track records at both Rillito (250 yards) and Sacramento (330 yards). Savannah Gray also

equaled the 330-yard track record at Hanford.

The year 1947 proved to be a banner year for Question Mark as two of his most outstanding offspring were foaled that year. These two stars were Grey Question and Question's Gold.

Grey Question was out of Lorane, by Zandy (a son of Zantanon). At 2, he gained fame by dead-heating with Bonnie Bert I for first place in the 220-yard Oklahoma Futurity. They also shared the honor of equaling the 2-year-old record for that distance and setting a record for the Enid, Okla., track.

The next year, Grey Question won the 330-yard Oklahoma Derby. Later, he equaled track records at Pomona (350 yards), Santa Rosa (330 yards), and Pleasanton (330 yards)—all in California. Later, this big, gray colt proved himself worthy as a sire.

Question's Gold was out of the unregistered mare Phillips' Del Rio, by Del Rio Joe. This palomino filly, who was at her best at 3 years of age and older, earned the titles of both Register of Merit and Supe-

rior race horse. As a 4-year-old, she placed second in the 350-yard Pacific Coast QHRA Handicap and third in the 400-yard Pacific Coast QHRA Championship. At 3, 4, and 5, Question's Gold set track records at Hanford (220 yards), Fresno (330 yards), and Sacramento (330 yards). She also equaled track records at Los Alamitos and Bay Meadows—both at 350 yards. Her lifetime earnings totaled $12,011.

Question Mark's biggest money-earner was Aero Mark. This 1950 sorrel filly edged out Question's Gold by accumulating $12,050. She, too, was both a race Register of Merit-qualifier and a Superior race horse. Two of Aero Mark's best races were at Bay Meadows, where she ran

Tulsa was another Palomino stronghold during the 1940s and 1950s. In this shot, taken at the 1950 Tulsa State Fair, Question Mark (right) is shown with a set of his blue-ribbon get.

Photo by Paul Yard, Courtesy of *The Quarter Horse Journal*

Dawson's Ballymark, a 1950 palomino gelding by Question Mark and out of Buckskin Dawson, was a halter and performance point-earner and a Register of Merit cutting horse. He was bred by pioneer Quarter Horse breeder John Dawson of Talala, Oklahoma. Dawson, incidentally, bred Oklahoma Star Jr.

Courtesy of *The Quarter Horse Journal*

Question Mark could throw working abilities as well as speed when crossed with mares of various types and bloodlines.

second in the 1957 Memorial Day Handicap at 440 yards and third in the 1955 Presidio Stakes at 400 yards. During her last year of racing, 1957, she also won 2 points in halter classes. Aero Mark was out of Dorothy Cates.

Mr. Cates, a 1952 palomino son of Question Mark, earned $9,639 from his 10 wins, 10 seconds, and 6 thirds out of 65 races. He also equaled the 350-yard track record at Stockton as a 3-year-old. Mr. Cates was out of Bertie Lou.

Another track record-setter by Question Mark was Jody Question. He set a 330-yard record at Santa Rosa in 1951. A sorrel gelding out of an unregistered daughter of Joe Blair (TB), Jody Question earned $5,757 from nine wins, eight seconds, and eight thirds.

Some other top money-earners among Question Mark's sons and daughters were:

Jo Ann's Baby (out of Paulita Murray by Bull), $7,742.

Snoops Hoodat (a filly out of Snooper C by Hard Tack), $5,922.

Del Mark (also a daughter of Phillips' Del Rio), $5,340.

Jasmine Cue (from the unregistered Minnie Blair), $5,244.

Ego Mark (an Appendix horse out of an unknown dam), $3,327.

No Money Down (out of June Baxter), $3,154.

Major Question (a son of Penny RO by Candy Kid), $3,059.

Question Mark's six qualifiers for Register of Merit in official AQHA shows indicated that he could throw working abilities as well as speed when crossed with mares of various types and bloodlines. Top working point-earners among these were Dawson's Ballymark (also a halter winner), out of Buckskin Dawson by the Jim Minnick-bred Comanche; and Jeep Honeycutt, out of M's Doodle Bug by Tommy Clegg. Others were Dynamo Power, out of Nowata's Smoke; Mr Question, full brother to the runners Aero Mark

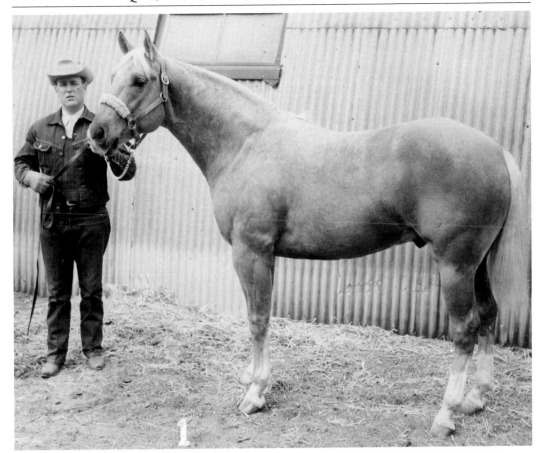

As evidenced by this shot of Trademark, the second generation of the Question Marks was every bit as good as the first. Foaled in 1948 and sired by Mark Master by Question Mark, Trademark is shown here in the early 1950s after being named grand champion stock-type Palomino at the Denver National Western Stock Show. Owner Roger Mellon of Johnstown, Colo., is at the halter.

Photo by Albert Corwin, Courtesy of the Palomino Horse Breeders of America

Here is Becky Lee, a 1956 mare by Bos'n and out of Josie Mark, and Buzzie Bars, her 1960 Sugar Bars son. Jack Anderson of Broken Arrow Ranch, Broken Arrow, Okla., owned the attractive pair, who had just won the mare and foal class at a 1960 Oklahoma Palomino show. Buzzie Bars went on to become one of the greatest sires in the history of the Palomino breed. The handler is Jimmy Hobbs and Mrs. Al Knight is presenting the trophy.

Photo by Jack Strayhorn, Courtesy of the Palomino Horse Breeders of America

Pioneer Palomino and Quarter Horse breeder Jack Anderson of Broken Arrow, Okla., with Josie Mark after she had been named grand champion Palomino mare at the 1960 Tulsa State Fair. Sired by Little Joe Jr. and out of Gold Question, by Question Mark, Josie Mark went on to become one of the Palomino association's greatest show champions and broodmares.

Photo by Jack Strayhorn, Courtesy of the Palomino Horse Breeders of America

and Questionnaire Lad; Young Question, out of an unregistered Cates mare; and Question Miss, out of Sue Hancock.

The progeny of Question Mark also made their marks in palomino shows. Among these was Miss Question Mark, who stood grand champion mare at Denver's National Western Stock Show. Another winner at the Denver show was his son Banjo. Quotation Mark compiled an enviable record as a trophy winner in numerous New Mexico Palomino shows.

Question Mark's sons, including Gray Question, Osage Red, and Dark Mark (a full brother to Savannah Gray), sired many capable foals; but it appears that

Question Mark's greatest impact on the Quarter Horse breed was through his daughters.

They produced 952 foals. Of these, 202 started in recognized races and earned $537,390. From the daughters' 76 performance point-earners there were 31 ROM-qualifiers. Daughters of Question Mark also foaled three horses who were to earn Superiors in their respective events. Five AQHA Champions also came from those daughters, along with 62 halter point-earners and two horses who earned the title of Superior halter horse.

The speedy Savannah Gray proved to be one of Question Mark's outstanding producing daughters. Her crowning achievement was producing Savannah Jr by the Thoroughbred Everett Jr. Rated Top AAA, Savannah Jr earned $277,005 while becoming the world champion 2-year-old colt and the world champion

Junior Reed, a 1954 palomino stallion by Leo and out of Lorane Question by Question Mark, was a AAA-rated stakes-winning race horse who went on to become a noted sire.

Photo by Orren Mixer, Courtesy of *The Quarter Horse Journal*

3-year-old colt. Possibly best-known for winning the 1965 All American Futurity, Savannah Jr also won the LaMesa Oklahoma Futurity, the Sunland Park Fall Futurity, and the 1966 Ruidoso Championship Stakes. He was third in the Rainbow Derby.

Savannah Jr very capably carried on the bloodline and family traditions by proving himself in the breeding shed. With his first crop of foals he showed the ability to sire a high percentage of racing Register of Merit qualifiers. He went on to sire such horses as Savannah Lark (stakes-winner of $122,249 with a speed index of 108), Southern Gentlemen (stakes-winner of $102,026 with a speed index of 103), Savannah Swinger (stakes-winner of $109,915), Savannah One Time (stakes-winner with a speed index of 108), and Donna Dodad (stakes-winner of $68,635).

Also among Savannah Jr's many talented get are two AQHA Supreme Champions: Sir Savannah (himself a noted sire) out of Last Bardial by Johnny

In this rare shot, taken in July 1961, 24-year-old Question Mark is shown with his last owner, Roland Pelt of Las Vegas, New Mexico.

Photo by Orren Mixer

Dial, and Savannah Tiger out of Bar Tawny by Bar Tonto.

Savannah Gray also produced the Top AAA Savannah's Deb and Savannah Cates. The latter of these two good fillies won the 1962 Sunland Championship and one division of the 1961 Sunland Stakes, as well as placed second in the Sunland Park Fall Derby. Savannah Cates also produced Savannah's Jet Jr, a sire of stakes runners.

Question Mark's unraced daughter Questionaire's Miss accomplished in the broodmare band what she didn't get a chance to demonstrate on the track. In addition to several other good foals (including the ROM-producing daughters Questionette, Question's Doolin, and Andra Star), she foaled the race ROM full brothers Leo's Question and Leotation. Both were sired by Leo and both placed in stakes.

Leo's Question became an important sire of outstanding horses in various fields. Although he sired several good race horses (including the AAA runners Baldy Pete, She's A Leo, and Van's Dumpy), Leo's Question also sired winners in performance arenas.

War Leo, a son of Leo's Question and War Bird by War Star, won the Nebraska Quarter Horse Association Futurity and then turned to the show arena. He became an AQHA Champion with 192 performance points and enough halter points

(72) to earn the Superior award in that field. War Leo was the 1963 AQHA High-Point Cutting Stallion and earned the NCHA Bronze Award for his success in open cutting horse contests.

Other descendants of Leo's Question who became prominent in working events are Mr Gun Smoke (AQHA Superior cutting horse, NCHA Certificate of Ability, and important sire of top cutting, reining, and working cow horses); Gun Smoke's Dream (NCHA Futurity champion); Two D's Dynamite (NCHA reserve world champion); Jae Bar Fletch (NCHA Hall Of Fame, with earnings of $349,401, as well as being the 1989 NCHA World Champion and 1985 World Champion Senior Cutting Horse); War Bond Leo (1969 AQHA High-Point Cutting Horse); War Leo Jr (1981 AQHA High-Point Cutting Horse); Jae Bar Gaby ($138,057 in cutting); Jae Bar Fame ($133,848 in cutting); Rondo Leo (AQHA Champion and noted sire of cutting horses); Dry Doc's Dottie (NCHA Futurity finalist), War Olee (Superior cutting); and Hollywood Smoke (All American Quarter Horse Congress reining champion).

Another of Question Mark's unraced daughters, Lorane Question, also proved important as a broodmare. Both she and her full sister, proven speedster Gray Question, were out of Lorane, a daughter of Zandy.

Bred to Vandy, Lorane Question produced Vandy's Question, who won a 440-yard derby at Pawhuska and set a 440-yard record for that Oklahoma track. Earlier, he had run second in the Pawhuska Futurity.

When bred to Leo, Lorane Question produced a AAA colt named Junior Reed. A track record-setter at 300 yards, Junior Reed also was an outstanding sire. His best-known foal was the Supreme Champion Mach I. In addition to his Top AAA running ability, Mach I clinched his title by earning points in team roping (both heading and heeling), reining, and western pleasure. Junior Reed also sired Smug Reed, who acquired a considerable reputation as a sire of team-roping horses.

Savannah Jr, a 1963 gray stallion by Everett Jr. (TB) and out of Savannah Gray by Question Mark, won $277,005 during his stellar racing career. The winner of the 1965 All American Futurity, he was also the 1965 Champion Quarter Running 2-Year-Old Colt and the 1966 Champion Quarter Running 3-Year-Old Colt.

Courtesy of *The Quarter Horse Journal*

Although there was a question mark stamped on his pretty head, there was never a question about the lasting contributions Question Mark made to both the Palomino and the Quarter Horse breeds. Outstanding horses bearing his blood are still winning.

14 TWO EYED JACK

By Frank Holmes

The word "versatile" truly applied to Two Eyed Jack and all his get, who amassed over 15,000 halter points and over 21,000 performance points. They rode as good as they looked, and this photo of Two Eyed Jack clearly shows where his offspring's looks and ability came from.

Photo by Alfred Janssen III, Courtesy of *The Quarter Horse Journal*

JUST LIKE THE playing card he was named after, Two Eyed Jack was a top draw. The famous sorrel stallion was bred by Herman Mass and was foaled on his Double H Ranch outside McHenry, Ill., on March 22, 1961. Sired by Two D Two and out of Triangle Tookie, his pedigree was rich in the blood of Old Sorrel, Grey Badger II, and Joe Hancock.

Herman Mass was one of the Midwest's premier pioneer Quarter Horse breeders. Traveling throughout the West and Southwest on horse-buying trips in the early to mid-1950s, he often brought breeding stock back to his northern Illinois facility by the boxcar-load.

On one of his trips, Mass came across a 5-day-old colt in California at Jack Schwabacher's ranch. Sired by Double Diamond and out of Double Life, the typey bay youngster impressed Mass enough that he gave $500 for him on the spot. Registered as Two D Two, he went on to become an AQHA Champion, a top breeding stallion, and the sire of Two Eyed Jack.

Triangle Tookie had been taken to Illinois from Texas by Mass even earlier—in 1952. Sired by Grey Badger III and out of Lady Hancock, the Burnett Estates-bred palomino was regarded by her owner as one of his very best broodmares.

In 1960 Mass made the first of several successful Two D Two-Triangle Tookie matings. Two Eyed Jack was the result. Subsequent crossings would produce Tookie's Two and Triangle Queen. All three would go on to become AQHA Champions.

According to Mass, as he was often

160

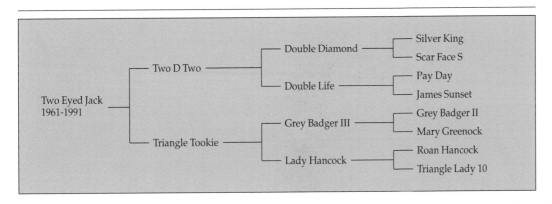

```
                          ┌── Silver King
             ┌── Double Diamond ──┤
             │            └── Scar Face S
   ┌── Two D Two ──┤
   │         │            ┌── Pay Day
   │         └── Double Life ──┤
   │                      └── James Sunset
Two Eyed Jack ──┤
1961-1991    │            ┌── Grey Badger II
   │         ┌── Grey Badger III ──┤
   │         │            └── Mary Greenock
   └── Triangle Tookie ──┤
             │            ┌── Roan Hancock
             └── Lady Hancock ──┤
                          └── Triangle Lady 10
```

quoted in later years, Two Eyed Jack was a picture-perfect colt—"an ideally conformed adult Quarter Horse in miniature." And the Illinois horseman wasted little time in seeing if the rest of the world would agree with him. Shown by Mass and his daughter Melinda, Two Eyed Jack began his show career with a win in the weanling stallion class at the Illinois State Fair. A number of wins as a yearling and 2-year-old halter stallion followed, and in 1963 he was sold to E.C. Coppola of Iowa.

Shortly thereafter, he sold again, this time to Joe Lindholm of Audubon, Iowa. By then, the big sorrel stallion had attracted quite a following; a Nebraska Sandhills breeder named Howard Pitzer was one of them.

Pitzer, a knowledgeable horseman, had already established a name for himself in the show ring with his Pat Star Jr. line of halter and working champions. By the time Two Eyed Jack was 3, Pitzer reasoned that he needed to find a way to get involved with him.

"We were at a show in Burwell, Neb.," Pitzer recalls, "and Joe had Two Eyed Jack there. I was hitting the show circuit pretty hard at this time, and I asked Joe to consider letting me show Jack. He agreed, and we did a little more talking, a little horse-trading, and I wound up with a half-interest in the horse.

"I showed Jack for the better part of a year and a half and put a bunch of halter points and some western pleasure points

Halter and Performance Record: Performance Register of Merit; AQHA Champion; Superior Halter, 217 points, 70 Grand Championships.

Progeny Record:

Foal Crops: 17	Halter Points Earned: 15,698.5
Foals Registered: 1,416	Superior Halter Awards: 74
AQHA Champions: 119	Performance Point-Earners: 577
Supreme Champions: 3	Performance Points Earned: 21,336.5
Youth Champions: 30	Performance Registers of Merit: 314
World Champions: 21	Superior Performance Awards: 102
Halter Point-Earners: 454	Superhorse: 1

on him. By the end of 1964 he had earned close to 50 grand championships."

In 1965 Pitzer and Lindholm decided that they needed to own Two Eyed Jack's sire, so they partnered once more and purchased Two D Two. A year later, they traded again, and this time Two Eyed Jack became the sole property of Howard Pitzer.

"I had made the decision that I was going to find a way to own Jack by myself, free and clear," Pitzer says. "I traded my half of Two D Two back to Joe, added some cattle, did a little more swapping and trading, and wound up with Jack. I'd wanted him from the first time I laid eyes

Two D Two was an AQHA Champion, but his main claim to fame was siring Two Eyed Jack.

Photo by Darol Dickinson, Courtesy of *The Quarter Horse Journal*

With 350 halter points and 216 working points, Jack's Tune was a true representative of her bloodline. This 1967 dun daughter of Two Eyed Jack and out of Little Music was an AQHA Champion and Superior halter and western pleasure horse. Kay Schleichardt, who worked for Howard Pitzer for several years, is in the picture, which was taken when Jack's Tune stood grand champion mare at a Lincoln, Neb., Quarter Horse show.

Photo Courtesy of *The Quarter Horse Journal*

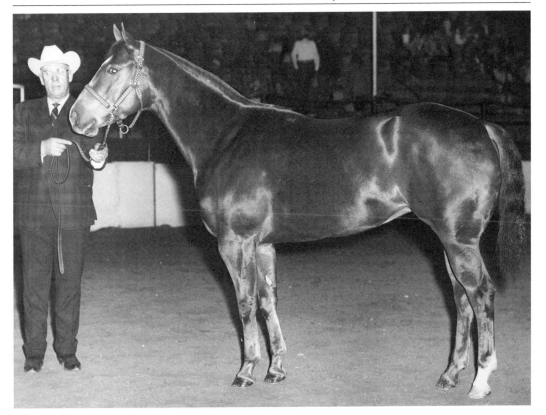

Howard Pitzer showed Miss Buckets to the grand champion mare title at the 1970 National Western Stock Show in Denver. A 1966 daughter of Two Eyed Jack and out of Cooksey Lady 2, Miss Buckets was an AQHA Champion and earned Superior awards in halter and western pleasure.

Photo by Darol Dickinson, Courtesy of *The Quarter Horse Journal*

Vallerina Miss was one of Two Eyed Jack's greatest daughters. Foaled in 1968 to Miss Monsieur, the outstanding show mare was the 1975 AQHA High-Point Halter Horse, High-Point Halter Mare, and World Champion Aged Mare. She earned Superior awards in halter, western pleasure, and youth showmanship, as well as open and youth AQHA Championships. Stretch Bradley is at the mare's lead in this photo.

Photo Courtesy of *The Quarter Horse Journal*

Miss Patty Jack was a highly successful show mare by Two Eyed Jack and out of Patty's Queen. The 1972 sorrel mare earned 100 halter and 74 performance points on her way to becoming an AQHA Champion and Youth Champion, the 1975 World Champion 3-Year-Old Mare, and winner of Superior awards in halter, western pleasure, and youth showmanship.

Photo by Harold Campton, Courtesy of *The Quarter Horse Journal*

on him and I eventually got him. I just had to get him a piece at a time."

Two Eyed Jack was shown until he was a 9-year-old. He stood grand at some of the most prestigious shows in the country and earned 217 halter points. A versatile, willing performer, he also accumulated 46.5 western pleasure, 7 hunter under saddle, 6 reining, 3 western riding, and 3 working cow horse points. He was awarded a Superior in halter and his AQHA Championship in 1964.

"Most people think of Jack strictly as a halter horse," Pitzer says, "and he certainly was a great one. But he was more that just that. He was an excellent performance horse and the only thing that ever kept him from achieving as many wins in performance as he had in halter was that we didn't show him that heavy. He was a big, heavily muscled horse, but he still moved real light on his feet. If you were standing in the corral with him, and had your back turned, he could walk up behind you and you'd never know he was there.

"One year at the Congress, he won the versatility class and ran the barrels in record time after only 2 weeks' training on them. You should have heard the roar from the crowd when he rounded that last barrel and headed for home.

"Another thing about Jack that I always admired," Pitzer continues, "was that he was always just so willing to do what you asked of him. And he'd do it with just the lightest little bit in his mouth. We used him for everything here at the ranch. He could work a cow as well as any of them.

"I've seen a lot of different families of horses over the years that I dearly loved to look at. They were good-looking. But, when it came time to ride them, you had to hang so much iron in their mouths to even get their attention that I just couldn't stand it. Two Eyed Jack was never like that. Neither were his descendants. He was just special that way."

Given the outstanding show record that Jack had accumulated, there was a certain amount of speculation on the part of the Quarter Horse show fraternity about

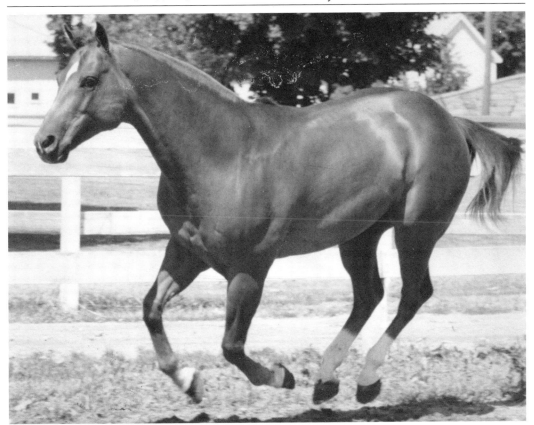

Two Eyed Revenue, a 1970 sorrel stallion by Two Eyed Jack and out of Midnight Gold, earned the titles of AQHA Champion and world champion aged stallion, and earned Superiors in halter and western pleasure.

Photo Courtesy of *The Quarter Horse Journal*

Deacon Jack, even at 22 months, shows off the unmistakable Two Eyed Jack look. He went on to become an AQHA Champion, Superior halter horse, and the 1977 World Champion 2-Year-Old Stallion. He was foaled in 1975 to Miss Rag's Royal.

Photo by Alfred Janssen III, Courtesy of *The Quarter Horse Journal*

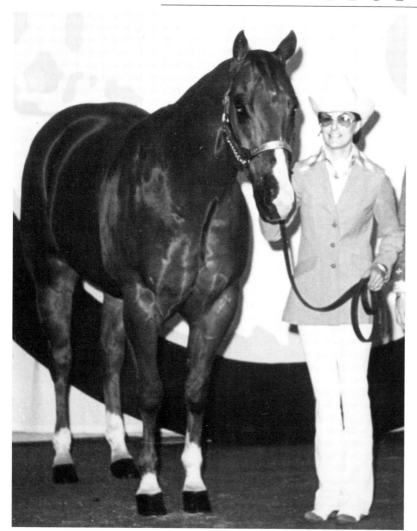

One of the top gelded sons of Two Eyed Jack in the mid-1970s, Two Eyed Dandy garnered 442 open and 159 youth halter points. Foaled in 1974 to Hilda Pat Star, he later became the 1974 World Champion Aged Gelding and an AQHA Champion.

Photo by Harold Campton, Courtesy of *The Quarter Horse Journal*

Miss Denver Dot, a 1970 daughter of Two Eyed Jack and out of Dot Pat Star, earned 412 halter points, 50 performance points, and an AQHA Championship.

Photo by Alfred Janssen III, Courtesy of *The Quarter Horse Journal*

whether he could succeed as a breeding stallion. That concern was put to rest in short order. From Jack's first small foal crop, which hit the ground in 1964, he sired Miss Sunbonnet, who earned 179 halter points; and Katie Two Eye, an AQHA Champion. His second crop included Two Eyed Scoot and Two Jack, both of whom were AQHA Champions and Superior halter horses. From there, it just took off.

To list just the open AQHA Champions sired by Two Eyed Jack, 119 of them, would require the better part of a small book. Add to that his 30 youth AQHA Champions, 176 open and youth Superior award winners, 31 open and youth world or reserve world championship winners, and 13 AQHA high-point winners, and the book size swells to large.

His open world champion get included Two Jack Two, Two Eyed Ted, Vallerina Miss, Two Eyed Dandy, Two Eyed Sox, Two Eyed Revenue, Miss Patty Jack, Mr Jack Prince, The Dallas Cowboy, Vickie Lee Pine, and Two Eyed Bartender.

Among his more accomplished open halter get were Miss Buckets (367 points), Denver Jack (504), Jack's Tune (350), Acres High (301), Vallerina Miss (924), Chubby's Doll (533), Two Eyed Dandy (442), Miss Denver Dot (412), Two Eyed Revenue

(175), Watch Joe Jack (225), Pep Up Jackie
(254), Boots Jack (190), Lin D Two (161),
and Vickie Lee Pine (237).

His top open performance point-earners
included Miss Buckets (271), Two Jack
Two (168), Denver Jack (136), Jack's Tune
(216), Jack's Pants (104), Two Eyed Bonus
(160), Vallerina Miss (187), Chubby's Doll
(107), Bucket Jack (143), Silver Poco Jack
(103), Two Eyed Revenue (153), Watch Joe
Jack (201), Two Eyed Donna (215), Two
Eyed Del (319), Two Eyed Patti (163), Mr
Jack Prince (594), Left Jack (165), Watch
Lucky Jack (217), Two ID Patty Queen
(119), Chubbys Jackie Jo (155), Two Eyed
Tyree (129), Prarie Tom Jack (167), Two
Eyed Blue Boy (167), Two Eyed Tune (113),
Two Eyed Lady Jack (129), Sansarita Jack
(140), Jackie Joann (137), Two Socks Jody
(217), and Two ID Bartender (164).

Vickie Lee Pine, a 1974 bay mare by Two
Eyed Jack and out of Poco Coed by Poco
Pine, was the 1978 AQHA World Show
Superhorse—the first such titlist.

Mr Baron Red, by Red Baron Bell and
out of Two Eyed Patti by Two Eyed Jack,
took the same award in 1983.

Numbers alone could never even begin
to tell the whole story of Two Eyed Jack
and the Quarter Horse dynasty he began.
Coming into existence as he did near the
end of the true all-around Quarter show
horse, his is one of the last great families of
horses that could and did excel as halter
and performance horses in many events.

And the Two Eyed Jacks were horses
whom almost anyone could get along
with. Put in the hands of top professionals,
they were capable of winning world
championships in a variety of events.
Relegated to ranch and rodeo status, they
excelled. Bred and trained by amateur
horsemen, they performed with amazing
consistency.

Two Eyed Jack passed away on March
2, 1991, just 20 days short of reaching his
30th birthday. His legend and his legacy
have been profound.

He sired 119 AQHA Champions. No
other sire has even come within sighting
distance of that mark. In today's climate of
the specialized performers, it seems a safe
bet to say that no horse ever will.

But then, Howard Pitzer's big sorrel son

Watch Joe Jack, a 1970 sorrel stallion by Two Eyed Jack and out of Watch Joe Moore, was a Cadillac pleasure horse in the mid-1970s, with over 200 points. He was the 1973 High-Point Western Pleasure Stallion. But, with 225 halter points, he also stood with the best halter horses in the country.
Photo by Alfred Janssen III, Courtesy of *The Quarter Horse Journal*

of Two D Two and Triangle Tookie was not
your run-of-the-mill foal, show horse, or
sire. No matter what playing card he was
named after, to all of those who were ever
connected with him, and to those who
have owned and ridden his descendants,
Two Eyed Jack was really a king.

15 MR GUN SMOKE

By Betsy Lynch

Mr Gun Smoke had a profound effect on the cutting, reining, and working cow horse industries, and two breeds—Quarter Horse and Paint. Once called a "poor man's sire" by his longtime owner Dale Wilkinson, the sorrel stallion went from breeding obscurity to a $10,000 stud fee in his lifetime.

Photo by Don Trout, Courtesy of Jeff Oswood

MANY TRULY GREAT horses were said to be "ahead of their time." This was perhaps never truer than it was of Mr Gun Smoke. In fact, the performance horse industry may still be trying to catch up to the athletic potential available through this explosively talented line. But it took an elite class of horsemen and women to figure out how best to capitalize on the Gun Smoke firepower.

One such horseman was Dale Wilkinson, a National Reining Horse Association and National Cutting Horse Association Hall of Fame member. Wilkinson owned Mr Gun Smoke for most of the stallion's 22 years. He called Mr Gun Smoke "a tremendous poor man's sire." He explained that the stallion so consistently passed on his own brand of courage, charisma, and cow sense that it didn't take an extraordinary mare to get an extraordinary foal.

In turn, Gun Smoke's progeny passed these traits on to their offspring, which is why Gun Smoke's trademark style is still so highly visible in the arena today.

Most notably, Mr Gun Smoke sired cutting, reining, and working cow horse winners. His AQHA get-of-sire record shows that his direct offspring have earned just shy of 2,000 performance points. Yet this doesn't begin to accurately reflect his influence on the performance horse industry.

Many of Mr Gun Smoke's best sons and daughters were never shown in AQHA events. Instead, they made their mark in National Cutting Horse Association (NCHA), National Reining Horse Association (NRHA), and National Reined Cow Horse (NRCHA) competition. The latter

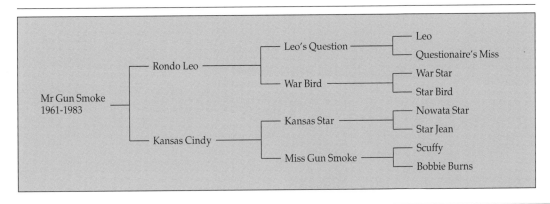

Mr Gun Smoke
1961–1983

- Rondo Leo
  - Leo's Question
    - Leo
    - Questionaire's Miss
  - War Bird
    - War Star
    - Star Bird
- Kansas Cindy
  - Kansas Star
    - Nowata Star
    - Star Jean
  - Miss Gun Smoke
    - Scuffy
    - Bobbie Burns

was formerly called the California Reined Cow Horse Association. Those associations didn't always keep complete performance records—let alone comprehensive sire and dam records—so it is impossible to piece together a complete picture.

Yet even a brief overview is impressive. Among Mr Gun Smoke's distinguished offspring are an NCHA Futurity champion (Gun Smoke's Dream), two NRHA Hall of Fame horses (Hollywood Smoke, Miss White Trash), an NRCHA Snaffle Bit Futurity champion (Kit's Smoke), an NRCHA Hackamore Maturity champion (Political Smoker), and multiple NRCHA bridle horse sweepstakes champions.

What's more, several of Mr Gun Smoke's most memorable get and grandget are registered Paint Horses. Mr Gun Smoke's propensity to produce Quarter Horses with excessive white enriched Paint Horse working lines tremendously.

Pedigree analyst, breeding consultant, and author Larry Thornton speculates that Mr Gun Smoke's pronounced ability to produce overo cropouts may have been inherited through his sire line. The Leos, which were linebred Joe Reed, were well-known for producing generous white markings. "But there could be other factors involved," Thornton acknowledged. Whatever the source, the characteristic Gun Smoke white trim has been a source of both pride and frustration for many cow-horse breeders.

Nevertheless, Harley and Mamie Price of Bazine, Kan., were batting a thousand when they chose to breed their stallion Rondo Leo to Kansas Cindy. The recipe was ripe with cow sense, athletic ability, and speed. Without question, Mr Gun Smoke proved to be a silver bullet for cut-

Halter and Performance Record: Superior Cutting; Performance Register of Merit; NCHA Certificate of Ability; NRCHA Cow Horse Hall of Fame.

AQHA Progeny Record:

Foal Crops: 20	Performance Point-Earners: 162
Foals Registered: 556	Performance Points Earned: 1,967.5
AQHA Champions: 1	Performance Registers of Merit: 48
Halter Point-Earners: 6	Superior Performance Awards: 5
Halter Points Earned: 43.5	

NRHA Progeny Record:

Performers: 95	World Champions: 1
Total Earnings: $77,137 (as of 1997)	Hall of Fame Inductees: 2
Leading Money-Earners: Miss Reed Smoke ($21,700)	

NCHA Progeny Record:

NCHA Futurity Champions: 1	World Champions: 1

NRCHA Progeny Record:

NRCHA Snaffle Bit Futurity Champions: 1
NRCHA Hackamore Maturity Champions: 1

APHA Progeny Record:

Registered Foals: 67	Halter Points: 100
Performing Foals: 16	Superior Halter Awards: 1
APHA Champions: 1	Performance Point-Earners: 22
World Champions: 1	Performance Points: 579
National Champions: 1	Performance Registers of Merit: 21
Halter Point-Earners: 4	Superior Performance Awards: 2

169

Dale Wilkinson cutting on Mr Gun Smoke. Dale said the horse had a tremendous desire to control a cow, and he considered it a personal challenge. He earned an AQHA Superior in cutting and a NCHA Certificate of Ability.

Photo by Fred Droddy

He provided a much-needed outcross for the King P-234 and Doc Bar families, and improved a host of other bloodlines as well.

ting, reining, and working cow-horse breeders. He provided a much-needed outcross for the King P-234 and Doc Bar families, and improved a host of other bloodlines as well.

Gun Smoke's sire, Rondo Leo, was an AQHA Champion with 20 halter points, 25 cutting points, and 11 reining points. He also had an impressive pedigree. He traced to Leo through Leo's Question, a AA race horse who earned a tremendous reputation as a cutting horse sire. Rondo Leo's full brother, War Leo, was also an AQHA Champion, an NCHA Top 10 horse, and the 1963 AQHA High-Point Cutting Horse, as well as a stakes race winner. Both stallions were out of War Bird, a line-bred Oklahoma Star mare who produced four AQHA Champions.

Mr Gun Smoke's dam, Kansas Cindy, was also line-bred Oklahoma Star through her sire, Kansas Star. Kansas Star was by Nowata Star and out of Star Jean. Oklahoma Star was a noted speed horse (as was Leo). In the early 1920s he was such a great match race horse that owner

Tommy Moore soon ran out of willing contenders. Oklahoma Star also passed on his speed. Nowata Star, for instance, sired nine ROM race horses.

The intensive Oklahoma Star breeding on both sides of Mr Gun Smoke's pedigree infused him with a double dose of dynamite. It may also be responsible for his prepotency as a sire, noted Thornton. It certainly contributed to his "breedy" build. Unlike the stout-muscled, compactly built Leos, Mr Gun Smoke matured at 15.1 hands and had a lean, elegant look.

"His conformation was just exactly the way you'd build one," said Wilkinson. "He had a little ol' narrow chest, a little pencil neck, high withers, short back, and his stifle just hung out there about 6 inches. He didn't have much gaskin, but he was made like a modern athlete.

"A characteristic of Gun Smoke horses is that they've got a lot of movement in the front end," Wilkinson continued. "I think that conformation complemented them so they could easily move the front end and do everything off of their hindquarters."

From Kansas to Ohio

Mr Gun Smoke was foaled in Kansas in 1961. The Prices didn't own the blaze-faced, stocking-legged sorrel for long,

Mr Gun Smoke was inducted into the NRCHA Hall of Fame in a ceremony during the 1980 NRCHA Snaffle Bit Futurity. Jeff Oswood, manager for GW's Futurity Farms, where Gun Smoke stood at the time, leads the stallion.

Photo by Fallaw, Courtesy of Deborah O'Brien

however. By the time he had reached his first birthday, Mr Gun Smoke had already been sold twice. The first exchange took him to Ohio, where he would spend almost his entire life—not exactly the first place that comes to mind when you think of premier cow horses.

Another sale put him into the hands of Bill Nicodemus, who formed a partnership with his brother-in-law, Tom Ryan. Nicodemus dabbled in racing and pleasure with Mr Gun Smoke before contacting Dale Wilkinson about training the colt for cutting. Nicodemus offered Dale one-third interest in the horse in exchange for his training fees. But Wilkinson wasn't ready to take the plunge on the unproven 3-year-old. Instead, he agreed to take Mr Gun Smoke for 2 months at his regular training fee, after which time he would reconsider the offer.

Dale admitted he was less than impressed with the looks of the horse. But all that changed when he slapped a saddle on his back.

"Mr Gun Smoke was very impressive from the beginning," Wilkinson said. "He was a very athletic horse, very physical, with a lot of uncontrollable moves. He was also very, very cowy. He could move *so* fast. Too fast," he chuckled. "He was really more than you could control."

Two months wasn't nearly enough time for Dale to figure out how to contain Mr Gun Smoke's extreme reactivity. Yet he was intrigued by the stallion's potential. Wilkinson accepted Nicode-

mus' offer, and took part ownership of Mr Gun Smoke. He admits he never did collect his training wages.

Unfortunately, not long into his schooling, Mr Gun Smoke sustained a front leg injury that sidelined his early show career. Wilkinson believes the stallion broke a bone in his ankle. As he was recovering from that, he developed ringbone in a hind leg. Over the next several years, Mr Gun Smoke vacillated between soundness and lameness.

Due to this injury, no one probably ever saw Mr Gun Smoke at the top of his form. Dale speculates that the ailment may have slowed the horse down just enough to allow the trainer to get a handle on his phenomenal talent. When Mr Gun Smoke was finally sound enough to compete, he was awesome.

Gun Smoke had undeniable power and presence. He was light to the rein and leg. And he could stop and turn with such force that it often prompted some good-natured ribbing. Wilkinson recalls western artist Lex Graham chiding him after watching Gun Smoke cut:

"Hey Dale, I sure wouldn't have any need for your horse."

"Oh, why is that?" Dale queried back.

"Well, I noticed you spent half your time just getting back on him," Graham laughed.

Wilkinson explained that Mr Gun

When Mr Gun Smoke was finally sound enough to compete, he was awesome.

Dale Wilkinson won the 1972 NCHA Futurity on Gun Smoke's Dream, a 1969 bay mare out of Lady Badger 71. After victories like that, breeders finally took Mr Gun Smoke seriously as a sire of cow horses.

Photo Courtesy of Dale Wilkinson

Smoke had a tremendous desire to control a cow. He considered it a personal challenge. And the horse's ground-driving stop was built-in. Dale said he never had to teach the stallion to stop with a cow. Mr Gun Smoke reacted instinctively. The stallion also quickly figured out where to position himself to keep his working advantage. If a cow would stop and face the horse, Mr Gun Smoke would crouch and challenge the animal, just daring it to make a move.

Dale relates, "We were at Columbus, Ohio, for a cutting. There was a small pen called the Cooper Arena and they would sprinkle the top of it with water to keep the dust down. Anyway, Ronnie Sharp worked first. The top of the dirt was wet and when Ronnie went in, he slipped around, almost fell down. After he quit and came out, he said 'That ground's dangerous. Somebody's going to hurt themselves.'

"I went in on Mr Gun Smoke, and when we got done cutting, I'd marked a 76," Wilkinson continued. "So I told him, 'Ronnie, there's lots a dry dirt down there if you just get down in there and get it.'

"You know, you can be a smart alec when you're riding one like that," Wilkinson chuckled. "But that was the difference with Mr Gun Smoke. . . . He was such a strong-stopping horse. When a cow would stop, he'd just drop his butt in the ground. It's one of the things I feel he's passed on."

Long before Mr Gun Smoke had his banner show year in 1967, the stallion had earned Wilkinson's respect. He was hot-blooded, light-footed, and exceptionally responsive. He was also extremely intelligent. According to Dale, he was a giant step ahead of many of the cooler-tempered horses who were popular at the time. His big eyes and alert, intelligent appearance prompted Texas cutting horse legend Pat Patterson to tell Wilkinson that his horse "looked like a truck driver on bennies." He cut cattle with intensity, and commanded a great deal of respect.

Wilkinson and others have often described Mr Gun Smoke as an athletic genius. Legendary reiner Bill Horn agrees. Horn is the first rider in the history of the NRHA to have won more than

172

Dale Wilkinson showed Marijuana Smoke, a 1975 stallion out of Miss Maria, at the 1978 NCHA Futurity. Notice that he is not wearing chaps, despite the prestige of that event. Dale explained that the Gun Smoke colts were very sensitive, especially about the belly area. At home, he never wore chaps on Marijuana Smoke when he worked him. He said: "When I got to Fort Worth, I figured it wouldn't be smart to start then . . . if that leather flopped against his belly, no tellin' where he'd go!"

Photo by Dalco, Courtesy of Dale Wilkinson

a million dollars in reining competition. More than a few Mr Gun Smokes contributed to that tally, including NRHA Hall of Famers Miss White Trash, Hollywood Smoke, and Trashadeous.

Horn rode with Dale during the early days when Wilkinson was training and showing Mr Gun Smoke. He says that the stallion was one of the most physically powerful horses he's ever seen. Unlike Dale, who said he was discouraged from reining on the Gun Smokes because they tended to be hot, Horn was one of the first horsemen to successfully channel that explosive energy in the reining pen.

White Trash

Due to fate, however, Horn's first Mr Gun Smoke became a cutter. In 1966, Horn bred his Quarter Horse mare Little Miss Hank to Dale's stallion. What he got was a flashy sorrel filly he named White Trash. That's because the mare's generous white markings made her ineligible for AQHA registration papers. They also kept her out of the NRHA Futurity. At

that time, the event was open only to registered Quarter Horses.

But White Trash was no throwaway in Horn's eyes. He competed with the mare at the 1970 NCHA Futurity, placing sixth in the most prestigious cutting event in the country. She won more than $10,000 in cutting before Horn turned her physical prowess to reining. From 1976 to 1980, Miss White Trash won a number of open reinings, earning more than $13,000 at a time when the prestige was a lot greater than the payback.

An even greater contribution to the industry is the one Miss White Trash made as a broodmare. She produced five offspring who won more than $150,000 in NRHA events. They are Patrasha, Im Not Trash, Mr White Trash, Mark Him Trash, and Trashadeous. She was inducted into the NRHA Hall of Fame in 1993.

Her most famous son is Trashadeous, a 1987 stallion by Be Aech Enterprise (AQHA). In spirit, appearance, and sheer unbridled talent, Trashadeous is the

Bill Horn was one of the first horsemen to successfully campaign the hotblooded Gun Smoke horses in reining. Here he is on Hollywood Smoke, a 1969 son of Mr Gun Smoke out of Pistol's Holly. The stallion, who was inducted into the NRHA Hall of Fame and also earned an AQHA ROM in cutting, started his own line of topquality reiners, including two NRHA Futurity reserve champions.

Photo Courtesy of Earl Cox

image of his grandsire. With Horn in the saddle, the Paint stallion electrified audiences every time he entered the show ring. He retired with more than $100,000 in NRHA earnings.

But Trashadeous' road to riches got off to a rocky start. Horn, who bred the stallion, says he knew from the start that Trashadeous was special. Horn personally took charge of breaking and training the colt. He was "cocky," according to Horn, but fragile as well. People who worked for Horn still like to tease him about his runaway colt.

"It was so easy to scare him," Horn said. "And for him to scare himself—he could do so much." For a year, Horn never touched Trashadeous with a spur. He just kept trying to build the colt's confidence and trust and get him under control. Horn felt certain that if he could just capture the colt's ability, he would be awesome in the

show pen. At his first show, Trashadeous reared straight up. Hardly an auspicious beginning for a future Hall of Famer.

But Trashadeous more than redeemed himself by winning the reserve championship in the 1990 NRHA Futurity. He finished a half-point away from the top spot.

After recovering from colic surgery, Trashadeous went on to win the NRHA Derby, NRHA Superstakes, NRHA Congress Open, and the Lazy E Classic Open. He became the NRHA's 1992 Open World Champion. In 1996, Trashadeous was inducted into the National Reining Horse Association Hall of Fame.

"I've got a lot of respect for Trashadeous and Bill . . . but maybe more for Bill," acknowledges Wilkinson. "Trashadeous was so much like Mr Gun Smoke. My God, he was so physical. You never knew where he was going to go or what he was going to do. But you did know he was going to do something."

Among horsemen, the Gun Smokes did have a reputation for being volatile. And in truth, they weren't for everyone. Yet in the right hands, they exhibited such courage, determination, and raw

Bill Horn is the first reiner to earn $1 million in NRHA competition and most of it was won on Gun Smoke-bred horses such as Trashadeous, shown here. The sorrel overo stallion is by Be Aech Enterprise and out of the Gun Smoke daughter Miss White Trash. He was the 1990 NRHA Futurity reserve champion and earned more than $100,000 in his career.

Photo by Waltenberry

physical talent that they were hard to beat. But getting along with them required patience and strategy rather than force. One needed to be careful about lighting matches while sitting on a powder keg.

"They took a little more of your time than a fellow really wants to spend on one," admits Wilkinson. "They took a lot of riding, a lot of quiet riding, a lot of sensible riding. As far as hurting them, that wasn't in their program at all. I don't think very many people won if they used that approach on them. Most of the Gun Smokes are very intelligent. Mr Gun Smoke himself was very intelligent."

Wilkinson also pointed out that many of the Gun Smokes matured a bit slower than horses from other popular performance lines—both physically and mentally. It didn't necessarily pay to be in a hurry.

A Transformation

When Dale first saw Mr Gun Smoke as a 3-year-old he thought the colt was scrawny, light-muscled, and as fractious as any youngster he'd ever started. By the time Mr Gun Smoke was a 5- and 6-year-old, he had made a remarkable transformation. Not only was he physically handsome, he was also mentally mature enough to be all business.

California horseman Pat Hubbert can relate to that assessment. He experienced a similar situation with his great Gun Smoke daughter Smokes Belle. The mare is out of Mac's Sujo and is a full sister to 1976 CRCHA Snaffle Bit Futurity Champion Kit's Smoke. Hubbert teamed up with Smokes Belle at the end of her 3-year-old year when his client bought her at the CRCHA Snaffle Bit Futurity Sale. Although Smokes Belle had finished in the snaffle bit futurity finals, she was on pretty shaky ground.

Hubbert said Smokes Belle was athletic and cat quick, but extremely flighty. And

Kit's Smoke, a 1973 mare by Mr Gun Smoke and out of Mac's Sujo, became the first horse to win the title of NRCHA Supreme Working Cow Horse. Benny Guitron rode her throughout her career. In this photo they are circling the cow during the finals of the 1979 Cow Palace stock horse classic in which they were the reserve champions.

Photo by Fallaw

she had so much stamina that there weren't enough hours in the day to wear her out. Training her was a mind game. Hubbert liked the challenge.

"She used to be my morning's work," Hubbert recalled. "I'd go out and saddle her up and ride her. I could see she was a basket case, but I didn't fight with her. I just tried to get something done with her every day."

His persistence paid off. She got better and better. In her second year of NRCHA hackamore competition, Smokes Belle won the hackamore division year-end award. In fact, Hubbert had begun to think so highly of the mare that when the opportunity came up to buy her, he and his wife Judy mortgaged the ranch and bought Belle and her full sister, Nuthin But Smoke.

By the time Smokes Belle was retired to the Hubbert broodmare band, she had won more than $57,000 and had earned her NRCHA Supreme Working Cow

Horse title. Nuthin But Smoke also did her part and earned more than $30,000 before she was given broodmare status. What's more, Smokes Belle has produced 12 foals who have won more than $150,000 in working cow horse, cutting, and reining competition.

Her daughter Smokinic, by Reminic, won the 1986 NRCHA Snaffle Bit Futurity and has lifetime earnings of more than $80,000.

Belle's cropout Paint son by Winnerinic, Smokes Dude, is an APHA world champion and the association's No. 1 lifetime leading working cow horse, at the time of this writing. He also has Superiors in cutting and reining.

Although Mr Gun Smoke's own performance career was short, Wilkinson made the most of it. He didn't haul very much because "there was too much work to be done at home," but Dale took the horse to fairs, fat stock shows, and the occasional Quarter Horse show. Mr Gun Smoke was shown approximately 30 times. He earned 71 AQHA performance points, an AQHA Superior cutting award, and received his NCHA Certificate of Ability with nearly $8,500 in winnings. In fact, Mr Gun Smoke

Like her full sister, Kit's Smoke, Smokes Belle earned the title of NRCHA Supreme Working Cow Horse. She and her owner-trainer Pat Hubbert are shown here winning the bridle horse sweepstakes at the 1980 CRCHA Snaffle Bit Futurity.

Photo by Fallaw

did well enough in 1967 with limited showing to place 11th in the NCHA's year-end standings.

Even prior to the stallion's show ring success, Wilkinson had a hankering to acquire sole ownership of Mr Gun Smoke. In early 1967, tight financial circumstances convinced Bill Nicodemus and Tom Ryan to part with their shares. Nicodemus set a price, but as part of the bargain, he also wanted the trophy he anticipated that Mr Gun Smoke would win at an upcoming show.

"I said all right, but there isn't any guarantee on the trophy," Wilkinson recalled with a laugh. "But I won the cutting and Bill got his trophy and $2,500."

For his part, Tom Ryan received a 2-year-old Mr Gun Smoke filly in trade.

Prior to 1967, Mr Gun Smoke had bred only a handful of mares. But once the stallion debuted on the show scene, his strong cutting performance and good looks began to generate some local interest.

Then, as the handful of Gun Smoke sons and daughters began to trickle into the show arena, serious cow-horse breeders couldn't help but notice. In 1970, Bill Horn and Miss White Trash finished sixth at the NCHA Futurity. In 1971, Two D's Dynamite, another Gun Smoke daughter, became the NCHA Non-Pro Futurity reserve champion. That same year, Smoked Out was on the AQHA's list of top 10 reining horses. The next year, Dale won the 1972 NCHA Cutting Futurity with Gun Smoke's Dream.

Mr Gun Smoke's ability to sire talented performance horses was obviously no fluke.

After Wilkinson won the NCHA Futu-

Trainer Pat Hubbert and his wife, Judy, mortgaged their ranch to buy Smokes Belle (left) and her full sister Nuthin But Smoke. With Smokes Belle is Smokes Master, and with Nuthin But Smoke is Nuthin Smokin. Both 1992 foals are by Master Remedy.

Photos by Linda Rosser, Courtesy of Jackie Robertson

rity, regional interest expanded to national interest. In what could hardly be considered a hot-bed of cutting, Mr Gun Smoke was breeding more than 3 dozen mares from all over the country. His book was starting to fill with a better class of mares, and his offspring were being saddled by some of the nation's better trainers.

Mr Gun Smoke's get continued to make inroads. In 1973 Two D's Dynamite was the AQHA high-point cutting horse. In 1974 she became the NCHA reserve world champion and world champion mare. The next year, she became the AQHA reserve world champion senior cutting horse.

In 1974, Gun Smoke's Dream

reasserted herself by winning the All American Quarter Horse Congress Cutting Maturity. That same year Smoke 49 won the Texas-New Mexico Cutting Horse Maturity. Smoke 49 went on to become an AQHA Champion, earning 25 halter points and 16 working points in cutting and English pleasure. Incidentally, Smoke 49 later sired the cropout Paint, Smokes Peppy San, a two-time APHA world cutting champion.

Off to California

With Mr Gun Smoke's increasing credentials as a sire, California horseman Charlie Ward recognized an opportunity to introduce new blood into the West Coast cow-horse industry. He invited Dale to stand Mr Gun Smoke at the Doc Bar Ranch in 1975. Dale sent the stallion west, and

Ward bred several of his good mares to the stallion. But to Ward's and Dale's disappointment, few other California breeders chose to take advantage of the service. Mr Gun Smoke was returned to Ohio.

Yet Ward had had the right idea. He was simply ahead of the game. The next year, trainer Benny Guitron won the 1976 California Reined Cow Horse Association Snaffle Bit Futurity riding Kit's Smoke. Guitron and partner Bert Crane had purchased the mare in Georgia, and Benny had just 4½ months of training on her when they claimed their snaffle bit victory by 4 points.

Suddenly reined cow-horse breeders recognized the name Mr Gun Smoke. They began clamoring for his get. The demand for breedings "was more than you could dream," recalled Wilkinson.

In 1978, Kit's Smoke, again with Benny Guitron riding, won the NRCHA A division year-end hackamore championship. In 1979, she claimed title to the 1979 CRCHA Bridle Horse Sweepstakes Championship, the All-Around Stock Horse Contest Championship, and won every major event she showed in that year. She was the first horse to accomplish this prestigious series of wins and became the first horse in CRCHA history to earn the special designation of Supreme Working Cow Horse.

By the time Kit was retired at age 6, she had earned more than $40,000 in competition. What's more, Kit's Smoke went on to produce Reminikit—a three-time AQHA world champion—and numerous snaffle bit futurity finalists.

By then, Guitron had begun to beat the drum about bringing the stallion back to the West Coast. The sire's age, however, deterred many would-be investors.

"I told a group of men, 'We ought to buy this horse,'" recalled Guitron. "But they said 'No, he's too old, he'll never pencil out.' I said, 'Well, he's going to come to California and he's going to haunt us. You guys are going to be sorry that you didn't do it.'"

Guitron finally found a receptive listener in California businessman Gary Wexler. Wexler was just getting started in the horse industry. With Guitron's enthusiasm for the Gun Smokes, the possibility of owning the stallion began to intrigue Wexler. The businessman also had the financial resources to make it possible. Wexler approached Wilkinson and the men negotiated a deal that would install Mr Gun Smoke at GW's Futurity Farms.

At about the same time, renowned Quarter Horse breeder B.F. Phillips contacted Wilkinson about bringing Mr Gun Smoke to Texas. Although tempted, Wilkinson said he declined Phillips's offer because he'd already shaken hands on a lease-purchase agreement with Wexler.

Back to California

When Mr Gun Smoke returned to California in 1979, it was to a far warmer reception than he had received the first time. Jeff Oswood, who was the stallion manager for GW's Futurity Farms, remembers that the response from mare owners was tremendous. Mr Gun Smoke bred more than 80 mares his first year standing at Wexler's Ranch in Temecula. His court included a number of well-bred Doc Bar, King Fritz, and Sugar Vandy mares. An advertisement for Mr Gun Smoke in the April 1991 *California Horse Review* magazine listed his breeding fee at $5,000. He was booked full.

It didn't hurt that the Gun Smokes continued to flex their muscles in cow-horse competition. In addition to Kit's Smoke's ongoing success, Aledo Smoke won the 1979 California Cutting Horse Futurity. Hol E Smoke was the 1979 RECHA Champion Novice Cutting Horse and the 1979 Jim Reno High-Point Award winner. Political Smoker won the 1981 CRCHA World

Suddenly reined cow-horse breeders recognized the name Mr Gun Smoke.

Docs Gunsmoke, a crop-out Paint son of Mr Gun Smoke out of Tykes Molly Reed, was highly successful in working cow horse, cutting, and reining competition. This 1994 photo, taken at an NCHA cutting, shows him with his owner, Nancy Sharer of Clovis, California.

Photo by Midge, Courtesy of Nancy Sharer

Championship Hackamore Maturity. Kit's Smoke's full sister, Smokes Belle, was both the 1980 and 1981 CRCHA Bridle Horse Sweepstakes Champion. And the list of winners continued to grow.

GW's Futurity Farms added more gun powder to its arsenal. Wexler stood two of Mr Gun Smoke's sons. One Gun was the 1977 AQHA Reserve World Champion Junior Cutting Horse and 1979 All American Quarter Horse Congress Open Cutting Champion. Hollywood Smoke was a Congress open reining champion, who also earned an NCHA Certificate of Ability and a ROM in AQHA cutting competition.

Bright Smoke, a grand champion at halter and a Congress novice cutting champion, also stood at GW's Futurity Farms and was owned by Triple A Stock Farm.

Hollywood Smoke, out of Pistol's Holly,

became an outstanding sire in his own right. He sired two NRHA Futurity reserve champions—Gunner's Brawny Lad in 1979 and Havegunwilltravel in 1984. Gunner's Brawny Lad also won the 1979 Congress Reining Futurity and was the 1980 NRHA Open Reserve World Champion Reining Horse.

Hollywood Smoke's daughter, Walk Away Rene, was the 1978 NRHA World Champion and the 1979 Congress Junior Cutting champion. White Is was the 1980 NRHA Open World Champion, and Path Of Smoke was the 1975 AQHA World Champion Junior Reining Horse.

When GW's Futurity Farms was dispersed in 1982, Mr Gun Smoke was sold to Rapps Quarter Horses. Oswood went with him and continued to manage Mr Gun Smoke until the time of the stallion's death. He had tremendous regard for the horse.

"Mr Gun Smoke was pretty laid back, pretty quiet. He was probably the kind-

Smokes Dude, Smokes Belle's cropout son by Winnerinic, is the APHA's lifetime leading working cow horse, as of 1997. He also excelled in reining and cutting, with Superior titles and championships to his credit. The bay overo stallion was trained and shown to his many wins by Pat Hubbert, who so ably showed his dam. Smokes Dude is owned by Jackie Robertson of Petaluma, California.

Photo by Osteen, Courtesy of Jackie Robertson

est horse I've ever been around," Oswood said. "He was a very friendly horse, very affectionate toward me. I was pretty much the only person who ever messed with him (in California), so he and I had a pretty good rapport."

Oswood had the honor of leading Mr Gun Smoke into the arena during the ceremony at the 1980 World Championship Snaffle Bit Futurity in Reno, when Mr Gun Smoke was inducted into the Cow Horse Hall of Fame. He also had the burden of being by the horse's side the day that the great stallion was humanely put down due to failing health. It was 1983 and Mr Gun Smoke was 22.

More Offspring

Gun Smoke's offspring continued their winning streak after he died. Docs Gunsmoke, for example, a cropout Paint stallion out of Tykes Molly Reed (AQHA), finished third in the NRCHA Snaffle Bit Futurity and was the high-scoring horse in the fence work. He earned more than

$30,000 at the event and went on to win the Idaho Reined Cow Horse Snaffle Bit Futurity. In 1987 Docs Gunsmoke was the NRCHA Snaffle Bit Futurity Hackamore Maturity Champion. Docs Gunsmoke also became an APHA national champion in cutting in 1987 and a two-time APHA reserve world champion in 1995. He has won more than $45,000 in prize money. He also sired an NRCHA Snaffle Bit Futurity reserve champion, Smokin Vogt, and an APHA World Show cutting futurity champion and reserve world junior cutting champion, Smokes Partee.

Docs Gunsmoke is joined by several other outstanding Paint sons and daughters of Mr Gun Smoke. Strait Smoke, for example, is an APHA youth world reining

Mr Gun Smoke's pre-potency to pass on bald faces and high stockings is clearly evident in this photo of his grandget, belonging to Nancy Sharer. The yearlings were sired by Sharer's stallion, Docs Gunsmoke, a crop-out son of Mr Gun Smoke.

Photo by Carol Enrietto, Courtesy of Nancy Sharer

champion. Smokes Last Spot, a gelding out of Chex Design, is a reserve world champion in reining and working hunter under saddle. Jester Smoke earned his Superior in cutting with 70 points. Kid Smoke is a reserve world champion in working hunter under saddle.

Miss Smokette became an APHA Champion with 79 points in halter and over 30 points in performance, including bridle path hack, reining, and western pleasure.

Bonnie Smoke, out of two-time Paint national champion working cow horse Ropers Calcutta, has won more than $27,000 in cutting and working cow-horse competition for owner-trainer Smoky Pritchett, and her offspring have won even more.

Mr Gun Smoke's 16 APHA performers have earned more than 400 APHA performance points and nearly 100 APHA halter points.

During his lifetime, Mr Gun Smoke sired 556 AQHA foals, 67 Paints, and 4 Appaloosas. In his last 2 years at stud, the horse Dale Wilkinson had called his "tremendous poor man's sire" commanded a breeding fee of $10,000.

The Grandget

Mr Gun Smoke's last foals were born in 1984. What's truly remarkable is that the dynasty continues to grow. NCHA performance records from the 1980s to the 1990s show that Mr Gun Smoke's grandget won more than $3 million in cutting competition during that period alone. Mr Gun Smoke continues to appear on the leading maternal and paternal grandsires lists for the NCHA, NRHA, and NRCHA. Even well into the 1990s some of his direct sons and daughters continue to accumulate performance points and awards.

The sheer number of great Gun Smoke horses becomes unfathomable as you start to trace pedigrees. For example, Boomernic, who won the 1992 NRHA Futurity, was out of Docs Leavum Smoke, an own daughter of Mr Gun Smoke.

The 1996 NRHA Futurity reserve cham-

Sanpeppy Smoke, who won the 1982 CRCHA Snaffle Bit Futurity with Kenny Pugh in the saddle, was Mr Gun Smoke's grandson through Mr Fools Smoke. His dam was Minnie Gal, by Peppy San. The stallion is now owned by Charlotte Pierce of California.

Photo by Skippen-Coy

pion was a Paint stallion named Colonels Smokingun, who is out of Katie Gun, a great-granddaughter of Mr Gun Smoke through One Gun.

Lenas Telesis, the 1991 NCHA Super Stakes champion, is a great-grandson of Mr Gun Smoke through Gun Smokes Dream.

Smokin Jose, the 1980 AQHA World Champion Junior Cutting Horse and a Masters Cutting champion, is a grandson of Mr Gun Smoke through Gunsmokes Ripple.

The CRCHA Snaffle Bit Futurity champion and California Cutting Futurity champion, Sanpeppy Smoke, is a Mr Gun Smoke grandson through Mr Fools Smoke. And that's just the tip of the iceberg.

Says Benny Guitron, who is now riding and winning on Kit's Smoke's grandget, "People may call me an idiot for saying this, but I think Mr Gun Smoke outsired Doc Bar, if you consider the number and caliber of mares who were bred to him. He sired winners in the major reining, cutting,

and reined cow-horse futurities. Doc Bar himself never did that.

"I made a prediction," continued Guitron. "I really believed in that horse so much that I said, 'If you don't have a Gun Smoke mare in your broodmare band, you ain't got a broodmare.' But it's a proven fact. You look at the stats at every major event and there will be a colt out of a Gun Smoke-bred mare in the finals."

"It's really strong breeding," confirmed Wilkinson. "Mr Gun Smoke contributed to all of us through his offspring. He was a tremendous, strong-willed horse. He's done some wonderful things for our industry. I feel fortunate to have been a part of his life."

16 HOLLYWOOD JAC 86

By Betsy Lynch

His drop-to-the-basement way of stopping literally revolutionized the style of reining.

DESPITE HIS NAME, Hollywood Jac 86 didn't look like a celebrity. He wasn't handsome. He wasn't big. He wasn't at all impressive at the end of a lead shank. He was a 14.3, sandy-colored palomino with a dark dorsal stripe and floppy ears. Yet when Hollywood Jac stepped to center stage, he had undeniable star power. His

drop-to-the-basement way of stopping literally revolutionized the style of reining. He passed this ability on so consistently that it became the signature trait of the Hollywood Jac family line.

Hollywood Jac 86 was bred by John and Mary Bowling of Sumner, Iowa. The Bowlings were well known for their

Richard Greenberg, a Chicago businessman, had tremendous success as a non-pro rider on Hollywood Jac 86. They are shown here after winning the reining championship at the 1974 Blue Ribbon International in Illinois. Greenberg owned the stallion through most of his career, and then formed a partnership with Sally Brown of Fox Meadow Farms, Maple Plain, Minn., when the palomino was 18 years old.

Photo by Mark Thomas, Courtesy of Richard Greenberg

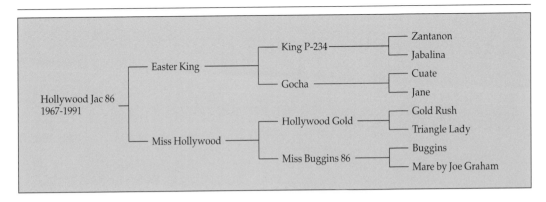

				Zantanon
		King P-234		Jabalina
	Easter King			
		Gocha		Cuate
Hollywood Jac 86				Jane
1967-1991				
		Hollywood Gold		Gold Rush
	Miss Hollywood			Triangle Lady
		Miss Buggins 86		Buggins
				Mare by Joe Graham

strong performance lines. They owned Jac's sire, Easter King, an own son of King P-234. Their broodmare band boasted more than 2 dozen daughters of Hollywood Gold, who was known in the 1950s and '60s as the "King of the Cutting Horse Sires." Among those daughters was Miss Hollywood, herself a Register of Merit-earner. In 1967, she foaled Holly-wood Jac 86.

Hollywood Jac was first sold to Pat Fitzgerald of Mondovi, Wis., but Fitzger-ald didn't own the weanling long before trainer Spain Prestwich came along, decided he liked the colt, and took him to Minnesota.

"Pat had made some kind of trade and there must have been 30 to 40 colts in that pen," recalled Prestwich. "When I told Pat I wanted the lop-eared colt, he laughed and said, 'That's the ugliest one in the bunch.' But I picked Jac out because I liked the way he stopped. He would run from one end of the pen to the other and just slide into the fence, roll back, and then run to the other end and slide."

Prestwich instinctively knew the colt would make a great reining prospect. He was not disappointed. He said that even as a yearling and 2-year-old, Jac continued to show this natural desire and ability to stop. Before he started riding Jac, Prest-wich worked him on the longe line. The horse could be bucking and playing and racing in circles, but when Spain called out "whoa," Jac would drop on his hindquar-ters, slide to a stop, sit there on his butt, and look around like a friendly pup. Prestwich had never seen anything like it, before or since.

"He looked like Bullwinkle the Moose

Halter and Performance Record: Performance Register of Merit; Superior Reining; NRHA Hall of Fame.

AQHA Progeny Record:

Foal Crops: 21
Foals Registered: 249
Halter Point-Earners: 3
Halter Points Earned: 5

Performance Point-Earners: 126
Performance Points Earned: 943
Performance Registers of Merit: 31
Superior Performance Awards: 3

NRHA Progeny Record:

Performers: 201
World Champions: 8

NRHA Derby Champions: 4
NRHA Futurity Champions: 6

Total Earnings: Close to $1.5 million, as of spring, 1997
Leading Money-Earners: Mr Melody Jac ($109,640)

ApHC Progeny Record:

Registered Foals: 3
Performance Point-Earners: 3
Performance Points: 60
Registers of Merit: 3

Bronze Medalions: 4
World Champions: 2
National Champions: 2

Buckskin Progeny Record:

1996 ABRA World Champion Amateur Reining

As a young horse, Hollywood Jac 86 showed talent for cutting, but owner-trainer Spain Prestwich wanted to develop him as a reiner. This photo was taken in 1970 in Anoka, Minn., just after Prestwich started Jac on cattle.

**Courtesy of
Spain Prestwich**

with his ears flopped out to the side," Prestwich said with a chuckle. "He used to do that a lot."

This peculiar talent remained with Jac when Prestwich started him under saddle.

"He was a really nice horse to train. He was a little studdy as a 2- and 3-year-old, which is normal for that age, but we didn't have any problems with him. He was really smart. He pretty much taught himself. And you couldn't make him miss a lead. In fact, we even showed him as a western riding horse," said Prestwich.

The trainer also started Hollywood Jac on cattle. He noted that the stallion had a lot of cow sense, which didn't surprise Prestwich, given the way the colt was bred. But Spain was more interested in developing Jac as a reiner. He occasionally

showed Jac in cutting to help fill classes. One time, Spain's father, an avid cutter, asked Spain to enter a class so the top horses could earn more points. He did and Jac placed second, beating the horse shown by Spain's dad. "He wasn't too happy about that," Spain smiled.

Prestwich began showing Hollywood Jac as a 3-year-old, and he started to accumulate reining points almost immediately. In his first trip to the Minnesota State Fair, one of the biggest reinings in the upper Midwest, Jac placed third in the junior reining. The next year as a 4-year-old, he won it. The following year he won it again as a senior horse. But on one of those occasions, Jac literally made an impact.

"We were showing at the Minnesota State Fair and he stopped so hard that he slid about 50 feet and hit the wall," recalled Prestwich. "Boy, those guys were really screaming. But the judge said, 'As long as he didn't fall down, he's going to win the reining.' And he did win the reining!"

It was during that same time when Hollywood Jac made a strong first impression on Tim McQuay, a reining horse

186

Hollywood Jac's sire, Easter King, was a 1951 son of King P-234. This photo was taken at the 1954 Colorado State Fair. The handler is unidentified, but the owner is listed as LaRue Gooch of Simla, Colorado.

Photo by Stewart's Photo

Although Jac didn't look like the kind of horse who could stir up controversy, he sure enough did.

trainer who has since become legendary himself for his association with this family line. Tim, who now lives in Tioga, Tex., was living in Minnesota at the time.

"I saw Hollywood Jac when Spain still owned him, and I fell in love with him then," McQuay acknowledged. "I don't know how to explain it. It was a different style back then. But he was a great stopper. He'd just curl up in a ball, bury his butt, and slide for what seemed like forever. He just had his own style."

McQuay remembers watching Prestwich and Jac win the tough senior reining class at the Minnesota State Fair. When the duo came back the next day to compete in the reining stake, Prestwich really called on the horse. When Spain asked Jac to back up, the horse went into reverse with so much speed that he lost his footing and went down. The glitch only served to heighten McQuay's respect for Hollywood Jac. He recognized that the stallion's talent was exceeded only by the size of his heart.

Although Jac didn't look like the kind of horse who could stir up controversy, he sure enough did. He had so much

ability and try that judges tended to look past his mistakes. Prestwich recalls another ruckus they caused at a northern Minnesota horse show.

"I remember it was a long arena, and when I came out of a rollback, my saddle slipped to the side. So I stood up and started to straighten it, and the horse just buried his butt and started sliding. There wasn't supposed to be a stop there, so I kicked him out of it. Well, there was one particular trainer who was mad because we won the reining anyway. He said for all rights and purposes, we'd broke pattern. The judge looked at the trainer and said, 'No, that horse scotched, so I knocked him 3 points because it was a bad scotch, but he still beat you by 2 points.'"

Richard Greenberg

Of course, the judges weren't the only ones taking stock of Hollywood Jac's

One of Hollywood Jac's trademarks, besides his tremendous stopping ability, was his floppy ears. Here, Richard Greenberg brings Jac to a hard stop.

Courtesy of Richard Greenberg

talent. Richard Greenberg was in the stands one day watching a versatility class in Madison, Wis., when Spain rode in on Jac. Clark Bradley, another respected reining horse trainer, sat beside him. As they watched Jac work, Bradley commented that the palomino looked like a pretty nice horse. Since Greenberg was in the market for a non-pro horse, Bradley suggested that Richard try to buy him.

Greenberg tracked down Prestwich after the class to ask if the horse was for sale. Although Prestwich and Greenberg have slightly different versions of what transpired, the bottom line was, Spain was in no hurry to part with Hollywood Jac 86. Prestwich had once sold Jac as a 3-year-old to a Minneapolis police officer named

Al Crepeau. When Crepeau lost interest 5 months later, Prestwich was happy to take the horse back.

Incidentally, Crepeau never transferred Jac's papers into his name, but he did briefly stand him at stud, advertising his services for a $75 fee.

However, it wasn't long after Greenberg made his inquiry that Prestwich's situation changed. He was purchasing a farm and needed capital. So he called Greenberg on a Monday morning to find out if he was still interested in buying the horse. The price was $3,000. He could deliver him that evening.

"Mind you, I'm in Chicago and he's in Minnesota. I didn't even know that Jac was a stallion," explained Greenberg. "But like everything else I do in my life, without thinking I said, 'I'll take him.' Sure enough, that night he (Prestwich) showed up with Jac.

"But by this time, I had started to worry that maybe something had happened to the horse that influenced Prestwich's deci-

Spain Prestwich noted Hollywood Jac's propensity to drop his hindquarters while stopping, even when the horse was a weanling. Generations later, this unique trait is still evident among the palomino stallion's get and grandget. This picture was taken in Norway, Mich., about 1972.

Photo by Bruce Peasley, Courtesy of Spain Prestwich

sion to sell him," Greenberg continued. "So after he took the horse out of the trailer, I said 'Okay, let me see him.' Prestwich proceeded to ride Jac around and do all kinds of stuff. When he got off, he asked me, 'Do I want to try the horse?'"

To make matters worse, this entire transaction was taking place at a large boarding stable where a local horse association meeting was in progress. The presence of a curious audience only added to poor Richard's discomfort.

"By this time I was so intimidated and felt so stupid by what I had done," Greenberg added, "I just said 'No.' I gave him his money and he left. I hadn't even gotten on the horse.

"So, Prestwich leaves and one of these very knowledgeable horse people comes up to me and says, 'You didn't buy that horse did you?' And not knowing that much about horses and, of course, respecting anybody who had an opinion, I said, 'Yeah.' To which he replies, 'Well, that horse is so unsound, he won't last the year.'

"So there I was. The trainer had gone. I'd given him my money. I now own Hollywood Jac. I'm $3,000 poorer. I have someone who has told me that the horse won't last the year. And I said to myself, 'Life goes on. Whatever is, is.'

"I guess I've made worse mistakes," Greenberg laughed years later.

But if Richard was feeling pangs of regret, it may have comforted him to know that so was Prestwich.

"I knew what I had there. I knew what he was. But it was just one of those things. I should have kept the horse and sold the farm," Spain laughed. "He was probably the best horse I ever rode."

Greenberg's doubts were soon alleviated. A week after he bought Jac, he trailered the horse and a mare to trainer Ed Cridge's farm for a lesson. Cridge not only gave Jac his seal of approval, he startled Richard with another revelation. When Greenberg

Tim McQuay is credited with proving that the Hollywood Jacs were good open horses, as well as non-pro mounts. Here he's on Mr Boggie Jac, a son of Hollywood Jac and out of Boggie's Last, who was the 1984 NRHA Derby Non-Pro Champion and the 1985 NRHA Open Reserve World Champion.

Photo by Don Trout, Courtesy of McQuay Stables

unloaded the horse, Cridge told him that he didn't think it was a good idea to haul his stallion next to a mare. Greenberg's response: "What stud?" Jac was so gentlemanly that Richard still hadn't noticed that the horse was still intact.

Cridge rode Jac and was duly impressed. He gave Greenberg some additional advice: Go have some fun with the versatile little horse. Richard took him at his word.

At their first show together, Richard showed Jac in 28 classes in a 2-day period—barrels, poles, pleasure, reining, and just about everything on the show bill.

"I think we missed the all-around by just a half-point," Greenberg laughed, "and he never took a lame step." The dire

prediction of the "horse expert" whose comments had worried Greenberg couldn't have been more wrong.

"He never took a lame step in the 20 years that I owned him," noted Greenberg. "He never had a cold. He never even threw a shoe."

Even so, Richard was lucky he didn't kill Hollywood Jac. One day, after leaving the Gold Coast Circuit, Greenberg's horse trailer came unhitched on a Florida interstate. He had forgotten to lock down the ball. The trailer did a double flip.

"We thought for sure the horses were dead," said Greenberg. "We had to get a fire truck and a welder to cut the trailer apart to get the horses out. The other horse, who was a big hunter jumper, was laying on top of Jac. We had to sedate him because he was thrashing around, but we didn't give Jac anything. Finally, after about an hour, we got them out. When we pulled Jac out of the trailer, he got up,

Hollywood Dun It qualifies as one of Hollywood Jac's best sons. Foaled in 1983 to Blossom Berry, the dun stallion proved he could slide in his father's shoes and then created his own dynasty of reining horses. Ridden by Tim McQuay, who now owns the stallion, Dun It was the 1986 NRHA Futurity Reserve Champion and the 1987 NRHA Derby Champion. His get entered the show ring in 1992 and in just five show seasons, they amassed over to $1 million in earnings. Like his father's get, Dun It's offspring have proven to be exceptional open and non-pro horses. In this photo Dun It and McQuay won the 1987 NRHA Superstakes. Cliff Steif, Barrington, Ill., Dun It's owner at the time, holds the bronze trophy. Dr. Tim Barlett, Superstakes chairman and later president of the NRHA, is to the left.

Courtesy of *The Quarter Horse Journal*

shook his head, walked over to the side of the road, and started eating grass.

"About an hour later my friend Dr. Tim Bartlett came along. He had an empty slot in his trailer and Jac jumped right in like nothing had happened. Tim brought him home for me," Greenberg said incredulously.

The near-tragedy illustrates the take-it-in-stride disposition that Hollywood Jac 86 was noted for. It is also a hallmark of his get.

Despite Richard's initial lack of horse experience, he and Hollywood Jac did become a fabulous team—once Jac straightened Greenberg out about a few things.

"The first time I went to a reining by myself with Jac, I was getting ready to walk into the pen. At that time I was just beginning to rein and I knew a lot less than I thought I knew," Greenberg confided. "So I reached up with my spur and poked Jac in the shoulder to get him to lighten up and turn around faster. Jac

turned around and bit my toe," he laughed. "That was the last time I ever rode Hollywood Jac with a pair of spurs.

"He had a tremendous amount of feel," Greenberg added. "He was a very easy horse to ride. He had an incredible combination of power and sensitivity. Yet you could put little kids on Jac and they couldn't even get him to trot."

Winnings

Richard's respect and affection for Hollywood Jac paid big dividends. Greenberg won 12 NRHA bronze trophies riding Jac and earned 2 NRHA non-pro world champion titles, one in 1974 and another in

With her reserve championship at the 1992 NRHA Futurity, Fancy Jac (registered as Stars Fancy Jac) pushed her sire's progeny record to over $1 million in NRHA earnings—the first stallion to accomplish this feat. Doug Milholland rode the red dun Hollywood Jac daughter, owned by Sally Brown. Fancy Jac is out of A Great Star, a multiple NRHA bronze winner and the 1985 NRHA Non-Pro World Champion.

Photo by Waltenberry, Courtesy of Sally Brown

1975. Greenberg retired Jac from the show ring with NRHA earnings of $6,089.

Appropriately, one of Hollywood Jac's biggest fans, Tim McQuay, judged the stallion the last time Greenberg ever showed him. It was at a jackpot reining at trainer Ken Eppers' place in Grayslake, Illinois.

"I remember it vividly," said McQuay. "He ran like he was going to win it that day. He was great, but he set up going to the last stop, so I placed him second."

"He was an unbelievable horse," said Greenberg, "He was just an unbelievable creature. He was ready to go when I bought him, and he always stayed ready to go."

Spain Prestwich showed Jac to his AQHA Superior award before turning over the reins to Greenberg in 1972. Jac earned 72 AQHA reining points. One of Prestwich's favorite stories about Jac is the time he showed him for Richard at a Quarter Horse show in Northbrook, Illinois. When Prestwich arrived, he unloaded the horse and noticed that Jac's sliding plates had broken in two. He tried to find a shoer. No luck. So Prestwich went to the nearby Libertyville Saddle Shop, bought some tools, and pulled Jac's shoes.

"I'd hauled him 400 miles so I thought, I'm just going to show him anyway. So I rode him barefoot and won the reining. He

Another outstanding Hollywood Jac 86 son and a great sire in his own right, Mr Melody Jac won the 1988 NRHA Futurity Championship. Among his many winning off-spring is Hesa German Melody, champion of the 1996 NRHA Limited Open Futurity. Mr Melody Jac, a 1985 bay stallion out of Dude's Bueno Gal, is owned by Peter Phinney, Cold Spring Farm, Maple City, Michigan. He has earned over $109,000 in NRHA competition, ridden by Tim McQuay.

Photo by Waltenberry, Courtesy of Peter Phinney

beat the horse that was leading the nation," Prestwich recalled gleefully.

Breeding Career

Despite Jac's own impressive performance in the show ring, when it came time to establish a breeding career for the stallion, Greenberg had difficulty convincing mare owners that his ugly duckling would produce swans. At first, Richard even tried to give away breedings. He had few takers. Nevertheless, he had such faith in his horse that Greenberg slowly began to build the stallion's reputation by breeding Jac to his own good show mares. He also had the good sense to put Jac's foals into the hands of people such as Tim McQuay, who believed in their potential.

McQuay cultivated a string of Hollywood Jac winners early on, starting with such horses as Crome Plated Jac and Jacs Little Pine. Over the years, McQuay has probably ridden 2 dozen or more sons and daughters of Hollywood Jac. Among the best known are NRHA Futurity champion Mr Melody Jac, and NRHA Derby and Superstakes champion and Futurity reserve champion Hollywood Dun It. But there have been many others with good solid reputations as winners.

Without reservation, Tim says he owes his career to the Hollywood Jacs. McQuay now owns Hollywood Dun It, who won over $65,000 in NRHA competition before being retired to stud. He has sired winners who will soon exceed the $1 million mark in NRHA earnings. Hollywood Dun It is chasing Hollywood Jac's own phenome-

Jac O Rima, a 1986 son of Hollywood Jac 86 and out of Torima, was the 1989 NRHA Limited Open Futurity Champion and reserve champion of the open division. He was ridden by Canadian Gaetan Gauthier.

Photo by Waltenberry, Courtesy of *The Quarter Horse Journal*

nal siring record, which boasts winners of nearly $1.5 million dollars in NRHA events, as of 1997.

In fact, McQuay believed so strongly in Hollywood Jac's merits that he introduced his client Sally Brown to Greenberg, precipitating the formation of the "Jac Pac."

Brown was changing gears from cutting horses to reining horses. She wanted to build a breeding program. Sally had seen McQuay work Jacs Little Pine and Jacs Ima Pine, and she liked what she saw. Based on that and McQuay's personal endorsement of Jac's get, Brown entered a partnership with Greenberg, without ever having seen Hollywood Jac 86 himself.

Brown saw Jac for the first time in 1984 when he was 18 years old.

"I wasn't the least bit disappointed," she recalled. "It wasn't uppermost that he be a handsome young thing. I had already heard the stories of him being floppy-eared. I had seen pictures of him. My interest was in finding a good breeding stallion. When I saw him, I thought he looked really good for his age."

Personality Quirks

She was also amused by his obvious personality. Jac was stabled in a renovated silo. He took great pleasure in putting his head out the window to watch the goings-on. He was also particular about his choice in female companionship. Brown and Greenberg both had gray mares. Jac loved Sally's mare, but had no passion for Richard's. To get Jac to breed Richard's mare, they had to entice him with Sally's mare. It was bait and switch. "It worked," Brown said, "but you only fooled Jac once." It was a good thing that Richard's gray mare settled the first time.

The initial Jac Pac agreement included Jac and 12 broodmares; Brown and Greenberg each had 6 mares to breed. They then continued to breed other good reining mares to Jac's court, giving him a better chance to prove himself as a sire. Many happened to be daughters of Great Pine. It was a nick that worked extremely well.

A 1993 article in the *Quarter Horse News*, "Breeding for Reining Horses," showed that the Hollywood Jac—Great Pine cross had produced offspring with winnings of more than $265,000 in NRHA competition. They included Kelinds Taffy Jac, who earned more than $47,000; Bees Honey Jac with just shy of $28,000; Stars Fancy Jac, more than $84,000; The Jac Be Nimble with nearly $30,000; A Little Shady Jac, over $16,000; Jac Hollywood Doll, more than $10,000; and 1996 NRHA Open World Champion Mr Gold Pine Jac with more than $26,000.

Jac also crossed well with the Nifty Bee line. But it's important to note that he also produced stellar offspring from a diverse range of families—from Doc Bar to Bueno Chex, Two Eyed Jack to Dun Berry.

"With Jac, it didn't seem to matter what you bred him to; his genetic pool was so strong that he consistently put athletic, good-minded babies on the ground," observed Brown. "Richard and I would check from year to year to see how many of Jac's babies showed up at the NRHA Futurity. Eighty to ninety percent who went into training made it to the Futurity. That's why people bred to Jac."

Brown herself has experienced the pleasure of having Futurity success with her Hollywood Jacs. One of her greatest delights happened when Fancy Jac won the NRHA Futurity open reserve championship in 1992 with rider Doug Milholland. Fancy Jac then went on to become the NRHA Superstakes reserve champion. The mare won approximately $84,000 before being retired to the broodmare band.

Although Brown and Greenberg had the foresight to assemble good mares to breed to Jac, the rest of the reining industry was slow to recognize the stallion's breeding potential. By the time the light finally dawned, it was almost too late for outsiders to capitalize on Hollywood Jac's genetic payload.

About the time the Jac Pac formed, Hollywood Jac's foals were finding their footing in the performance pen. Greenberg himself was having terrific results with some of the Jac offspring he had raised. He won the NRHA Non-Pro Futurity on Ms Maggie Jac, and claimed two more world titles, one on Hollywood Bandido and another on Ms Yellow Jac.

Other riders were also starting to share his success. But because some of the significant early wins were with non-pro riders, many people chose to label the Jacs as strictly non-pro-caliber horses.

It was a huge misconception. There was plenty of ability to be tapped, and soon

Although Brown and Greenberg had the foresight to assemble good mares to breed to Jac, the rest of the reining industry was slow to recognize the stallion's breeding potential.

Bees Honey Jac, a 1988 daughter of Hollywood Jac 86 and out of Bee's Great Pine, proved how well the Hollywood Jac-Great Pine—Nifty Bee cross worked. The pretty palomino placed fourth in the 1991 NRHA Futurity and went on to produce Whizard Jac, a winner of that prestigious event. Doug Milholland is in the saddle.

Courtesy of Sally Brown

open competitors would feel the Hollywood Jac sting. Mr Boggie Jac, Jacs Little Pine, Hollywood Dun It, Ms Poco Roco Jac, Mr Melody Jac, Jac O Rima, Denim Jac, Fancy Jac, and others would win big at major NRHA events.

Credit to McQuay

Greenberg gives trainer Tim McQuay much of the credit for being among the first to prove just how tough the Hollywood Jacs could be in open competition. What's more, McQuay began to win with horses that other trainers had rejected. Tim noted that perhaps the Hollywood Jacs just suited his style.

"When I started riding them," says Tim, "everybody said that they were just really nice non-pro horses, not open horses. But they've worked out great for me. They stayed quiet. Ninety percent of them were really good lead-changers. All of them really wanted to stop. And although I had to work with some of them a little bit to get them to turn around, it wasn't necessarily because they couldn't do it. I just had to teach them where to put their feet. Ever since I started riding them, I'll bet I've won a half-million dollars or more.

"And if they didn't all make open horses, they made something," McQuay asserted. "They were just very useful horses."

One criticism of the Hollywood Jacs is that they're not noted for being especially pretty movers. They tend to have a certain degree of knee action at the lope. That never concerned Hollywood Jac fans. It never affected their soundness, and McQuay noted that when they're asked to

Bees Honey Jac's son by Topsail Whiz, Whizard Jac, won the 1996 NRHA Futurity with Mike Flarida riding. The sorrel stallion is owned by Dawn and William Pohl, Centerville, Ohio.

Photo by Waltenberry, Courtesy of Sally Brown

run fast circles, they look like they're really flying.

By the time Jac's get hit their stride in open competition, Greenberg and Brown had already raised his fee to $4,000. It was the highest in the industry for a reining horse sire. It scared off some would-be breeders and added to the monopoly that the Jac Pac partners had on the family line, although it wasn't by intent. They simply believed in their product. In retrospect, the breeding fee looks like a bargain. And all those who declined those early free breedings are probably kicking themselves.

Regrettably, Hollywood Jac 86 sired only 249 registered Quarter Horses, but of those, 126, or more than half, were performers. Not many stallions can claim that half of their foals are, or were, point-earners. Hollywood Jac's get earned 943 points, 31 Registers of Merit, and 3 Superior performance awards.

Additionally, Jac sired three Appaloosas, and every one of them made it big in the show ring as reiners. Hollywood Taps GN was the ApHC World and National Champion Senior Reining Horse in 1994. Crack Back The Jac was the 1993 World Champion

Snaffle and Hackamore Champion, and Hollywood Jake was the 1997 National Champion Senior Reining Horse. Among them, those three horses accounted for 60 performance points, 3 Registers of Merit, and 4 Bronze Medallions.

Jac also has several offspring registered with the Buckskin and Palomino associations rather than the AQHA because they were the result of breedings with frozen semen. (AQHA does not register foals resulting from breedings using frozen semen. In the mid-1990s, the association did change its rules to recognize breedings using chilled or cooled semen, but not frozen semen.) The majority of those foals

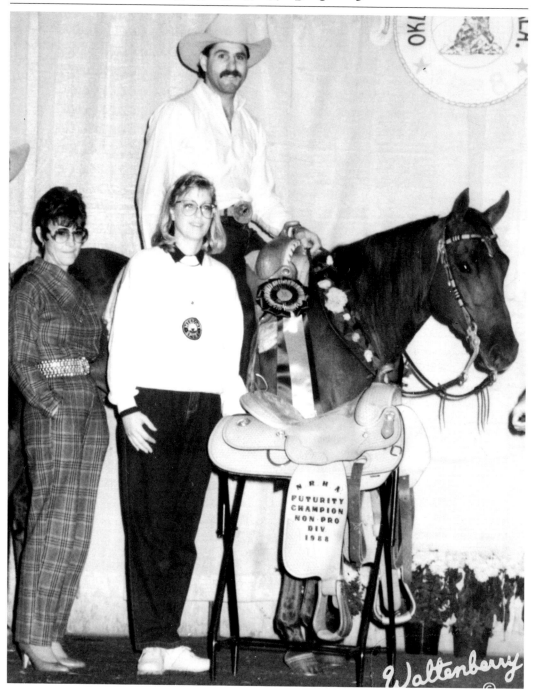

1988 was quite a year for Ms Jessie Jac, a 1985 daughter of Hollywood Jac and out of Juniper Jessie. With her owner, Charlie Wiederholt, Hastings, Minn., she won the non-pro divisions of the All American Quarter Horse Congress Futurity and the NRHA Futurity. In the photo are Sally Brown (far left) and Charlie's wife, Cheryl.

Photo by Waltenberry, Courtesy of Sally Brown

were born when Jac was in his late teens and early 20s. Even then, Jac was breeding only 30 to 40 mares a year.

Hollywood Jac died in 1991 at age 24 due to kidney failure. His last official foal crop was born in 1992. But several Hollywood Jac 86 foals have hit the ground since then, due to the use of frozen semen. Sally Brown, who got three such foals, had fun naming them: Jacs Pipedream, Ice Man Jac, and Subzero Jac.

Jacs Pipedream, cleverly named because frozen semen is contained in pipettes called "straws," was a buckskin filly who was the 1996 American Buckskin Registry Association World Champion Amateur Reining Horse.

Sally Brown and Richard Greenberg saved six straws each of Hollywood Jac's frozen semen for breeding purposes after the great stallion died. One of the results was this 1996 palomino colt, Sub Zero Jac, out of A Great Star, owned by Brown.

Courtesy of Sally Brown

Fewer Foals, More Winners

Even though Hollywood Jac had fewer foals than many of his contemporaries, he has sired more NRHA Futurity champions and NRHA world champions than any other stallion (as of this writing). In the late 1980s and early '90s, he topped the NRHA leading sire list for 5 of 7 years. He was displaced during one of those years by his son Hollywood Dun It, now owned by Tim McQuay.

As for earning power, Hollywood Jac was the first stallion whose get earned over $1 million in NRHA events. In the spring of 1997, that figure increased to nearly $1.5 million.

Jac sired four NRHA Non-Pro Futurity champions: Bit O Holly (registered as Ms Hollywood Jac) in 1978, Ms Maggie Jac in 1983, Ms Jessie Jac in 1988, and Mi Hollywood Darlin in 1994. Chasin Eighty was the 1989 NRHA Non-Pro Futurity Reserve Champion.

Mr Melody Jac won the open division of the NRHA Futurity in 1988. Jac O Rima won the 1989 NRHA Limited Open Futurity and was also the Open Futurity Reserve Champion.

Hollywood Dun It, Denim Jac, and Fancy Jac were also reserve champions of the open division of the NRHA Futurity in 1986, '91, and '92 respectively.

Hollywood Jac has sired eight NRHA world champions and nine reserve world champions and there are probably more in the making.

The roster of Hollywood Jac's winners is so long and impressive that's it's impossible to list them all without risk of forgetting some of the great ones. However, other notables include Mr Boggie Jac and Hollywood Dun It, NRHA Derby and Sweepstakes champions. Some other big-money winners include Bees Honey Jac, Hollywood Rerun, Hollywood Eighty Six, Boggies Flashy Jac, Boggies Last Jac, Jac Be Quick, Jacs Little Pine, Kelinds Taffy Jac, Marthas Mega Jac,

Jacspin is a second-generation Hollywood Jac horse who not only looks like a "Jac," he rides like one too. Owner Charlie Wiederholt, Hastings, Minn., rode the 1988 red dun son of Jacs Little Pine and out of Miss Teepee Glo to victory in the 1991 NRHA Non-Pro Futurity, after an exciting runoff. Jacspin's sire, Jacs Little Pine, a 1981 dun stallion by Hollywood Jac, was the 1986 NRHA Open Reserve World Champion.

Photo by Waltenberry, Courtesy of *The Quarter Horse Journal*

Mr Gold Pine Jac, Ms Majestic Jac, The Jac Be Nimble, and many more.

Hollywood Jac 86's AQHA get of sire record, while minor compared to his NRHA record, is still substantial. His sons and daughters had earned more than 948 AQHA points by the mid-1990s. All but 5 of the points were in performance. He's had several horses in the reining year-end top 10. In 1994, Jac Daniels Neat was second in the nation in junior reining for the AQHA high-point award. In addition, Hollywood Jac 86 has sired more than 30 performance Register of Merit-earners.

Hollywood Jac's siring record continues to rise at a remarkable rate. What's more, he has a surprising number of good sons and daughters with outstanding offspring. Jac has consistently topped the list of leading grandsires of NRHA money-earners. It's easy to see why. For example, the 1996 NRHA Futurity Champion, Whizard Jac

(bred by Sally Brown's Fox Meadow Farm), is out of the great Hollywood Jac mare Bees Honey Jac.

The 1996 Futurity Limited Open Champion, Heza German Melody, is also a Hollywood Jac 86 grandson by 1988 Futurity Champion Mr Melody Jac.

Mr Tori Kid, who won the Southwest Reining Horse Association Futurity and who also had the highest composite score of the 1996 NRHA Futurity and earned more than $50,000, is a Hollywood Jac grandson through Miss Torima Jac.

In fact, it's not unusual for the list of NRHA Futurity finalists to look like a Hollywood Jac family reunion.

Richard Greenberg and Sally Brown have each kept one of Jac's sons to use in their breeding programs. Fox Meadow Farm kept Master Cowboy Jac, and Greenberg kept Jacs Aledo Bar. They have also kept a number of Hollywood Jac's best daughters to perpetuate the line. Sally Brown laughed that each one is so special to her that when she takes visitors on a tour of the herd, she sounds like a broken record

The Jac Be Nimble, a sorrel stallion by Hollywood Jac and out of Ruckers Shady Pine, won 12 NRHA bronze trophies and over $37,000 in NRHA events. He was the reserve champion of the 1991 NRHA Derby and Champion of the NRHA Super Stakes, as well as the 1992 NRHA Limited Open Reserve World Champion. He is shown here with Tim McQuay in the saddle.

Photo by Waltenberry, Courtesy of McQuay Stables

with "special" being the catch-phrase.

It's also important to note that the Hollywood Jac story is far from finished. One very significant Hollywood Jac characteristic is longevity.

"They are good, old soldiers," observed Brown. "They just keep going and going and going."

Brown and McQuay both noted that a number of Hollywood Jac sons and daughters had exceptionally long show careers. Dirty Jac 86, for example, who was the third Hollywood Jac foal to be born, was still being shown into his 20s. Many others were shown for 10 years or more. Silver Jac, Pearly Jac, and Hesa Co Jac , for instance, each changed hands several times and won for all their owners.

"There are some old horses who were sure hard-knocking," confirmed McQuay.

The Hollywood Jacs are also well-known for their heart. Sally Brown tells how Charlie Wiederholt and Ms Jessie Jac won the 1988 All American Quarter Horse Congress Non-Pro Futurity and the NRHA Non-Pro Futurity. Both events required a runoff, but the NRHA Futurity win was even harder fought. After what

had already been a demanding week of competition, Wiederholt and Ms Jessie Jac tied with Dr. Jim Morgan's horse in the finals. During the run-off for the championship, they tied again. In the third run of the day, Ms Jessie Jac again gave it her all and finally cinched the title.

Almost the exact scenario occurred at the 1991 NRHA Futurity when Wiederholt and Morgan battled again for the non-pro championship. They had to break a tie in another exciting finals runoff. Wiederholt won again, but this time he was riding a Jac grandson, Jacspin, by Jacs Little Pine and out of Miss Teepee Glo.

It's fitting that Hollywood Jac's sons and daughters continue to add pages to the colorful story of this powerful little horse. He may not have been much to look at, but in the end, he proved to be larger than life on reining's silver screen.

AUTHOR PROFILES

Diane Ciarloni.

**Photo by
John R. Woodrum**

DIANE CIARLONI authored the original *Western Horseman* book *Legends* under the byline of Diane Simmons.

Diane grew up in an agricultural area outside Memphis and began her career in journalism with the Scripps-Howard newspaper chain, while still working on her degree at Memphis State University.

She began her career as a free-lance writer in 1975, concentrating on horse-related subjects. By 1980, Diane's work had been carried in 12 publications, including *Western Horseman, American Horseman, Horse of Course, Horse & Rider, California Horse Review, Paint Horse Journal, Rodeo News, Horse Illustrated,* and *Speedhorse.*

She was one of the first equine journalists to begin working directly with veterinarians, providing medical and health articles in layman's terms for a number of magazines. She has also written feature material for *Art West* on equine and/or western artists.

Although Diane's writing accomplishments have involved almost every segment of the horse industry, she has concentrated on racing since 1978.

Now living in north Texas, she currently serves as editor for *Speedhorse/The Racing Report*. Her race-related editorials have won her several awards, including the American Quarter Horse Association Sprint Award twice, and her work was also reviewed in *The Best American Sports Writing of 1991.*

Jim Goodhue.

JIM GOODHUE is highly qualified to write on any subject dealing with the history of the American Quarter Horse.

Jim went to work for AQHA in 1958, immediately after receiving an advanced degree from Oklahoma State University. Originally hired to work for *The Quarter Horse Journal*, Jim went on to spend 11 years as head of the association's performance division and 22 years as AQHA registrar. For years, Jim wrote monthly columns for the *Quarter Running Horse Chart Book* and *Journal*. He also contributed feature material to the *Journal* on a regular basis.

A great deal of Jim's historical knowledge of the Quarter Horse breed was gained on a firsthand basis. He remembers, for instance, his first exposure to Grey Badger II, one of the horses profiled in *Legends 2.*

"It was in the late 1940s, and Walter Merrick was match-racing Grey Badger II in Oklahoma," he recalls. "Walter was down on the track, getting the horse ready to go, and Tien, his wife, was up in the stands, taking bets. Tien had bills wrapped around every finger and she was sure doing her best to see that anybody who wanted to lay some money down on the race had the opportunity to do so."

Having retired from AQHA in 1991, Jim now lives with his wife, Robin, in Corrales, N.M., where he enjoys such retirement activities as reading, participating in the local community theater, and, by his own admission, "doing too much yard work."

KIM GUENTHER was raised around horses in north-central Texas and has been writing about the western horse industry for 15 years. Her articles and features on top trainers, outstanding horses, and issues pertaining to the working horse world have appeared in magazines throughout the United States, Canada, Europe, and Australia.

An English major in college, Kim pursued a career as a free-lance writer. She had her first article published in *Paint Horse Journal* in 1982, and for a time she was assistant editor for that magazine.

Kim and her husband, Dean, moved to Australia, where Kim worked with a group of commercial photographers, and was a free-lance writer for the Australian publications *Hoofs and Horns* and *Hoofbeats*. During that time, her work appeared in various publications in the United States and Canada, including *Appaloosa Journal*.

In 1989, Kim and her husband returned to the United States, and for the past several years Kim has had her articles published in *Western Horseman*, *Quarter Horse News*, *The Quarter Horse Journal*, the Italian magazine *Western Side*, and the German magazine *Western Horse*.

Kim, who lives in Foresthill, Calif., is now focusing her work on the history and training techniques of the Spanish vaqueros, and the strong influence these traditions continue to have on today's reined cow horse.

Kim Guenther.

FRANK HOLMES has been writing historical articles involving the western horse for almost 30 years.

He sold his first feature article involving Quarter Horses to *Hoof and Horns* magazine in 1965. Frank is also considered one of the foremost historians of the Appaloosa breed, and his historical articles have been a regular fixture in *The Appaloosa Journal* for years. He has also written a children's book with horses as its main theme.

After 18 years of working for the federal government, Frank pursued a full-time career as a free-lance writer for 3 years. Then, between 1994 and 1996, he was employed by *WH* as a staff writer. During that time he wrote the *WH* book *The Hank Wiescamp Story*.

Frank left the magazine in 1996 to become the features editor of the *Paint Horse Journal* in Fort Worth. There, through his articles and photographs, he combines his love for history, horses, and the horsemen behind them. When he's not pursuing history or pedigree research, Frank lives in Gainesville near Fort Worth.

"There is a common thread that is shared by the major stock horse breeds," he notes. "Often, while pursuing research on one breed, I find myself gaining insight into the history of another.

"It is interesting to take note of the common heritage shared by the different breeds and to observe how they branched off to form the separate and distinct breed registries that exist today."

Frank Holmes.

Betsy Lynch.

BETSY LYNCH heads up her own marketing and communications firm, Third Generation Communications, which specializes in horse-related products and services. She is the managing partner and editor for Class Act Publications, which produces *Showtime Reports,* and co-author of the book titled *Bits: Power Tools for Thinking Riders.*

Betsy has a degree in agricultural journalism and has been involved in marketing, advertising, public relations, special events management, consulting, and publishing. At various times she has worked for the *California Horse Review, Horseman Magazine,* and *Appaloosa Journal.* During her free-lance career, her articles have appeared in numerous magazines in the United States and abroad, including *Western Horseman,* *Horse & Rider, Paint Horse Journal, Performance Horse, Cutting Horse Chatter, The Reiner, Team Penning USA,* and the German magazine *Western Pherde Journal.*

While growing up, Betsy had the opportunity to watch riders such as Dale Wilkinson, Bill Horn, and Clark Bradley set the arena ablaze. She remembers the thrill of meeting Wilkinson and Mr Gun Smoke during a 4-H tour of Wilkinson's farm. Those early experiences made a lasting impression in many ways. When the opportunity arose, Betsy took a hiatus from journalism to work on a cutting ranch in Texas.

She and her husband and their family now live near Fort Collins, Colo., where Betsy raises and rides a couple of her own reining and cow-bred horses.

Larry Thornton.

LARRY THORNTON started with a serious interest in equine pedigrees in the mid-1960s and wrote his first article for *Speedhorse* in 1984. He then became a regular contributor to that magazine, writing a monthly column and features. His interest in performance horses led to a series of stories for the National Cutting Horse Association's *Cutting Horse Chatter* on famous cutting horse bloodlines.

Since 1989, Larry has written a column for *Southern Horseman* called "The Working Lines," which is also published in several other horse magazines. Larry's book, by the same name, is a compilation of some of his articles on great horses and breeders.

"I credit any success I have as a writer to the people I have interviewed," states Larry about his writing career. "B.F. Phillips Jr. was the first great horseman and breeder to give me an interview, and it was his input that made my first story a success. I've been able to visit with many of the great horsemen in our industry, giving me an opportunity to learn about famous breeding programs and great horses.

"It seems that with every article, I find something new and interesting," says Larry. "Learning something new and then reporting on what I find is a very rewarding way to be a part of the horse industry."

Larry, a graduate of the University of Nebraska, is a vocational agriculture instructor at Lamar High School in Lamar, Arkansas. He lives in London, Ark., with his wife and children and is putting together a small band of mares for breeding good cutting and reining horses.

NOTES

PHOTO INDEX

The *Western Horseman*, established in 1936, is the world's leading horse publication.
For subscription information: 800-877-5278. To order other *Western Horseman* books: 800-874-6774.
Western Horseman, Box 7980, Colorado Springs, CO 80933-7980. Web-site: www.westernhorseman.com.

Books Published by Western Horseman Inc.

ARABIAN LEGENDS by Marian K. Carpenter
280 pages and 319 photographs. Abu Farwa, *Aladdinn, *Ansata Ibn Halima, *Bask, Bay-Abi, Bay El Bey, Bint Sahara, Fadjur, Ferzon, Indraff, Khemosabi, *Morafic, *Muscat, *Naborr, *Padron, *Raffles, *Raseyn, *Sakr, Samtyr, *Sanacht, *Serafix, Skorage, *Witez II, Xenophonn.

BACON & BEANS by Stella Hughes
144 pages and 200-plus recipes for delicious western chow.

BARREL RACING by Sharon Camarillo
144 pages and 200 photographs. Tells how to train and compete successfully.

CALF ROPING by Roy Cooper
144 pages and 280 photographs covering roping and tying.

CUTTING by Leon Harrel
144 pages and 200 photographs. Complete guide on this popular sport.

FIRST HORSE by Fran Devereux Smith
176 pages, 160 black-and-white photos, about 40 illustrations. Step-by-step information for the first-time horse owner and/or novice rider.

HEALTH PROBLEMS by Robert M. Miller, D.V.M.
144 pages on management, illness and injuries, lameness, mares and foals, and more.

HORSEMAN'S SCRAPBOOK by Randy Steffen
144 pages and 250 illustrations. A collection of handy hints.

IMPRINT TRAINING by Robert M. Miller, D.V.M.
144 pages and 250 photographs. Learn to "program" newborn foals.

LEGENDS by Diane C. Simmons
168 pages and 214 photographs. Barbra B, Bert, Chicaro Bill, Cowboy P-12, Depth Charge (TB), Doc Bar, Go Man Go, Hard Twist, Hollywood Gold, Joe Hancock, Joe Reed P-3, Joe Reed II, King P-234, King Fritz, Leo, Peppy, Plaudit, Poco Bueno, Poco Tivio, Queenie, Quick M Silver, Shue Fly, Star Duster, Three Bars (TB), Top Deck (TB), and Wimpy P-1.

LEGENDS 2 by Jim Goodhue, Frank Holmes, Phil Livingston, Diane C. Simmons
192 pages and 224 photographs. Clabber, Driftwood, Easy Jet, Grey Badger II, Jessie James, Jet Deck, Joe Bailey P-4 (Gonzales), Joe Bailey (Weatherford), King's Pistol, Lena's Bar, Lightning Bar, Lucky Blanton, Midnight, Midnight Jr, Moon Deck, My Texas Dandy, Oklahoma Star, Oklahoma Star Jr., Peter McCue, Rocket Bar (TB), Skipper W, Sugar Bars, and Traveler.

LEGENDS 3 by Jim Goodhue, Frank Holmes, Diane Ciarloni, Kim Guenther, Larry Thornton, Betsy Lynch
208 pages and 196 photographs. Flying Bob, Hollywood Jac 86, Jackstraw (TB), Maddon's Bright Eyes, Mr Gun Smoke, Old Sorrel, Piggin String (TB), Poco Lena, Poco Pine, Poco Dell, Question Mark, Quo Vadis, Royal King, Showdown, Steel Dust, and Two Eyed Jack.

LEGENDS 4
Several authors chronicle the great Quarter Horses Zantanon, Ed Echols, Zan Parr Bar, Blondy's Dude, Diamonds Sparkle, Woven Web/Miss Princess, Miss Bank, Rebel Cause, Tonto Bars Hank, Harlan, Lady Bug's Moon, Dash For Cash, Vandy, Impressive, Fillinic, Zippo Pine Bar, and Doc O' Lena.

PROBLEM-SOLVING by Marty Marten
248 pages and over 250 photos and illustrations. How to develop a willing partnership between horse and human to handle trailer-loading, hard-to-catch, barn-sour, spooking, water-crossing, herd-bound, and pull-back problems.

NATURAL HORSE-MAN-SHIP by Pat Parelli
224 pages and 275 photographs. Parelli's six keys to a natural horse-human relationship.

REINING, Completely Revised by Al Dunning
216 pages and over 300 photographs showing how to train horses for this exciting event.

ROOFS AND RAILS by Gavin Ehringer
144 pages, 128 black-and-white photographs plus drawings, charts, and floor plans. How to plan and build your ideal horse facility.

STARTING COLTS by Mike Kevil
168 pages and 400 photographs. Step-by-step process in starting colts.

THE HANK WIESCAMP STORY by Frank Holmes
208 pages and over 260 photographs. The biography of the legendary breeder of Quarter Horses, Appaloosas, and Paints.

TEAM PENNING by Phil Livingston
144 pages and 200 photographs. How to compete in this popular family sport.

TEAM ROPING WITH JAKE AND CLAY
by Fran Devereux Smith
224 pages and over 200 photographs and illustrations. Learn about fast times from champions Jake Barnes and Clay O'Brien Cooper. Solid information about handling a rope, roping dummies, and heading and heeling for practice and in competition. Also sound advice about rope horses, roping steers, gear, and horsemanship.

WELL-SHOD by Don Baskins
160 pages, 300 black-and-white photos and illustrations. A horse-shoeing guide for owners and farriers. The easy-to-read text, illustrations, and photos show step-by-step how to trim and shoe a horse for a variety of uses. Special attention is paid to corrective shoeing techniques for horses with various foot and leg problems.

WESTERN HORSEMANSHIP by Richard Shrake
144 pages and 150 photographs. Complete guide to riding western horses.

WESTERN TRAINING by Jack Brainard
With Peter Phinny. 136 pages. Stresses the foundation for western training.